International Perspectives on Children's Play

International Perspectives on Children's Play

Edited by
Jaipaul L. Roopnarine, Michael M. Patte,
James E. Johnson and David Kuschner

 Open University Press

Open University Press
McGraw-Hill Education
McGraw-Hill House
Shoppenhangers Road
Maidenhead
Berkshire
England
SL6 2QL

email: enquiries@openup.co.uk
world wide web: www.openup.co.uk

and Two Penn Plaza, New York, NY 10121-2289, USA

First published 2015

A catalogue record of this book is available from the British Library

ISBN-13: 978-0-335-26288-5
ISBN-10: 0-335-26288-0
eISBN: 978-0-335-26289-2

Library of Congress Cataloging-in-Publication Data
CIP data applied for

Typeset by Transforma Pvt. Ltd., Chennai, India

Praise for this book

"This welcome volume brings together new scholarship on culturally situated play in 16 diverse global contexts. The child rights-based foundation of the volume and nuanced perspectives are a powerful counter-narrative to the narrowing construction of childhood to one of academic readiness and test scores. The authors' collective narratives and research will contribute to many disciplines concerned about children, childhoods, culture and policy."

Dr. Elizabeth Swadener, *professor of Justice and Social Inquiry and associate director of the School of Social Transformation at Arizona State University, USA*

"In this research-based book, four international play scholars organize, author, and edit the work of their academic peers to weave a historical, developmental, cultural account of children's play around the globe. They examine the 'culturally constituted' child and explore first-hand accounts of real children's play in real places, extracting novel perspectives about historical and socio-cultural traditions and contexts for play. Here is the evidence that adults who influence children need for deeper understanding of play and developmental approaches to child rearing and early education. Scholars, teachers, parents, policy makers - this book is for you!"

Joe L. Frost, *Parker Centennial Professor Emeritus University of Texas, USA and Author of* A History of Children's Play and Play Environments.

"This timely and outstanding volume addresses the influences that shape children's play experiences in diverse cultural contexts. The inclusive chapters thematically explore how parental beliefs, socialization practices, cultural change, technology, and other factors shape children's play at home, school, and in the community. This volume makes a wonderful contribution to our understanding of play as a universal yet culture-specific activity that serves as a learning context and guides children's developmental outcomes. The selection of varied geographic regions and cultural groups that receive scant attention make this text a unique contribution to the field. Readers interested in children's experiences, cultural psychology, early childhood education, and anthropology will find this text stimulating and rewarding."

Dr. Robyn Holmes, *Professor of Psychology at Monmouth University, UK*

Contents

Figures

Tables

About the Editors

Jaipaul L. Roopnarine (Ph.D., University of Wisconsin, Madison) is Jack Reilly Professor of Child and Family Studies and Director Jack Reilly Institute for Early Childhood and Provider Education, Department of Child and Family Studies, Syracuse University, Syracuse, New York, USA, and Adjunct Professor of Education and Research Scientist at the Family Development Centre, The University of the West Indies, Trinidad and Tobago. He was Fulbright Scholar to The University of the West Indies, Trinidad and Tobago and has published extensively in the areas of child development and early childhood education and is currently the Editor of the journal *Fathering*. His recent book is Roopnarine, J. L. and Johnson, J. E. (Eds.). (2013). *Approaches to Early Childhood Education* (6th ed.). New York: Pearson Education.

Michael M. Patte (Ph.D., The Pennsylvania State University) is Professor of Education, College of Education, Bloomsburg University, Bloomsburg, Pennsylvania, USA. He is a Distinguished Fulbright Scholar, Co-editor of the *International Journal of Play*, Past President of *The Association for the Study of Play*, and board member of *The International Council for Children's Play*. His recent book is Brown, F. and Patte, M. M. (2013). *Rethinking Children's Play*. London: Continuum Press.

James E. Johnson (Ph.D., Wayne State University) is Professor of Early Childhood Education, College of Education, The Pennsylvania State University, University Park, Pennsylvania, USA and Adjunct Professor of Education, The University of the West Indies, Trinidad and Tobago. He was Fulbright Scholar to Taiwan. He is a leading expert on children's play and is currently Editor of the *Play & Culture Studies* series for The Association for the Study of Play. His recent book is Johnson, J. E., Christie, J., and Wardle, F. (2005). *Play Development and Early Education*. Boston, MA: Allyn & Bacon.

David Kuschner (Ed.D., University of Massachusetts, Amherst) is Associate Professor Emeritus of Early Childhood Education, College of Education, University of Cincinnati, Cincinnati, Ohio, USA. He is a leading expert on early childhood education and children's play. His recent book is Kuschner, D. (2009). *From Children to Red Hatters: Diverse Images and Issues of Play*. Lanham, MD: University Press of America.

List of Contributors

Ilka Dias Bichara
Department of Psychology
Universidade Federal da Bahia
Bahia
Brazil

Erika L. Bocknek
Early Childhood Education
Wayne State University
Detroit
Michigan
USA

Michelle Buchanan
Elementary and Early
Childhood Education
University of Wyoming
Laramie
Wyoming
USA

Ana Maria Almeida Carvalho
Department of Psychology
Universidade de São Paulo
São Paulo
Brazil

Pei-Yu Chang
Department of Child Development and
Education
Minghsin University of Science and
Technology
Xinfeng Township
Hsinchu County
Taiwan

Nandita Chaudhary
Department of Human Development
and Child Studies
Lady Irwin College
University of Delhi
New Delhi
India

Margaret Cooney
Elementary and Early Childhood
Education
University of Wyoming
Laramie
Wyoming
USA

Gwenda Beed Davey
Cultural Heritage Centre for Asia
and the Pacific
Deakin University
Melbourne
Australia

Susan Gaskins
Department of Educational
Psychology
Northeastern Illinois University
Chicago
Illinois
USA

Yumi Gosso
Department of Psychology
Universidade de São Paulo
São Paulo
Brazil

Janice E. Hale
Early Childhood Education
Institute for the Study of the African
American Child (ISAAC)
Wayne State University
Detroit
Michigan
USA

Nesrin Isikoglu Erdogan
Faculty of Education
Early Childhood Education Program
Pamukkale University
Denizli
Turkey

Yoko Ito
The Faculty of Education
Chiba University
Chiba City
Japan

Asiye Ivrendi
Faculty of Education
Early Childhood Education Program
Pamukkale University
Denizli
Turkey

Satomi Izumi-Taylor
Department of Instruction and
Curriculum Leadership
University of Memphis
Memphis
Tennessee
USA

James E. Johnson
Department of Curriculum and
Instruction
The Pennsylvania State University
University Park
Pennsylvania
USA

Eunjoo Jung
Department of Child and
Family Studies
Syracuse University
Syracuse
New York
USA

David Kuschner
Early Childhood Education
University of Cincinnati
Cincinnati
Ohio
USA

Anne Lillvist
School of Education, Culture and
Communication
Mälardalen University
Västerås
Sweden

Smita Mathur
Department of Early,
Elementary and Reading
Education
School of Education
James Madison University
Harrisonburg
Virginia
USA

Rain Mikser
School of Doctoral Studies
Tallinn University
Tallinn, Estonia

John T. Ng'asike
Early Childhood Education
Kenyatta University
Nairobi
Kenya

Michael M. Patte
Department of Teaching and Learning
Bloomsburg University
Bloomsburg
Pennsylvania
USA

Jaipaul L. Roopnarine
Department of Child and Family Studies
Syracuse University
Syracuse
New York
USA

Anette Sandberg
School of Education, Culture and
Communication
Mälardalen University
Västerås
Sweden

Shashi Shukla
Department of Human Development and
Child Studies
Lady Irwin College
University of Delhi
New Delhi
India

Aino Ugaste
Early Childhood Education
Tallinn University
Tallinn
Estonia

Elizabeth Wood
School of Education
University of Sheffield
Sheffield
England

Foreword

Danny is six, Ella is four. I ask Ella, 'what do you like best about Kinder?' 'Playing', she says, then pauses – 'and patting the white rabbit.' 'Danny, what do you like best about school?' 'Playing with my friends', he says. Both children return to their drawings, but Danny has something more to say: 'I wish we had a rabbit at school.'

The primacy of play and intimacy in children's hierarchy of importance – this is just one of the threads that can be found in this admirable compilation of narratives from the four corners of the world about the environments, the characteristics and the functions of play in children's lives. While there is now a rich library of books about children's play, some of them ground-breaking works of scholarship, it is uncommon to find a volume that deliberately uses a range of nationalities and cultures as an organising principle. The editors have encouraged their writers to go beyond the description and analysis of children's play in their particular domain (though the examples chosen of children's playlore are fascinating and revealing) to explore the economic, social and cultural contexts which both frame and influence play ways. Some writers offer a historical perspective on the changing patterns of play in their country or community; others elucidate play practices from a particular theoretical vantage point. Most acknowledge what I call the double helix of play: the inherited, adapted and invented games, rhymes, riddles, insults, etc – the enduring and universal panoply of children's play – and the multiple variations in play that result from the accident of place, time, gender, class and culture into which a child is born. One of the intellectual pleasures of this book is to compare and contrast the play experiences from chapter to chapter, each different, each with elements of commonality.

The focus of the majority of the writers is on the play of early childhood, and their narratives enable the reader to consider the significance of matters of real relevance to young children's opportunities to play, including education policies and family cultural traditions. The latter may range from non-interference – play is what children are expected to do – to a conviction that play comes only after work and study. A strength of the writing in this area is its respectful understanding of the origins of these adult perspectives: there is no flourish of 'we know best'.

As for the discussion of education policies, there is material in this book to gladden the heart and to grind the teeth. While almost everywhere those who shape education policy pay lip-service to the developmental importance of play for children, and there are examples of genuinely innovative and edifying early childhood programs, a number of writers point to contradictions between words and deeds. Children in some of the so-called 'developed' nations are finding their opportunity to play at school and their freedom to play as they choose grow ever more limited – threatened by the steamroller of increasing assessment and measuring of 'outcomes'. Play resists such measurement, and 'outcomes' are ambiguous. Yet education bean-counters appear to follow the fearsome example of the mythological Greek Procrustes, trying to fit play neatly into the curriculum bed by chopping off some of its essential qualities. As this compilation makes clear, children and play are not so easily separated.

When the historian Peter Laslett wrote in 1965 of 'the crowds and crowds of little children... strangely absent from the written record', the number of scholarly books in English devoted to children's play was fewer than the fingers on our two hands. Now there are books aplenty, together with journals and conferences and university courses. This book is of a range and quality that ensures it will enrich readers' understanding and appreciation of children's play – this wonderfully resilient, multifaceted and universal phenomenon.

June Factor
University of Melbourne
July 26, 2014

Acknowledgements

This volume grew out of our mutual interest in play and childhood development, children's right to play, and the education of children across the world. Jaipaul L. Roopnarine appreciates the support offered by his wife Nancy Beth and his children Miles, Maya, and India during the different phases of this project. Michael M. Patte acknowledges the exceptional support, understanding, and patience that his wife Sarah and his children Harrison, Oliver, and Lillian exhibited while he worked on this book. James E. Johnson owes a deep sense of gratitude to his wife, Karen, and David Kuschner thanks his wife, Leslie, for accepting this project as part of life in retirement.

Finally, we thank Kimberly L. Davidson, doctoral candidate in the Department of Child and Family Studies, Syracuse University, for her assistance with the manuscript. We thank the anonymous reviewers who provided feedback on this volume while it was being conceived.

1   Play as culturally situated: diverse perspectives on its meaning and significance

Jaipaul L. Roopnarine

Introduction

Within a child rights framework (e.g., Article 31 of the UN Convention on the Rights of the Child) and with increasing attention to the lost developmental potential of children due to difficult family social and economic circumstances (e.g., UNESCO 2006; Engle et al. 2007), there is growing global emphasis on child-centered approaches to child-rearing and the education of young children. A few primary goals across cultures include eradicating childhood poverty, improving the health conditions of children (see the UN Millennium Development Goals), and providing quality early childhood education programs at the family and community levels, all with an eye toward human capital development. At the same time, there is increasing awareness of the need for indigenous voices that outline cultural beliefs, practices, and goals on how we care for and educate children in different regions of the world (see Gupta 2013, 2014; Logie and Roopnarine 2013). Acknowledging the aforementioned issues as important for advancing the moral cause and well-being of children, play and early stimulation activities have been identified as having tremendous promise in laying the foundation for maximizing the life chances of children. This book was conceived in the spirit of these larger global issues of meeting the culturally, developmentally appropriate needs of young children by cataloging the diverse expressions and meanings of play as a major activity of childhood. It is meant to give the reader a glimpse into the rich and diverse play and playful activities of children in ecological niches across developing, recently developed, and developed societies.

As is evident from the chapters in this volume, while universally accepted as an activity of childhood, the processes and mechanisms whereby children's play and playful activities are expressed in different cultural communities and the degree to which governmental bodies, parents, early childhood educators, and other caregivers embrace play as a viable means for influencing childhood development are far from uniform. Over the years, a major challenge has been to articulate exactly how play in different cultural settings influences intellectual, physical, socio-emotional, and cultural development in young children. This volume begins to address this challenge by presenting the works of a multidisciplinary group of play scholars (e.g., early childhood education, child development/developmental psychology, anthropology, folklore, cultural psychology) who are from within the cultures themselves or have conducted groundbreaking work in different cultural communities.

Drawing upon the expertise of authors from diverse disciplines in order to consider how play in cultural communities falls along different points on Human Development Indices (HDI) sits squarely with calls within the fields of psychology and education for greater scientific integration of knowledge systems from the developed and "majority world" (Moghaddam and Taylor 1989; Kağitcibaşi 2007; Gupta 2014; Berry in press a, b; Thompson in press). It also honors indigenous perspectives on early childhood development (e.g., Nsamenang 2008). As will become apparent to the reader, play activities and their expressions in everyday settings are tied to prevailing cultural practices within the specific developmental niche. Play is embedded in the social, political, and economic structures of societies and the changing ethos of childhood itself. This volume eschews a comparative or cross-cultural approach to play and instead highlights their modes and properties within the cultures themselves—a cultural approach to understanding play and early development and education. In essence, play is viewed as a cultural activity and participating in it is an avenue through which development is facilitated during the critical early childhood years (see Vygotsky 1978; Rogoff 2003). In this vein, attempts are also made throughout the chapters to discuss how prominently play is woven into the (re)conceptualization of early childhood care and education in different cultural communities.

Conceptualizing and defining play across cultures

In deliberations of play across cultures, there are two interrelated issues that warrant some attention: theoretical frameworks and the definition of play. Traditionally, play has been conceptualized within a narrow band of theories on cognitive and social development (e.g., Piaget's cognitive developmental theory; Parten's play typologies) that were presumed to have universal applications. More recent conceptualizations of childhood development in the areas of cultural psychology and early education (e.g., Greenfield et al. 2003; Chaudhary and Tuli 2010) have proposed different cultural pathways to achieve common developmental goals across cultures. Following these newer perspectives on different developmental pathways, the chapters in this volume draw from a broad range of theoretical perspectives to frame play during the early childhood years. In most cases, the theoretical perspectives converge or intersect regarding play as a universal cultural activity. However, they do diverge on the developmental significance of play. Its benefits for the development of cognitive and social skills in children in different cultural settings are only now beginning to be discerned. The chapters in this book extend the discussion on the evolving meanings of play in meeting the developmental needs of young children in a global community marked by changes in parental socialization patterns, expectations of children, and population movements within and between countries for economic, sociopolitical, and educational reasons. Whereas, in some cultural communities, a strong case is made for the connection between play activities and practicing and learning culture-specific modes of behaviors, in others, children learn through a mixture of work and play or by observing others and replicating their activities.

The diverse theoretical planks and frameworks employed to contextualize play (e.g., ecocultural, life history, developmental niche, funds of knowledge, Vygotskyian, the individualism and collectivism continuum, Bronfenbrenner's ecological model) in this volume offer a platform for greater scientific integration of the play literatures from cultural, cross-cultural, and indigenous perspectives. It also invites broadening parochial definitions of play to include playlike and playful activities (e.g., rough joking, shaming games; see Gray 2009) not ordinarily considered as play by conventional academic criteria (see Johnson et al. 2005; Smith 2010). In his seminal writings on play, Sutton-Smith (1997) brought to the fore the diverse human activities that may be considered play: from mind and subjective play (e.g., fantasy, imagination), solitary play (e.g., hobbies, collections, bird watching), and playful behaviors (e.g., playing tricks, playing around) to informal play (e.g., joking, parties, dancing) (Figure 1.1). These and

Figure 1.1 The elaborate fantasy play observed in these girls in North America is seen in several other cultural settings.

the other themes discussed by Sutton-Smith (1997) are captured in this volume and will hopefully move the dialogue along on the nature and meaning of the diverse play and playful activities of *homo sapiens* across a wide spectrum of cultural communities and physical settings.

The contents of the book

Turning to specific aspects of the volume, care was taken to select cultures that are at different levels of economic and technological development, and from major geographic regions around the world. The cultural groups represented in this volume have had different familial and community or population level socio-historical experiences (e.g., oppression, marginalization, political domination, progressive child development policies) that have influenced childrearing practices, utilitarian, and psychological values associated with children and childhood, and the nature and quality of play. Part I of the book covers play in diverse groups in Brazil (e.g., Parakanã Indians, Combu Island children, children in caiçara communities, Xocó and *quilombo* children, see Chapter 3), the Mayans of Mexico (Chapter 2), African and Indo Caribbeans (Chapter 4), and diverse ethnic groups in the United States (Chapters 5, 6, 7, 8). Of note in this Part is the play of marginalized groups (e.g., African Americans, Native Americans, Parakanã Indians, children of Mexican migrant workers) that have and continue to receive scant attention in scholarly circles, as does the play of newer immigrant groups in the United States. A few immigrant groups (e.g., Asian Americans) tend to hold on to ideas about play and education that are closely aligned with value systems in the ancestral or natal culture. It appears that ethno-theories about childrearing, play, and early childhood development travel with families as they become immersed in new cultural communities or new locales around urban centers. How these ethno-theories change as families come into contact with competing beliefs about childrearing and the role of play in early education is matter of speculation at this time. The chapters on play among children of migrant farm workers, Caribbean families, and Asian immigrant families in the United States touch on these issues.

In Part II, a lone chapter that furnishes new observational data on play in Africa points to the glaring need for more research on topics regarding the care and education of young children in the diverse cultural communities in the African continent (Chapter 9). As with some other developing nations, the Turkana pastoralist children in Kenya are able to balance early work responsibilities within their families and still have ample time for play. The seemingly unsupervised play of these children does not go unnoticed by parents or by the wide range of adult caregivers and relatives who constitute their social milieus. These children readily observe and replicate with great precision adult modes of engagement in economic and cultural activities in their play themes. The adaptive strategies these and other children in developing societies (e.g., Brazil, India, the Caribbean) employ provide windows into the complex nature of children's social worlds and the manner in which they negotiate their way through challenging environmental circumstances using local materials. Hitherto, the play of children in developing societies has been viewed as deficient.

    Parts III and IV of this volume provide equally detailed intellectual excursions into play in the Asia and Pacific regions and play in Turkey and Europe. As indicated already, one aim of this volume was to present descriptions of play in developed and developing societies. Chapters 10–13 on play in India, Taiwan, Japan, and Australia each delve into socio-historical accounts of children's play as rooted in the philosophical and religious traditions of cultural communities that embody the contrasting realities of life in developed and developing economies. Again, situating play in beliefs about children and childrearing (e.g., *yudo hoiku, jiyu hoiku, suano,* and *ganbaru* in Japan, see Chapter 11) and edicts from religious traditions about the role of parents and the responsibilities of children toward parents (e.g., tenets of Confucianism, unilateral respect and obedience in Taiwan) permit insights into the struggles and paradoxes that parents encounter in accommodating contemporary demands on childrearing and education in meeting the play and stimulation needs of children. This is ever so present in emerging economies such as India and more developed nations such as Taiwan where there is a movement toward more organized parent–child activities through commercially available programs that offer space and materials for play. In multicultural Australia, and in some Asian societies (e.g., India), ethnic and regional differences require careful attention to the preservation of languages and traditional modes of play. This responsibility may reside with national policies and early childhood development and early education training programs as is clear from Chapters 10 and 12 on Taiwan and India.
    In Part IV, in Chapter 14, the progressive view of play in Sweden is in contrast to continued attempts to reshape and (re)conceptualize the meaning of childhood and appropriate early childhood education practices that are at work in enhancing the democratization of Estonian society after years of influence from the former Soviet Union (Chapter 16). Like Estonia, Turkey is also in the throes of redefining how children are viewed and educated at the national level. In Chapter 17, in Turkey, industrialization, urbanization, and women's participation in the labor force have all led to profound changes in family size, socialization goals (e.g., autonomous-relational self), availability of play spaces, and play patterns between adults and children. Along with attempts to preserve and catalog play activities and materials through children's toy museums, systematic revisions of early childhood curricula in Turkey have brought play to the center of early childhood education practices. In Chapter 15, in communities in England, Wales, Scotland, and Northern Ireland, play policies and pedagogy are featured prominently in early childhood curricula, and playwork is obvious in communities across the British Isles.
    In short, a few salient features of this volume include but are not limited to:

- considerations of sociodemographic characteristics and changes in cultural ecologies as they relate to early socialization, play, and early education;
- diverse theoretical perspectives and frameworks on play in cultural communities;
- discussion of play in the context of prevailing cultural childrearing goals and expectations and/or the early education of children;
- numerous examples of children's play activities and games *in situ*;

- current state of play research and possible meanings for childhood development and/or early education across cultures that fall on different levels on Human Development Indices;
- implications and future directions for understanding play and, in most cases, the education of young children.

It is our hope that the narratives in this volume will increase discourses among academicians, policymakers, early childhood educators, and the lay public in the direction of a pan-cultural or pan-human understanding of play and development. This might best be achieved through looking at children's social activities through a wider cultural lens and from a resilient-adaptive perspective that take into account children's diverse social worlds, the immediate ecological conditions, economic modes of production, and the beliefs and practices of socialization agents and early childhood educators.

References

Berry, J. W. (in press a). Global, indigenous and regional perspectives on international psychology. In J. L. Roopnarine and D. Chadee (Eds.), *Caribbean psychology: Developmental, health, social, and clinical.* Washington, DC: American Psychological Association.

Berry, J. W. (in press b). Achieving a global psychology. *Canadian Psychology, 54*(1), 55–61.

Chaudhary, N. and Tuli, M. (2010). Elective interdependence: Understanding individual agency and interpersonal relationships in Indian families. *Culture & Psychology, 16,* 477–496.

Engle, P., Black, M. M., Behrman, J. R., Cabral de Mello, M., Gertler, P. J., Kapirri, L. et al. (2007). Strategies to avoid loss of developmental potential in more than 200 million children in the developing world. *Lancet, 369,* 229–242.

Gray, P. (2009). Play as a foundation for hunter-gatherer social existence. *American Journal of Play, 2,* 476–520.

Greenfield, P. M., Keller, H., Fuligni, A. and Maynard, A. (2003). Cultural pathways through universal development. *Annual Review of Psychology, 54,* 461–490.

Gupta, A. (2013). *Early childhood education, postcolonial theory, and teaching practices and policies in India: Balancing Vygotsky and the Veda* (2nd ed.). Basingstoke: Palgrave Macmillan.

Gupta, A. (2014). *Diverse early childhood education policies and practices: Voices and images from five countries in Asia.* New York, NY: Routledge.

Johnson, J., Christie, J. and Wardle, F. (2005). *Play, development, and early education.* New York: Allyn & Bacon.

Kağitcibaşi, C. (2007). *Family and human development across countries: A view from the other side* (2nd ed.). Hove: Psychology Press.

Logie, C. and Roopnarine, J. L. (Eds.) (2013). *Issues and perspectives in child development and early education in Caribbean countries.* La Romaine, Trinidad and Tobago: Caribbean Publishers.

Moghaddam, F. M. and Taylor, D. M. (1989). What constitutes an "appropriate psychology" for the developing world? *International Journal of Psychology, 21*, 253–267.

Nsamenang, A. B. (2008). (Mis)Understanding ECD in Africa: The force of local and global motives. In G. Marito, P. Alan and J. L. Evans (Eds.), *Africa's future, Africa's challenge: Early childhood care and development in Sub-Saharan Africa* (pp. 135–146). Washington, DC: The World Bank.

Rogoff, B. (2003). *The cultural nature of human development.* New York: Oxford University Press.

Smith, P. K. (2010). *Children and play.* Chichester: Wiley-Blackwell.

Sutton-Smith, B. (1997). *The ambiguity of play.* Cambridge, MA: Harvard University Press.

Thompson, A. (in press). Caribbean psychology: context, imperatives and further directions: The need for a psychology of human diversity: global and regional responses. In J. L. Roopnarine and D. Chadee (Eds.), *Caribbean psychology: Developmental, health, social, and clinical.* Washington, DC: American Psychological Association.

UNESCO (2006). *Strong foundations: early childhood care and education—2007 education for all global monitoring report.* Paris: UNESCO.

Vygotsky, L. S. (1978). *Mind in society: The development of higher psychological processes.* Cambridge, MA: Harvard University Press.

Part I

Americas and the Caribbean

2 Yucatec Mayan children's play

Suzanne Gaskins

A group of four little girls and a little boy are playing in a yard together behind a house, under a tree. They have set up a group of broken boxes and discarded pieces of wood on rocks and filled them with empty bottles and jars, to make a pretend store. The oldest girl, age 8, is sitting behind the "counter" receiving two others as customers. One customer is busy arguing about the rightful price of a potential "purchase" when the other one "enters" holding a baby doll. There is a lively discussion about how much quantity should be included in the order for the stated price, culminating with an agreement to price and payment with leaves used as pretend money. Next to the "storekeeper" is her "assistant," who is younger than the others; she attentively watches the other three have their lively exchange. She is seated next to the little boy, who is 3 years old. The boy does not pay much attention to the unfolding story; rather, he spends his time smashing small fruits in an old tortilla press that has been incorporated into the play stage set and then eating them. Along with watching the other girls, the younger girl also watches to make sure that he does not smash his fingers and to help him if the task gets frustrating.

This observation was made in a small, Yucatec Mayan village in eastern Mexico. It represents a typical domestic play event in the lives of the children of the village. At first glance, it seems similar to children's play in many other places in the world. In this chapter, however, the understandings and commitments that lie behind such play events will be explored, with the goal of demonstrating how children's play is culturally organized and shaped by the everyday activities of the family and the beliefs and values of the particular culture.

The cultural organization of Yucatec Mayan play

Cultural beliefs about children's play

The Yucatec Maya view play as a natural activity of childhood; they take pleasure in seeing their children playing and enjoying themselves, as long as children do not get in the way, shirk their responsibilities, or use up precious resources while playing. They report valuing play because it occupies their children (giving adults time to work) and it indicates that their children are healthy (Gaskins 1996). But they do not view play as an important contributor to their children's development or learning, nor devote much time or many resources to supporting or actively mediating children's play. Since play is understood as a spontaneous activity of childhood, adults do not see themselves as play partners or as play organizers (Gaskins 1996, 2013).

Relative importance of work and play

While play is not viewed as a negative behavior in and of itself, it is discouraged when it interferes with children's contribution to family work (Gaskins 2009, in press a). The high cultural value placed on children's learning to be productive workers leads adults to curtail play when there is work to be done, in contrast with cultures where play is either actively cultivated or merely accepted (Gaskins et al. 2007). Children themselves appear to share this cultural value, volunteering to do chores (Gaskins 2000, in press a) and usually complying when called away from playing in order to work. From this perspective, play becomes a residual activity for children when there is nothing "useful" for them to do, either because the household's work is done or because they do not have the necessary skills to participate in the current tasks.

Cultural and theoretical perspectives on play

Play and development

Developmental psychologists argue that play supports development in children (e.g., Singer et al. 2006) but, there is, in fact, somewhat modest controlled experimental evidence to support that position (Smith 2009; Gaskins in press b), raising the issue of whether the consensus stems from assumptions growing out of cultural beliefs about the centrality of play in childhood (Fleer 2005; Gaskins et al. 2007). The classic play theorists (Mead 1934; Freud 1950; Bateson 1955; Piaget 1962; Vygotsky 1978) argue that play (especially pretend play) supports cognitive, social, language, and emotional development (Göncü and Gaskins 2011; Gaskins 2013) by providing practice for mastery, social negotiations, coping mechanisms for frustrations and fears, and coordination between cognitive and metacognitive thinking. While it is assumed that play provides unique opportunities for such activities, there is little evidence to distinguish between whether its impact comes from unique characteristics of play or from play being the dominant activity of childhood (for middle-class Euroamericans) (Gaskins in press b).

Play is not a privileged activity of childhood for the Yucatec Maya, and this case study provides evidence to suggest that play may be less uniquely important when children spend much of their time in other activities, such as family work (Gaskins in press a). Some characteristics of play may in fact be unique, for instance, the potential for fantasy and imagination. But missing is evidence of the specific developmental impact of these particular characteristics of play, separated out from all the rest (that are in fact shared by work), e.g., social interaction, communication, problem solving, and metacognition.

Play and learning

It is also often assumed that play serves as a unique medium for children's learning. Here, the distinction between exploration (which can be playful or not) and play itself is often lost. Constructing new understandings about the world and one's place in it through trial and error or through practice to mastery is thought to be an important consequence of exploratory play (e.g., Piaget 1954), but is not tied solely to play. In fact, this commitment to the power of play in learning is so strong, that despite arguing for the importance of child agency in play, proponents of learning through play often argue simultaneously for the value of adult organization of children's play to maximize learning (Bodrova and Leong 1995; Singer et al. 2006). Adults should scaffold children's play both by providing objects and activities that maximize learning and by directing and expanding on children's play routines. Often, adults are encouraged to be active play partners to achieve both ends.

The Yucatec Mayan case provides interesting perspectives on play and learning. First, as in many cultures, while children learn a lot through playful practice, they also learn a lot by observing and participating in ongoing activities in their everyday worlds (Gaskins and Paradise 2010). Many discussions of observational learning include practice as part of observation, but in fact, they are two logically separate processes that can support one another; practice also can exist outside of a play frame, either independently of, or embedded in, work. Second, in the Yucatec Mayan case, since adults do not mediate or participate in children's play, there is little scaffolding that occurs in play, beyond what older or more knowledgeable children provide. Play for these children, then, is really just for having fun. Much of the learning that goes on in everyday activities is achieved during observation of others and through work, not through play (Gaskins and Paradise 2010; Gaskins in press a).

Open attention

Gaskins and Paradise (2010) have suggested that in communities strongly committed to observational learning, children also commit to a particular form of attention called open attention (Figure 2.1). In this style of attention, one pays attention to more than one thing at a time (wide-angled) and can sustain attention for long periods of time (abiding). It is particularly important for observational learning, where one must take in information from ongoing activity that is unstructured and not designed to teach. (See also Rogoff et al. 2007). Open attention has consequences for play. Practicing open attention when playing, children always have one foot in the play frame and one foot in the real world. This limits the extent to which they may be transported through play to another psychological reality. Significantly, this distributed attention allows them to attend to their younger siblings while playing, but it also allows them to pay attention to everything else going on around them.

Figure 2.1 Children engage in open attention to adult activities.

Commitment to the non-fictional world

Finally, particular cultural beliefs and values can select particular kinds of play as inappropriate or even immoral. Carlson et al. (1998) report that Mennonite parents do not like their children to engage in inventive pretend play, with themes that are not realistic. The Yucatec Maya and related groups (e.g., the Mopan by Danziger 2006) likewise are committed to telling stories about real events that happened (Gaskins 2013). All stories are assumed by them to be non-fictional. This cultural stance includes stories seen on television, such as soap operas and cartoons (though as children receive more education, they may come to realize that some stories are "made up" and may not reflect reality). Given this cultural commitment to true narratives, it is not surprising that children limit their pretend play to interpretations of events and activities they have observed or heard about (Gaskins 2013).

The independence of children

While children are expected to contribute to household work and other shared social goals, how they do that is left largely up to them (Gaskins 1999). Children are given a great deal of leeway to decide their activities from moment to moment, as well as to make major decisions for themselves. This respect for children's agency, when paired with beliefs about the relative unimportance of play and the inappropriateness of adult engagement in play, ensures that play is motivated by and organized by children— usually the oldest children in the immediate play group. Disputes are settled and danger avoided based on the social hierarchy of responsibility of siblings which gives older children responsibility to keep younger children content and younger children responsibility to obey their older siblings (Gaskins and Lucy 1986).

Going beyond direct observation of play activity

How cultural commitments organize children's play can be understood better through more detailed analysis about how play occurs in Yucatec Mayan children's everyday lives.

Where play takes place

Children usually play within the family compound, within earshot (and sometimes within sight) of adults and older children, but they are not being directly supervised. (If someone is hurt or becomes unhappy, adults will be able to see these developments and respond if needed.) In many cultures, children's play is not "parallel activity" to other activity in the household, either occurring away from any direct supervision or under the direct supervision (and sometimes the participation) of adults (Gaskins et al. 2007).

Yucatec Mayan children are encouraged to play outside to give more space (and more tranquility) to the adults who are working inside. Yet they are also expected to stay within their compound for a number of reasons: they are within calling distance, if their help is needed; they are able to incorporate younger children into their play without taking them away from their mothers' supervision; and they are unlikely to cause trouble with neighbors (Gaskins 1996).

While limited to the compound, the various spaces within the yard provide a wide range of physical and social spaces for children to choose from. The girls in the example at the beginning of the chapter chose to play quite a distance from the house, in a relatively private and secluded setting. At other times, children may choose to play nearer the house or in view of the street. Boys playing a game of marbles, for instance, would need a large open space with flat ground that was cleared of rocks and weeds. Once play is over, the spaces used for play revert to being of general use, with little evidence that any play had taken place.

With whom children play

Yucatec Mayan children's social worlds are primarily made up of relatives, not friends (Gaskins 2006a), reflecting the general cultural norm of socializing with family and *compadres* ("ritual" family). This one cultural preference has many consequences for their social interactions during play (Gaskins 2006a). First, their play partners are not all the same age. Multi-aged groups require that the play be flexible enough to include varying capacities and interests. Second, children's playmates are consistent—there is a shared knowledge of and continuity to the play experience that can be relied on and social bonds that endure beyond the play activity. There is no negation about what must be done to secure another child's friendship. Third, the children who are playing together retain their responsibilities and obligations that they have to one another as older and younger siblings (Gaskins and Lucy 1986).

Which objects are used in play

Yucatec Mayan children conduct their play using very few "toys." With the exception of the baby doll carried by the one girl, all of the props used in the pretend store were items from the natural world (e.g., rocks, leaves, and fruit) or discarded (bottles and jars, pieces of wood, tortilla press). A game of marbles would use one inexpensive and durable toy, the marbles themselves; boys could have earned enough money to purchase the marbles. If they had no marbles, they might choose to play a rock tossing-and-catching game similar to jacks. Baseball can be played with a stick and unripe orange if there is no bat and ball. The minimal use of commercial toys reflects a cultural norm of investing little in supporting children's play.

At the same time, the fact that toys are bought at all, given a family's limited resources, indicates that adults are not opposed to play and enjoy providing toys to make their children happy. Purchased toys are given to a particular child, but children are expected to share their toys with other children in the family. As children lose interest in a particular toy, it is saved for use by those who are younger who do not seem to mind toys' wear and tear. (The baby doll in the pretend store above was a valued hand-me-down possession even though it was missing clothes, an eye, and most of her hair.)

Types of play

While Yucatec Mayan children engage in all types of play, the character of that play is sometimes different from what one sees in middle-class American children's play. Small-motor manipulation is often aimed at developing competence within some practical, real-world task (Figure 2.2). Pretend play is limited to interpretive play based on real-world scenarios they have seen or heard about, not inventive play about fantasy scenarios about things that are not known or could not happen (Gaskins 2013). And rule-based play is necessarily modified to accommodate to the differing levels of skill represented in the playgroup, with the goal often defined as a joint accomplishment through collaboration rather than individual accomplishment through competition.

Activities competing with play

Yucatec Mayan children spend some of each day at play, but they also have many other competing activities. Those who are attending school spend about 6 hours a day in school, plus they have homework they must do in the afternoon or evening. In families who own a television or DVD player, children also enjoy watching cartoons and other shows. And perhaps most significantly, children of all ages are engaged in doing chores (Gaskins 2009, in press a). These contributions to household work are significant in time spent and contribution made, and children's work obligations increase as their competence increases. Between the ages of 4 and 11 years, about two-thirds of

Figure 2.2 Toddler plays with real-world objects.

children's days are spent in work and play; as work responsibilities increase, time spent playing decreases. So while children aged 4–7 years old spend more time playing than working, those aged 8–11 years old spend more time working than playing (Gaskins 2000).

How adults mediate play

Yucatec Mayan adults' priority throughout the day is to get their work done (Gaskins 1999), and supervision of children reflects this priority. They spend little time and few resources mediating children's play. While infant care takes significant adult resources, once children can walk, they spend more of their time with other children than with adults, and much of their play takes place at a distance away from adult work. Children are not "kept busy" or "entertained," but rather left to organize their own time and activities during the day. Adults' lack of involvement in children's play in particular reflects their beliefs about the minimal role of play in children's development and learning.

Understanding play as culturally organized behavior

Developmental psychology is committed to universal developmental processes and outcomes, which makes it difficult to interpret cultural differences (Gaskins 2006b, in press a). A second tenet is that the systematic experiences of children's everyday lives influence development. The only way these two positions can co-exist is to interpret any differences in experience from the Euroamerican middle-class ideal as leading to deficits or negative outcomes. Unless one is willing to suspend the claim of universal development, there is little room for interpreting cultural variation as anything but non-normative and detrimental (Gaskins 2006b, in press a). This is the model that has often been applied to research on differences in children's play, especially when studied in minority groups within the United States (e.g., Smilansky 1968).

By studying children's play in cultures with different understandings of the value and meaning of play, trying to understand the system of meanings and behaviors from the participants' perspective, not that of the researchers, the conclusions about play variation leading to developmental deficit are called into question. In particular, this Yucatec Mayan case study of children's play illustrates that play may be only one primary activity in children's lives, and that its importance for development and learning will be reduced when other activities, such as participation in family work, are highly valued and represent a large part of a child's day. Thus, play should be considered one important medium for children's development and learning, not the one and only medium. Learning to negotiate, take the perspective of others, and communicate effectively and learning to solve problems can happen outside of play as much as inside play, if children are meaningfully engaged in other activities. In addition, this case study identifies characteristics of play that should not be seen as universal, but rather culturally specific. Currently, with the majority of research on children's play limited to a single cultural tradition, it is not possible to understand how universal characteristics of their play are interwoven with culturally specific ones.

A particularly important characteristic is who the playmates are. Assuming that same-aged peers are the primary playmates who shape our expectations about the nature of play, age-graded play is significantly different from multi-aged play, in terms of who is in charge and what play can hold the participants' interest. Likewise, the quality of social interaction among relatives, who are permanent playmates who share all other aspects of one's life, creates a very different play environment, in terms of what must be negotiated (and what may not be), the degree of shared knowledge, and more (Gaskins 2006a).

This study also demonstrates that adults' mediation of and participation in children's play can vary dramatically across cultures. Within our own culture, parents today value play much more highly as a childhood activity with important consequences than they did one hundred years ago (Mintz 2004; Chudacoff 2007), and as a result, they are more likely to be significantly involved in their children's play (e.g., Haight and Miller 1993; Lancy 2007; Lillard 2007). This involvement reduces children's agency in play, a concept that is basic to most of the current theories about how play uniquely influences development. For the Yucatec Maya, they spend little time thinking about children's play and furnish few resources to support it. As a result, while play is a residual activity for children, especially as they become more competent at the skills needed for work, it is also completely within children's shared, collaborated control.

Broader cultural beliefs and understandings also influence the nature of children's play. A particularly strong example of this cultural effect for the Yucatec Maya comes from the analysis of their pretend play (Gaskins 2013), which is qualitatively different than that seen in Euroamerican middle-class children. They engage in interpretive pretend play with great enthusiasm, constructing, elaborating on, and commenting on activities and roles they have observed or heard about. But they do not engage in inventive pretend play, where they construct narratives that go beyond their experience and understandings of the way the world is. This pattern is in harmony with the larger cultural commitment to true narratives about the real world. It has consequences for the role that play may have in the children's development, especially in the domains of emotion and imagination. Play has been conceived of as a way for children to deal with frustrations and fears by pretending about a "what-if" world (Freud 1950; Piaget 1962; Vygotsky 1978). Gaskins and Miller (2009) have argued that pretend play for the Yucatec Maya does not fulfill this purpose, and in fact, their everyday experiences may construct an emotional environment in which they have less need to do so. A second cultural factor that contributes to a commitment to interpretive play is the high value placed on open attention (Gaskins and Paradise 2010). This culturally organized attentional stance, sustained during play, makes it difficult to enter into an imaginative world, since children are expected to continue to pay attention to the here and now.

Implications of understanding play as cultural behavior

Interpreting the role of play in Yucatec Mayan children's everyday lives through respecting the Maya's own understandings allows us to see that their style of play is culturally appropriate, embedded in a wider range of activities, and motivated by cultural values and understandings. (As an added benefit, it allows us to see middle-class European children's play and our theories and research about play from the same relative perspective). It leads us to look not just at what they do not do in play that would be expected as ideal from our cultural-centric understandings of play, but also what they do accomplish in play and in other activities, especially work. When this perspective is taken, Yucatec Mayan children appear to be thoughtful, creative, and motivated to learn. Their behavior is understood as productive, socially sophisticated, and responsible. In their play, they demonstrate and explore their understandings of how their physical and social worlds work, they use play to further their skills, they sustain and build their primary social relationships, they pay open attention to what is going on around them, and they enjoy themselves. But play is not the only important thing that they do in a day; they also spend a great deal of time participating in family work and in learning through observing what goes on around them.

This culturally relative perspective on play would lead early childhood educators to develop a radically different curriculum than the play-based curriculum that is the norm for middle-class Euroamerican children (an outcome recognized by early childhood educators who work from within a sociocultural perspective, e.g., Brooker and Edwards 2010). While Yucatec Mayan children enjoy playing, their time in school might be more productive if it focused more on allowing the children to be productive doing real work, which they are eager to do, and preparing them more explicitly for the unique expectations of the primary school classroom. A play-based curriculum is likely not to have the effect expected by European and American educators, nor is it likely to be valued or supported by parents. A culturally motivated work/skill curriculum would be particularly at odds with the recommendations made by many early childhood educators in the United States who are alarmed at the increasing time spent on classroom skills (e.g., Elkind 2007; Singer et al. 2006; Gray 2013).

Finally, understanding play to be culturally organized leads to new insights about the limitations and inaccuracies of current theories and claims about play as the leading activity for development and learning in early childhood. While the ethnographic record supports the idea that in all cultures, children play and enjoy doing so (Schwartzman 1979; Lancy 2008), it also demonstrates that there are important quantitative and qualitative differences in children's play across cultures, stemming from cultural understandings and practices. From this perspective, we may look at children's everyday behavior more open-mindedly and build more accurate understandings about the contributions of play to development and learning and the circumstances that support play's significance in children's lives.

References

Bateson, G. A. (1955). A theory of play and fantasy. In G. A. Bateson (Ed.), *Steps to an ecology of mind* (pp. 177–193). New York: Chandler.

Bodrova, E. and Leong, D. J. (1995). *Tools of the mind: The Vygotskian approach to early childhood education*. Upper Saddle River, NJ: Prentice Hall.

Brooker, L. and Edwards, S. (Eds.) (2010). *Engaging play*. Maidenhead: Open University Press.

Carlson, S. M., Taylor, M. and Levin, G. R. (1998). The influence of culture on pretend play: The case of Mennonite children. *Merrill-Palmer Quarterly, 44*(4), 538–569.

Chudacoff, H. P. (2007). *Children at play: An American history*. New York: NYU Press.

Danziger, E. (2006). The thought that counts: Interactional consequences of variation in cultural theories of meaning. In N. S. Enfield and S. C. Levinson (Eds.), *Roots of human sociality: Culture, cognition, and interaction* (pp. 259–278). Oxford: Berg.

Elkind, D. (2007). *The power of play*. Philadelphia, PA: Da Capo.

Fleer, M. (2005). Developmental fossils – unearthing the artefacts of early childhood education: The reification of 'child development.' *Australian Journal of Early Childhood, 30*(2), 2–7.

Freud, S. (1950). *Beyond the pleasure principle*. New York: Liveright.

Gaskins, S. (1996). How Mayan parental theories come into play. In S. Harkness and C. Super (Eds.), *Parents' cultural belief systems: Their origins, expressions, and consequences* (pp. 345–363). New York: Guilford Press.

Gaskins, S. (1999). Children's daily lives in a Mayan village: A case study of culturally constructed roles and activities. In A. Göncü (Ed.), *Children's engagement in the world* (pp. 25–81). Cambridge: Cambridge University Press.

Gaskins, S. (2000). Children's daily activities in a Mayan village: A culturally grounded description. *Journal of Cross-cultural Research, 34*(4), 375–389.

Gaskins, S. (2003). From corn to cash: Change and continuity within Mayan families. *Ethos, Journal of the Society for Psychological Anthropology, 31*(2), 248–275.

Gaskins, S. (2006a). The cultural organisation of Yucatec Mayan children's social interactions. In X. Chen, D. French and B. Schneider (Eds.), *Peer relationships in cultural context* (pp. 283–309). Cambridge: Cambridge University Press.

Gaskins, S. (2006b). Cultural perspectives on infant-caregiver interaction. In N. J. Enfield and S. Levinson (Eds.), *The roots of human sociality: Culture, cognition, and human interaction* (pp. 279–298). Oxford: Berg.

Gaskins, S. (2009). Work before play for Yucatec Maya children. In R. A. Shweder, R. Thomas, A. C. Bidell, S. Dailey, S. D. Dixon, P. J. Miller and J. Modell (Eds.), *The child: An encyclopedic companion*. Chicago: University of Chicago Press.

Gaskins, S. (2013). Pretend play as culturally constructed activity. In M. Taylor (Ed.), *Oxford handbook on the development of the imagination* (pp. 224–247). Oxford: Oxford University Press.

Gaskins, S. (in press a). Childhood practices across cultures: play and household work. To appear in L. Jensen (Ed.), *The Oxford handbook of culture and development*. Oxford: Oxford University Press.

Gaskins, S. (in press b). Cross-cultural play and play research. To appear in L. Brooker, S. Edwards and M. Blaise (Eds.), *Handbook of play and learning in early childhood*. London: Sage Publications.

Gaskins, S., Haight, W. and Lancy, D. F. (2007). The cultural construction of play. In A. Göncü and S. Gaskins (Eds.), *Play and development: Evolutionary, sociocultural and functional perspectives* (pp. 179–202). Mahwah, NJ: Lawrence Erlbaum Associates.

Gaskins, S. and Lucy, J. (1986). Passing the buck: Responsibility and blame in the Yucatec Maya household. Paper presented at 85th Annual Meeting of the American Anthropological Association, Philadelphia, PA, December.

Gaskins, S. and Miller, P. J. (2009). The cultural roles of emotions in pretend play. In C. D. Clark (Ed.), *Transactions at play* (pp. 5–21). Lanham, MD: University Press of America.

Gaskins, S. and Paradise, R. (2010). Learning through observation. In D. F. Lancy, J. Bock and S. Gaskins (Eds.), *The anthropology of learning in childhood* (pp. 85–117). Lanham, MD: Alta Mira Press.

Göncü, A. and Gaskins, S. (2011). Comparing and extending Piaget's and Vygotsky's understandings of play: Symbolic play as individual, sociocultural, and educational interpretation. In A. D. Pellegrini (Ed.), *Oxford handbook of the development of play* (pp. 478–457). Oxford: Oxford University Press.

Gray, P. (2013). *Free to learn: Why unleashing the instinct to play will make our children happier, more self-reliant, and better students for life.* New York: Basic Books.

Haight, W. and Miller, P. J. (1993). *Pretending at home: Early development in a sociocultural context.* Albany, NY: State University of New York Press.

Lancy, D. F. (2007). Accounting for variability in mother-child play. *American Anthropologist, 109,* 273–284.

Lancy, D. F. (2008). *The anthropology of childhood: Cherubs, chattels, changelings.* Cambridge: Cambridge University Press.

Lillard, A. (2007). Guided participation: How mothers structure and children understand pretend play. In A. Göncü and S. Gaskins (Eds.), *Play and development: Evolutionary, sociocultural, and functional perspectives* (pp. 131–153). Mahwah, NJ: Lawrence Erlbaum Associates.

Mead, G. H. (1934). *Mind, self, and society.* Chicago: University of Chicago Press.

Mintz, S. (2004) *Huck's raft.* Cambridge, MA: Harvard University Press.

Piaget, J. (1954). *The construction of reality in the child.* New York: Basic Books.

Piaget, J. (1962). *Play dreams and imitation in childhood.* New York: Norton.

Rogoff, B., Moore, L., Najafi, B., Dexter, A., Correa-Chávez, M. and Solís, J. (2007). Children's development of cultural repertoires through participation in everyday routines and practices. In J. E. Grusec and P. D. Hastings (Eds.), *Handbook of socialisation* (pp. 490–515). New York: Guilford.

Schwartzman, H. B. (1979). *Transformations.* New York: Plenum Press.

Singer, D. G., Golinkoff, R. M. and Hirsh-Pasek, K. (Eds.) (2006). *Play = learning: How play motivates and enhances children's cognitive and social-emotional growth.* New York: Oxford University Press.

Smilansky, S. (1968). *The effects of sociodramatic play on disadvantaged school children.* New York: Wiley.

Smith, P. K. (2009). *Children and play: Understanding children's worlds.* Malden, MA: Wiley-Blackwell.

Vygotsky, L. S. (1978) *Mind in society: The development of higher mental processes.* Cambridge, MA: Harvard University Press.

3 Brazilian children at play: reviewing relationships between play and culture

Yumi Gosso, Ilka D. Bichara and Ana M. A. Carvalho

Three 3–4-year-old girls are making cakes with mud, dressing them with leaves, sticks, bottle corks, etc. They chat between them: "The cake is ready, now we're placing the cherry . . ." "Yes, and placing it in the oven." One of them asks the researcher: "Do you like my cake? It's a meat cake." "Mine is a chocolate cake," says the other. The first girl offers the researcher a scribbled sheet of paper: "Here, take it, it's the cake recipe."

Introduction

Like many large countries, Brazil is very diverse in terms of its physical and sociocultural settings, ethnicity (strongly characterized by miscegenation) and socioeconomic conditions. In large metropolitan areas, slums with precarious dwelling conditions, scarce health and educational facilities can neighbor upper socioeconomic level residential areas where families can afford private medical and educational services and live in large houses or condos with private gardens. In rural areas, many families work as hired hands engaging in temporary work on large farms, while others strive to make a living through subsistence agriculture or small cattle breeding on their own little plot of land, often in very isolated and resourceless locations. Yet in other cases, a group of families may constitute a self-sufficient community, located in remote areas from larger population centers: Indian communities which still preserve to some degree their cultural traditions and ways of living; Afro-Brazilian communities — *quilombos* — founded by fugitive slaves before slavery was abolished in the late nineteenth century; communities organized around a shared subsistence activity, like coconut collectors in the state of Piauí or fishing communities in the large coastal areas. In the case of these communities, there is tremendous variation in patterns of life and childrearing beliefs and practices that are rooted in their socio-historical backgrounds and histories of exploitation (e.g., slavery, colonialism). At the same time, the outskirts of large cities are frequently occupied by families who migrate from rural areas. These communities are neither typically rural nor really urban; older members stick to rural values and ways of living while the new generations are already acculturated with respect to urban values, aspirations, and ways of life.

The physical and geographical characteristics of Brazil also influence economic activities and subsistence patterns, often interacting with characteristics of the people who occupy the different ecosystems: from the tropical Amazon rain forest to dry inland areas of the Northeast region; from the floodlands in the Central region to the coastal area, which extends for over 8,000 km with marked climate differences; and from large urban areas, mainly in the richer South and Southeast regions, to smaller towns with different cultural and socioeconomic dynamics.

Despite the huge diversity in ethnic groups, geography, economic and subsistence patterns, and cultural practices, an outstanding similarity can be observed in some aspects of children's social activities; whatever the immediate context they live in, children do play. How much, when, how, which play activities and with whom children play are likely to vary according to physical, social and cultural circumstances. This notwithstanding, the "deep structure" of games such as hide-and seek, chasing, marbles, kites, make-believe, and use and construction of play artifacts is clearly recognizable.

The diversity of Brazilian contexts of child development provides a wealth of opportunities for comparative reflections on the Brazilian research literature on children's play. Although not every sociocultural context is reflected in this literature, we select from the available research those instances that highlight cultural-regional diversity and "universal" aspects of games and play activities in different contexts, exploring relationships between play and culture in two interdependent senses: the creative appropriation of macroculture and the construction of peer cultures. The studies are typically focused on free play in natural settings (pre-school yards, playgroups, community spaces near the children's homes) and used ethnographic/ethological observation procedures. These methodological options are compatible with the perspective from which we look at play in childhood and its connection to cultural practices, as ontogenetic adaptations that evolved along the process that produced *Homo sapiens* as a biologically sociocultural species (Bruner et al. 1976; Cole 2002; Seidl-de-Moura 2005; Bichara et al. 2009).

Conceptual frameworks

Culture and play

Our focus here is on play as a cultural activity. Play is influenced by the economic context, by adults' views on ludic and non-ludic activities and by the way values are transmitted to children by the adults (Göncü et al. 2007). Conceptions and values regarding childhood and play vary between different cultures and sub-cultures. Adults may attribute an important developmental role to play activities and thus encourage them and engage as playmates with children. But in a number of cultural groups, play is considered a typical childhood activity that children perform spontaneously, with no need for adult guidance or participation. Because it is a spontaneous activity, it is perhaps less valued than other more "serious" activities, a devaluation that can lead to limitations of time and space for free play (Gaskins et al. 2007; Gaskins, Chapter 2 in this volume).

Children at play reproduce and recreate the specificities of their cultural environment (Corsaro 2003; Gosso 2010). One of the factors that influences how (and to what extent) they do so is the degree to which they are exposed to adult life experiences. In some societies, children's participation in adult activities is sparse, while in others it is witnessed abundantly. Children often spontaneously replicate what they observe, creating miniature objects and situations to represent the adult world they are allowed to share (Mead 1975; see Ng'asike, Chapter 9 in this volume). Children from American Indian societies, rural communities, and some small remote villages who observe and participate in adult activities and represent them in their play activities may have a smoother and more gradual transition from play to adult occupations as they grow up (Gosso and Otta 2003). Nunes (2002) believes that in postmodern societies children are isolated from the adult social world, which has the potential to impair the integration of cultural activities into play. In some cultural communities, children acquire a better understanding of the social world through freedom to experience time and space independent of adult concerns about stimulating play activities. Nevertheless, since they participate in the adult world, children often represent it in their play activities. Observing rural children at play, Leite (2002) noticed that play and work coexist; children perform several tasks while giving them a ludic character. By contrast, urban children who have less direct contact with the adult world may represent it in less elaborate ways. As an example, a 4-year-old boy pretending to be the father leaves the "house," saying "Bye, I'm leaving to work." He leaves with his "briefcase," stops at a distance from the "house" and waits. After a few minutes, he comes back, "Hello, I'm back" (Morais and Carvalho 1994).

Another salient aspect of children's play activity that is imported from their sociocultural context involves gender stereotypes. These stereotypes may be expressed in differential choice of games, in attribution of roles in pretend play (Morais and Carvalho 1994), or in perceptions about gender appropriateness of play activities (Smith et al. 1992).

Play is, thus, deeply embedded in the sociocultural context and is itself a cultural phenomenon. Through the creative appropriation ("interpretive reproduction" in Corsaro's terminology) of their sociocultural world, playmates create particular peer cultures, a "micro-aspect" of that sociocultural world (Corsaro 1985, 2003).

Children's play within the collectivism–individualism continuum

The prevalence of collectivistic or individualistic values and ways of subsistence in different societies is an interesting angle for the comparative analysis of play. Individualistic cultures value independence, privacy, competition, egotism, self-fulfillment, close relations with a limited number of people, and free expression of emotions (Oysermann et al. 2002). Collectivistic cultures value intra-group relations over individual fulfillment, have closer social ties and relationships, emphasize group harmony and cooperation rather than competition, restrict the expression of negative emotions, and place group above individual welfare (Kitayama et al. 1997; Conway et al. 2001; Takahashi et al. 2002; Gosso et al. 2007).

An interesting example of the potential impact of collectivist and individualistic values and ways of subsistence on children's behavior was reported by Gosso (pers. comm., February 2014). While working as a teacher for middle-class children in an urban school, and for Parakanã Amerindian children at their village school, she suggested to both groups an activity that involved finding the card with the correct word among several cards scattered on the ground. She was impressed by the different reactions in each group; while urban children competed fiercely to be the first to grasp the correct card, all of the Indian children looked toward the correct card, but did not move from their places to grasp it.

Large- and small-scale contexts for play

The conception of time in communities that express collectivistic and individualistic tendencies can be peculiar. For instance, among the Xikrin Indians of Pará State, a child who interrupts the father's work by seizing his tool is not scolded or required to return it. Instead, the father patiently waits until the child stops using the tool to recover it and resume work. When Xikrin Indian children wash their objects and do not clean them properly, adults will not perform the task for them; they believe that children will eventually learn how to do it properly and for the time being did it as well as they could. Among the Xikrin, many adult tasks depend on weather conditions; on a rainy day, one must be patient and wait for the rain to stop—and children follow the same routine. These children do not have industrialized toys and generally have fewer toys than do urban children, either self-made (mud puppets, straw baskets) or made by their parents (bow and arrow, small sculpted wooden canoes). In some of these communities, children do have access to TV but usually spend most of their time on external activities, playing with age-mates or helping adults. Play is considered a childhood activity that does not require adult stimulation and offers no reason for concern. Children play, just as adults work (Cohn 2002). Cohn's observations apply equally to several other Indian communities (Nunes 2002; Gosso et al. 2005).

A very different picture emerges in large urban centers, where the rhythm of life is accelerated and most activities are not dependent on weather conditions. Children's activities, including play, are programmed for certain times and spaces. Adults and children often live separate lives. There is significant concern about the future and about achievements in childhood in order to attain better occupational positions in society. Parents look for the best schooling options and closely monitor children's school performance. When play is considered as contributing to child development, parents stimulate it, mainly through the acquisition of industrialized toys and related activities. Under these circumstances, children have fewer opportunities for playing with peers and play more often with adults, either parents or other caregivers. Families are smaller, and interaction with peers is frequently limited to the school environment. The higher the socioeconomic level of the family, the greater the concern with the child's cognitive development, with more stimulation provided and more exposure to electronic devices (Beraldo and Carvalho 2003, 2006; Lordelo and Carvalho 2003, 2005, 2008).

Diamond (2012) states that in small-scale societies, children's education is more natural and informal, resulting from intense social interaction, while in modern societies even simple courtesy rules require formal teaching. For instance, in towns where adults are usually not acquainted with their neighbors, vehicular traffic is intense and people are exposed to kidnapping and other forms of violence, children are not free or safe to play with their peers. As a consequence, there is a need for special environments where children are taught to play with peers, where adults mediate children's relationships with other children and teach them basic rules of social interaction.

As a general trend, in small-scale societies, people are closer to one another, and no or fewer restrictions are imposed on children's lives. Children move around freely, observe what happens around them and take part in it, whereas in modern societies, children's participation in the life of adults is limited and may even include separate environments for them. However, even in large urban areas like Salvador, in the state of Bahia, Brazil, children—particularly the poorest—collectively and creatively appropriate for their play activities urban spaces that are not theirs, playing marbles or flying kites on landscaped median strips of large avenues or football on the sidewalks of busy streets. All these childhood activities are examples of creative re-signification of components of adult culture by the play group (Cotrim et al. 2009).

Considering the different degrees of contact children have with adult activities in small-scale and modern societies, it is not surprising that symbolic play themes in the former more often mirror adult daily life as compared to the latter: child care, domestic chores, diverse subsistence chores (hunting, fishing, collecting and selling fruits, riding on horseback or using boats or carts for transport). In small-scale societies in which children do not have access to TV (Indian communities) and do (caiçara communities, i.e. coastal communities), play themes are linked to everyday life rather than to TV and other fantasy characters. Support for such a contention is detailed in the next section.

Children's play in different Brazilian sociocultural contexts

Combu Island children

Some 375 families live in four small communities on Combu Island, on the Guamá river, about 1.5 km from the urban area of Belém, the capital of Pará state, Brazil. There is no electric energy supply or sanitation; some houses have electric generators, others use oil lamps; clean water is collected from a public tap in the city of Belém and carried home in plastic bowls. The main economic activity in these communities is the collection of açaí, the fruit of a palm tree whose juice is valued in the North region. Other produce such as cacao, mango and cashew are also collected and transported to be sold in Belém. Observations of 13 children from two communities in this area (Teixeira and Alves 2008) revealed that these children took part in practically all aspects of community life and imported it into their games (Figure 3.1). In their play they pretended to collect water from the river to wash objects representing dishes and pottery or took them to the river shore to be washed. Pretend play was often about collecting and selling açaí.

Figure 3.1   Parakanã children play with bow and arrow, replicating adult activities.

Parakanã Indian children

Parakanã Indians live in five villages in the Southeast of Pará state, in an Indian designated area, with limited contact with other cultural groups. Children, elders and most
women only speak their native idiom. There is no electric energy supply. They preserve their social organization and hierarchy, rituals, many cultural traditions such as
hunting, collecting, several rituals, and practice small-scale agriculture (planting manioc and corn). Men are responsible for hunting and making important decisions (marriage arrangements, moving the village to a new site, location of a new area for
agriculture, etc.). Women are in charge of body painting, gathering, preparing manioc
flour, and carrying animals killed by their husbands back to the village. Agricultural
tasks are divided between men and women.

In Parakanã Indian villages, each family has its own house, used basically for
sleeping in home-woven hammocks. The houses are built with wooden walls and straw
roofs with a single entrance facing the center of the village. Families usually have a
separate building to use as a kitchen where they light bonfires to roast or smoke-cure
the meat. Some kitchens are built with straw walls. There are no toilets inside the
houses. All the villages are built next to rivers. Although fishing is not a particularly
relevant activity for Parakanã Indians, rivers are very important for them. It is where
they bathe and wash their things; they use them also for transport to more distant locations and to visit other villages in canoes sculpted from a single tree trunk.

About a hundred people lived in each village when our study was conducted
(Gosso et al. 2005; Gosso et al. 2007). School-age children attended the village school
and, in their free time, played by the river and around the village with mixed-aged

Figure 3.2 Parakanã children diving in the river.

peers. Typical play activities included diving, swimming and fishing in the river; play-chase and hide-and-seek around the village; hunting with bows and arrows (boys); sculpting mud into bowls, animals, and human figures and weaving baskets (mostly girls) (Figure 3.2). From a young age, children take part in productive activities, help-ing parents in agricultural and hunting/fishing tasks.

Children in caiçara communities

Ubatuba is a coastal area in São Paulo state, between the mountains of Serra do Mar and the Atlantic Ocean, with a series of beach areas interrupted by steep cliffs. Many caiçara or coastal communities are located in isolated regions with no access except by boat or by foot. Some families still live on fishing and subsistence agriculture, while others are hired as domestic help in weekend houses kept by affluent São Paulo city dwellers. Certain caiçara traditions such as local music, fairs, regional and religious celebrations are still practiced by many families. Although many families own a TV set, the habit of sitting on the doorstep to chat with neighbors in the early evenings while their children play outdoors is strongly rooted in these families.

In cataloging the play of poor caiçara children during school breaks, Morais and Otta (2003) found differences in pretend play themes of caiçara and children living in urban areas of Brazil. Caiçara children's play themes focused on riding on horseback, introducing snakes in the plot, swimming in the river and bathing in the waterfall, among others, that were not found in urban children and reflected differences between the two groups' immediate environments. Also noticeable was the variety of games and activities created by caiçara children, which may be attributed to the absence of structured toys. On the whole, pre-school children in some large urban centers in Brazil display more fantasy play themes during make-believe play (particularly among boys, Morais and Carvalho 1994) than caiçara children do (Morais and Otta 2003) or children in Indian communities (Gosso and Otta 2003). Perhaps this is due to the closer contact that caiçara children and Indian children have with the adult world (compared to urban children, particularly with the "male" world, or the world of work outside the home) and to the challenging and stimulating environment they are exposed to compared with urban children. The Indian and caiçara children are surrounded by forests to explore, trees to climb, and rivers or the ocean to swim in. They may not need to resort to imaginary adventure themes during play because that is a part of their daily reality. Furthermore, in comparison to low socioeconomic, urban children who are often viewed poorly by teachers, caiçara children were seen by teachers as clever, lively and attentive. Again, these differences may be related to differences in daily life such as frequent interaction with the natural environment, time and space for free play, a safe and accessible social network of peers, relatives and neighbors, and a stable set of social norms and values characteristic of a traditional sub-culture (Morais and Otta 2003).

Xocó and quilombo children

Focusing on the creative use of environmental and social resources in cultural communities in Brazil, Bichara (2003) studied two communities that have settled for over two hundred years by the shores of São Francisco river, in the state of Sergipe, Brazil: a Xocó Indian village (about two hundred and fifty people) and a *quilombo* (about a hundred Afro-descendant families). Both are poor communities that subsist on fishing, agriculture and some cattle breeding. Although largely enculturated and cross-bred, Xocó Indians preserve some cultural traditions such as the production of pottery and Indian ornaments, the medical use of plants, and the Toré dance, which is a celebration in which the participation of children has been observed (Bichara et al. 2012). A small beach area and shallow waters are available to Xocó children on their island, in contrast to the steep and muddy shores available for *quilombo* children. Otherwise, daily life is similar in the two communities.

Children play freely around the village and cultivated areas by the river and in its waters. In both groups, around 20 percent of the observed play activities took place in the river or at its shores, particularly during the dry summer season: swimming and diving, jumping over obstacles in the water, playing football, play-chasing, building prisons, castles and other edifices or objects with sand, mud, water and other available materials and developing make-believe plots around them (thieves and police, princess in the castle). Girls were often observed intermingling play activities with washing clothes or pottery in the river. The river is also a central character in games related to transport; a wood board or a tree trunk is used to navigate the river as a canoe, a boat or a horse.

Further examples

Another well-known example of creative adjustment to available material in the development of play activities is the variety of local resources adapted to traditional games. Cotrim et al. (2009) report the use of plastic bottle corks in the game of marbles in Salvador, Brazil. The general play literature suggests a variety of other objects with the same function: from marbles made from marble in Ancient Egypt and glass marbles in Ancient Greece and Rome, to mud pellets and cashew nuts in different Brazilian regions (Carvalho and Pontes 2003). Plastic bottles are used as "safe harbors" in one of the varieties of Pira (the local designation for a chasing game practiced in the streets of a poor district of Belém, in the state of Pará), called Pira na garrafa (Pira in the bottle); other varieties are Pira in the high (where the chased child escapes by climbing a street post or similar structure), Pira on the timberwork (where the rule is to escape by climbing the wooden structure of an unfinished house), Pira help (where children who are caught help the pursuer to catch other partners) and Pira glue (where children who are not caught can help those that are "frozen" by the pursuer by touching and "ungluing" them). This complex set of games, while preserving the structure of play-chasing, was embellished and diversified in this particular context using its available resources, becoming a component of the playgroup's culture (Magalhães et al. 2003).

The two last variants of Pira also indicate the creative use of social circumstances. Pira is usually played by a mixed-age and mixed-gender group. A recurrent observation in this sort of social group is the existence of different rules for older and younger children—called "little angels," or "milk-and-coffee," in different playgroup cultures—who can take part in play activities in a protected or less exposed way. Magalhães et al. (2003) propose the notion of bridge toys to refer to artifacts—such as plastic bags or small sheets of paper—compatible with younger children's abilities to "fly kites," allowing them to gradually be trained into the use of real kites. Specific rules and artifacts exemplified here are usually specific to particular peer cultures. Similar examples are found in Corsaro's ethnography on peer cultures in other parts of the world (Corsaro 1985, 2003).

In some of the relatively isolated contexts discussed here where play themes still largely mirror the local culture and habits, reflections of mainstream industrialized culture on children's play may also occur. Besides the already quoted examples of the use of plastic bottles, an interesting instance of interpenetration between themes and resources from different cultural contexts is an episode offered in the work of Seixas et al. (2012) at Frades Island, on the coast of Salvador, Brazil. A group of boys from the local fishing community organized a boat race with sailboats made of synthetic trays that markets use as food containers. The boats were carried to the sea and released on the waves' crest to compete for time of arrival at the shore. In this case, as in others, the theme and development of the game were deeply merged in the local culture, but the material from which the boats were made was not part of it.

Final reflections

The variability and complexity of developmental and play contexts in a large country such as Brazil evoke some reflections on the ways of life constructed by human beings, particularly in the last two centuries, with the urbanization model imposed by the industrial revolution. Life in small-scale societies such as those of the Parakanã Indians seems to be embodied in the concept of the human environment of evolutionary adaptation, which is strikingly different from what is observed in large urban centers in Brazil today. As far as play is concerned, an inversion of priorities seems to have occurred. In our opinion, a devaluation of play in large societies is apparently in progress.

Does such devaluation affect the adaptive value of play in ways that may result in different developmental outcomes for children? The answer to this question requires resuming the discussion on play's adaptive value. Assuming what has been proposed by several researchers since the nineteenth century that the adaptive value of play is training for adult life (Pellegrini and Smith 1998), the current trend in large urban contexts to train children in cognitively oriented activities for life in a competitive world does not seem incongruous. Could it be that playing make-believe competitive games in a virtual world is perhaps as adaptive in a contemporary world as playing hunting in the forest? But assuming that play is an ontogenetic adaptation, that is, a behavioral system that enhances adaptation in immature stages of life (Pellegrini and Smith 1998; Spinka et al. 2001), the devaluation of play activities might have unforeseen consequences. From this perspective, opportunity for peer interactions and relationships, better sense of mastery, the development of competence and self-effectiveness through children's experiences with novel activities, versatile movements to deal with unpredicted events such as falls and loss of balance, and versatile emotional resources to deal with stressful and unexpected situations would be the main consequences of opportunities for free play, regardless of context.

If the aforementioned thesis is true, does childhood as lived in large urban centers, lacking playmates of different ages, unsupervised play and unrestricted access to adults, make a difference for the future? Regardless of whether it is a small-scale or urban setting, when interacting in groups, children reinterpret their societies and their cultures in creative ways. However, the conception of children as active agents of their development from an early age seems too often mistranslated as cultural practices regarding children's choice of time, space, play partners and play activities, and a critical examination of this would be timely.

References

Beraldo, K. E. A. and Carvalho, A. M. A. (2003). Na cidade grande [In the big city]. In A. M. A. Carvalho, C. M. C. Magalhaes, F. A. R. Pontes and I. D. Bichara (Eds.), *Brincadeira e cultura: Viajando pelo Brasil que brinca* (vol. 1, pp. 157–185). São Paulo: Casa do Psicólogo.

Beraldo, K. E. A. and Carvalho, A. M. A. (2006). Ouvindo educadoras de creche sobre suas experiências de trabalho [Listening to pre-school educators talking about their work experiences]. *Temas em Psicologia, 14*, 35–49.

Bichara, I. D. (2003). Nas águas do Velho Chico [In the waters of the São Francisco river]. In A. M. A. Carvalho, C. M. C. Magalhaes, F. A. R. Pontes and I. D. Bichara (Eds.), *Brincadeira e cultura: Viajando pelo Brasil que brinca* (vol. 1, pp. 89–107). São Paulo: Casa do Psicólogo.

Bichara, I. D., Lordelo, E. R. and Carvalho, A. M. A. (2009). Brincar ou brincar: a perspectiva da Psicologia Evolucionista sobre a brincadeira [To play or . . . to play: Evolutionary Psychology's perspective on play]. In E. Otta and M. E. Yamamoto (Eds.), *Fundamentos de Psicologia Evolucionista* (pp. 104–113). Rio de Janeiro: Guanabara-Koogan.

Bichara, I. D., Lordelo, E. R., Santos, A. K. and Pontes, F. A. R. (2012). Play and gender issues in rural and urban Brazilian contexts. In A. C. Bastos, K. Uriko and J. Valsiner (Eds.), *Cultural dynamics of women's lives* (pp. 197–208). Charlotte, NC: Information Age Publishing, Inc.

Bruner, J. S., Jolly, A. and Sylva, K. (1976). *Play: Its role in development and evolution.* Harmondsworth: Penguin.

Carvalho, A. M. A. and Pontes, F. A. R. (2003) Brincadeira é cultura [Play is culture]. In A. M. A. Carvalho, C. M. C. Magalhaes, F. A. R. Pontes and I. D. Bichara (Eds.), *Brincadeira e cultura: Viajando pelo Brasil que brinca* (vol. 1, pp. 15–30). São Paulo: Casa do Psicólogo.

Chen, X. (2011). Culture, peer relationships, and human development. In L. A. Jensen (Ed.), *Bridging cultural and developmental approaches to psychology: New syntheses in theory, research, and policy* (pp. 92–112). New York: Oxford University Press.

Cohn, C. (2002). A experiência da infância e o aprendizado entre os Xikrin [The experience of childhood and learning among the Xikrin]. In A. L. Silva, A. V. L. S. Macedo and A. Nunes (Eds.), *Crianças Indígenas: ensaios antropológicos* (pp. 117–149). São Paulo: Global.

Cole, M. (2002). Culture and development. In H. Keller, Y. H. Poortinga and A. Schölmerich (Eds.), *Between culture and biology: Perspectives on ontogenetic development* (pp. 303–319). Cambridge: Cambridge University Press.

Conway, L. G., Ryder, A. G., Tweed, R. G. and Sokol, B. W. (2001). Intranational cultural variation: Exploring further implications of collectivism within the United States. *Journal of Cross-Cultural Psychology, 32*(6), 681–697.

Corsaro, W. A. (1985). *Friendship and peer culture in the early years.* St. Louis, MO: Ablex.

Corsaro, W. A. (2003). *We´re friends, right? Inside kid's culture.* Washington, DC: Joseph Henry Press.

Cotrim, G. S., Fiaes, C. S., Marques, R. L. and Bichara, I. D. (2009). Espaços urbanos para (e das) brincadeiras: um estudo exploratório na cidade de Salvador (BA) [Urban play spaces: An exploratory study in Salvador]. *Psicologia: Teoria e Prática, 11*(1), 50–61.

Diamond, J. (2012). *The world until yesterday: What can we learn from traditional societies?* New York: Viking Penguin.

Gaskins, S., Haight, W. and Lancy, D. (2007). The cultural construction of play. In A. Göncü and S. Gaskins (Eds.), *Play and development: Evolutionary, sociocultural and functional perspectives* (pp. 179–202). New York: Lawrence Erlbaum Associates.

Göncü, A., Jain, J. and Tuermer, U. (2007). Children's play as cultural interpretation. In A. Göncü and S. Gaskins (Eds.), *Play and development: Evolutionary, sociocultural and functional perspectives* (pp. 155–178). New York: Lawrence Erlbaum Associates.

Gosso Y. (2010). Play in different cultures. In P. K. Smith (Ed.), *Children and play* (pp. 80–98). New York: John Wiley & Sons, Inc.

Gosso, Y., Morais, M. L. S. and Otta, E. (2007). Pretend play of Brazilian children: A window into different cultural worlds. *Journal of Cross-Cultural Psychology, 38*(5), 539–558.

Gosso, Y. and Otta, E. (2003). Em uma aldeia Parakanã [In a Parakanã village]. In A. M. A Carvalho, C. M. C. Magalhaes, F. A. R. Pontes and I. D. Bichara (Eds.), *Brincadeira e cultura: Viajando pelo Brasil que brinca* (vol. 1, pp. 33–76). São Paulo: Casa do Psicólogo.

Gosso, Y., Otta, E., Morais, M. L. S., Ribeiro, F. J. L. and Busab, V. S. R. (2005). Play in hunter-gatherer society. In A. D. Pellegrini and P. K. Smith (Eds.), *The nature of play: Great apes and humans* (pp. 213–253). New York: Guilford.

Kitayama, S., Markus, H. R., Matsumoto, H. and Norasakkunkit, V. (1997). Individual and collective processes in the construction of the self: Self-enhancement in the United States and self-criticism in Japan, *Journal of Personality and Social Psychology, 72*(6), 1245–1267.

Leite, M. I. F. P. (2002). Brincadeiras de menina na escola e na rua: reflexões da pesquisa no campo [Girls' play activities at school and on the streets]. *Cadernos Cedes, 56*, 6–80.

Lordelo, E. R. and Carvalho, A. M. A. (2003). Educação infantil e psicologia: Para que brincar? [Early childhood education and psychology: What is play for?] *Psicologia, Ciência e Profissão, 23*, 14–21.

Lordelo, E. R. and Carvalho, A. M. A. (2005). Infância hoje—e sempre? [Childhood today—and forever?] *Pátio – Educação Infantil, 32*, 1168–1170.

Lordelo, E. R. and Carvalho, A. M. A. (2008). Infância roubada: brincadeira e educação infantil no Brasil [Stolen childhood: Play and early education in Brazil]. In L. V. C. Moreira and A. M. A. Carvalho (Eds.), *Família e educação: Olhares da psicologias* (pp. 119–138). São Paulo: Paulinas.

Magalhães, C. M. C., Souza, A. R. and Carvalho, A. M. A. (2003). Piras no Riacho Doce [Play-chasing in Riacho Doce]. In A. M. A. Carvalho, C. M. C. Magalhaes, F. A. R. Pontes and I. D. Bichara (eds.), *Brincadeira e cultura: Viajando pelo Brasil que brinca* (vol. 1, pp. 77–880). São Paulo: Casa do Psicólogo.

Mead, M. (1975). Children's play style: Potentialities and limitations of its use as a cultural indicator. *Anthropological Quarterly, 48*(3), 157–181.

Morais, M. L. S. and Carvalho, A. M. A. (1994). Faz de conta: temas, papéis e regras na brincadeiras de crianças de quatro anos [Pretend play: Themes, roles and rules in 4-year-old children], *Boletim de Psicologia, 44*, 1–17.

Morais, M. L. S. and Otta, E. (2003). Entre a serra e o mar [Between the mountains and the sea]. In A. M. A. Carvalho, C. M. C. Magalhaes, F. A. R. Pontes and I. D. Bichara (Eds.), *Brincadeira e cultura: Viajando pelo Brasil que brinca* (vol. 1, pp. 127–156). São Paulo: Casa do Psicólogo.

Nunes, A. (2002). No tempo e no espaço: Brincadeiras das crianças A'uwe-Xavante [Time and space: A'uwe-Xavante children at play]. In A. L. Silva, A. V. L. S. Macedo and A. Nunes (Eds.), *Crianças Indígenas: Ensaios antropológicos* (pp. 64–99). São Paulo: Global.

Oysermann, D., Coon, H. M. and Kemmelmeier, M. (2002). Rethinking individualism and collectivism: Evaluation of theoretical assumptions and meta-analyses, *Psychological Bulletin, 128*(1), 3–72.

Pellegrini, A. D. and Smith, P. K. (1998). The development of play during childhood: Forms and possible functions. *Child Psychology and Psychiatry Review, 3*(2): 51–57.

Seidl-de-Moura, M. L. (2005). Bases para uma psicologia do desenvolvimento sociocultural e evolucionista [Bases for a sociocultural and evolutionary developmental psychology]. In F. A. R. Pontes, C. Magalhães, R. Brito and W. Martin (Eds.), *Temas pertinentes à construção da psicologia contemporânea* (pp. 16–41). Belém: EDUFPA.

Seixas, A. A. C., Becker, B. and Bichara, I. D. (2012). Reprodução interpretativa e cultura de pares nos grupos de brincadeira da Ilha dos Frades/BA [Interpretive reproduction and peer culture in play groups in Frades Island, Bahia]. *Psico, 43*(4), 541–551.

Smith, P. K., Hunter, T., Carvalho, A. M. A. and Costabile, A. (1992). Children's perceptions of playfighting, playchasing and real fighting: A cross-cultural interview study. *Social Development, 1*(3), 211–229.

Spinka, M., Newberry, R. C. and Bekoff, M. (2001). Mammalian play: Training for the unexpected. *The Quarterly Review of Biology, 76*(2), 141–168.

Takahashi, K., Ohara, N., Antonucci, T. C. and Akiyama, H. (2002). Commonalities and differences in close relationships among Americans and Japanese: A comparison by the individualism/collectivism concept. *International Journal of Behavioral Development, 26*(5), 453–465.

Teixeira, S. R. S. and Alves, J. M. (2008). O contexto das brincadeiras das crianças ribeirinhas da Ilha do Combu [The context of riverine children's play at Combu Island]. *Psicologia: Reflexão e Crítica, 21*(3), 374–382.

4   Play in Caribbean cultural communities

Jaipaul L. Roopnarine

> It was the August school holidays in Guyana. The boys were free to play on the banks of the canal in the farmlands behind their homes. They dug mud from the edges of the canal and made animal figures. After shaping the figures, they would leave them to dry in the hot midday sun. During the entire holiday season, they would return to the same spot to make different mud figures and to swim in the cool, murky water of the canal.

Introduction

As the anecdote above suggests, young Caribbean children from diverse ethnic backgrounds engage in different levels of play in community parks, on the streets, on beaches, on the banks of streams and rivers, and in yards (Figure 4.1). Some childhood games and play activities are seen across Caribbean communities; others are confined to specific locales. Despite such activities among children, however, and despite research data on the benefits of play stimulation for at-risk children, play remains at the periphery of parent–child activities and early childhood education practice in Caribbean cultural communities. This chapter discusses beliefs about play and development in English-speaking Caribbean cultural communities (e.g., Guyana, Jamaica, Trinidad and Tobago, St. Lucia), cultural models that may apply to understanding play in Caribbean communities, the meager literature on the play of Caribbean children, and implications for early childhood education and teacher training in the Caribbean context.

Theoretical considerations

Taking into account economic and social conditions, the ecocultural model (Whiting and Whiting 1975) and life history theory (Kaplan et al. 2000) offer the best propositions for understanding patterns of socialization and play activities of children in Caribbean cultural communities. The ecocultural model stresses the roles of environment and history, maintenance systems (e.g., subsistence patterns, modes of production, etc.),

Figure 4.1 Caribbean children play in diverse settings including beaches.

learning environments of the child (e.g., settings, caregivers), the behavioral tendencies and beliefs of the adult, and projective-expressive systems (e.g. religion and ideology) as influencing both childrearing strategies and the nature and quality of parent–child interaction patterns. It is argued that the learning environment is the major mechanism for determining the types of social activities and behavioral patterns of children in cultural context (Whiting and Whiting 1975). Following this model, factors in the developmental niche of Caribbean cultural communities—parental beliefs systems, childrearing customs, and the setting—shape parent–child activities and developmental pathways in children (Super and Harkness 1997). However, it is likely that the priorities parents establish in harsh ecologies with poor material resources may entail greater focus on survival and children's health rather than on social and cognitive stimulation via play activities (LeVine 2004). Striking a balance between meeting the child's more immediate needs and learning for future gains can be complex and depends upon a range of sociodemographic and inter- and intra-personal factors (Bock 2002).

Cultural context for early childhood development

The family context for childhood socialization and caregivers' beliefs and practices have long been known to have profound effects on childhood development (Sigel and McGillicuddy-DeLisi 2002). In Caribbean cultural communities, parent–child socialization practices occur in diverse mating and marital systems: visiting unions, common-law unions, married couples, mother–daughter alliances, and grandparent households, among other family constellations (see Anderson 2007; Leo-Rhynie and Brown 2013). Despite variations in the levels and quality of emotional and cognitive caregiving in different ethnic groups, socioeconomic strata, and family systems (Anderson 2007), a few basic socialization practices and goals appear pervasive across the Caribbean and could shed light on the importance of play in childhood development. For instance, disciplinary practices are often harsh and are rooted in biblical injunctions about shaping the child's behavior or are viewed as essential to maintain control over children (Brown and Johnson 2008); praise and rewards for "good behavior" are used sparingly (Leo-Rhynie 1997). Obedience and unilateral respect are highly valued by adults (Barrow and Ince 2008; Wilson et al. 2003). Early developmental expectations of basic social and cognitive skills in children are evident among less educated parents from low-income backgrounds (Leo-Rhynie and Brown 2013). Ethnic and religious socialization is prevalent across groups (Roopnarine et al. 2013a).

Recent research on families in Guyana and Trinidad substantiates the use of a combination of warmth and control in childhood socialization (Roopnarine et al. 2013b). What is less clear is the extent to which these methods of childrearing permit cognitive and emotional elbow room for parents and children to engage in playful interactions. Just as in other cultural settings, these newer studies suggest that harsh parenting and poor neighborhood quality seem to affect children's prosocial skills negatively—a major ingredient for social participation in play activities with peers. Moreover, these studies indicate that children displayed high levels of antisocial behaviors in classroom settings, possibly a result of controlling parenting practices that further undermine children's attempts at play with others (Roopnarine et al. 2013b).

Quality of caregiving environments

There is ample evidence that children who grow up in home environments with high doses of stimulation and that are adequately furnished with play materials and books perform significantly better cognitively than those in home environments with deficient cognitive stimulation and poor material resources (Pungello et al. 2010). The risks associated with poor home environments in the Caribbean may be exacerbated with deteriorating community conditions (Krishnakumar et al. 2014). Although most Caribbean countries are classified as middle income, high rates of poverty in some countries (e.g., Guyana and Jamaica) prevent parents and other caregivers from providing educational materials and toys for young children. Not surprisingly, a study of socialization patterns in Trinidad and Dominica (Barrow and Ince 2008) and two others conducted in Jamaica found that there was a lack of books and toys for engagement in play among poor families (Landman et al. 1983; Samms-Vaughan 2006). When present, toys were viewed as valuable commodities; they were kept away from children except when offered under adult supervision (Barrow and Ince 2008). Worse yet, parents were seemingly unaware of their role in early cognitive stimulation (Leo-Rhynie and Brown 2013). A study of 179 rural mothers in Grenada indicated that

46 percent had no information on the early stimulation process (Charles 2004). Many early childhood education settings also lacked basic play materials, and caregivers/ early childhood teachers had limited knowledge of child development (Charles and Williams 2006).

The availability of toys was more abundant in families with good material resources, and parents tended to "have a more relaxed attitude to the wear and tear" toys receive during use by children (Barrow and Ince 2008). In more economically privileged families, parents begin to introduce educational toys when children are 2–3 years of age. Presumably, this is done to enhance early cognitive training—a phenomenon noted among Asian immigrants in the United States (Parmar et al. 2004). A perceived advantage is that introducing educational toys gives children a head start for entry into preschool programs that emphasize learning numbers, letters, and words (Barrow and Ince 2008). But children from all economic backgrounds are encouraged to use non-manufactured materials from the near environment. Good examples are the nationwide effort by the Guyana National Early Childhood Programme (GNEP) to mobilize "local artisans and furniture makers to design and produce wooden, cloth, and plastic educational toys" for use in classroom settings (Harding 2013: 176) and the routine use of local materials (e.g., Tapia House) for play enrichment at the Family Development and Children's Research Centre at the University of the West Indies in Trinidad and Tobago.

Beliefs about play and early education

As I have stated in other papers on children's play across cultures (e.g., Roopnarine 2011), parental beliefs represent the internal working models or schemas about the care and education of children. These psycho-cultural schemas are accepted by cultural communities as central to the achievement of socialization goals (Super and Harkness 1997). They vary across cultural/ethnic groups and by socioeconomic status and are susceptible to influences from sources outside of the family (e.g., institutional demands, other patterns of childrearing). For instance, Caribbean mothers' and fathers' internal working models about childhood development may change after migration from the Caribbean to North America and Europe where emphasis is placed on democratic childrearing practices (Roopnarine and Jin 2012). Parental belief systems, whether they pertain to everyday socialization goals or the importance of play in children's development, often guide the structuring of cognitive and social activities and may determine the modes and levels of input parents provide to children during these activities (Super and Harkness 1997; Sigel and McGillicuddy-DeLisi 2002).

Contrary to middle-class aspirations in North America (Morelli et al. 2003), play is rarely viewed in terms of school readiness and social adjustment (Figure 4.2). Because Caribbean parents construct and interpret their childrearing roles in the context of facilitating academic preparation, learning manners, being obedient to adults, and in providing food, clothing, and basic school materials for children, there is less of an emphasis on fostering curiosity and creativity through play (Brown 2003). Jamaican mothers believe that children should avoid messy play and be neat

Figure 4.2 Girls at play during community cultural event.

and tidy (Landman et al. 1983). Furthermore, they see play as having a time and place. Early childhood settings are for academic work and the outdoors are for play to shore up physical and socioemotional development (Long 2013). In the same vein, mothers in Trinidad and Dominica opined that play is a distraction and is sometimes problematic in that it has the potential to make children and the home environment messy. Play is tolerated if performed quietly (Barrow and Ince 2008). Even though they recognized the importance of play for learning, Dominican mothers believed that play should be curtailed (Impact Study of the Roving Caregivers Programme Research Findings 2008).

Findings of parents' and teachers' perceptions of what children should learn in preschool also show a lack of emphasis on play and learning. The majority of mothers in Jamaica, Guyana, and St. Vincent and the Grenadines indicated that the most import-ant things children should learn in preschool include: writing and spelling their names, recognizing the letters of the alphabet and accompanying sounds, number recognition, and counting. Early childhood teachers in these countries also subscribed to the same beliefs (Leo-Rhynie et al. 2009). By contrast, mothers and fathers in Caribbean immi-grant families in the United States had more diverse views about play and childhood development than their counterparts in the Caribbean (Roopnarine and Jin 2012). It is possible that these families, having been exposed to more child-centered preschool programs in the United States, may be changing the internal working models about play and early education they knew in the Caribbean.

Play in Caribbean children

What we do know about play in Caribbean families and community settings comes from descriptive accounts of children's games and from intervention studies of children at risk for developmental delays. I piece together some of this literature here in order to offer a glimpse of play in Caribbean cultural communities.

Parent–child play

Interviews with low-income mothers and fathers in common-law unions in Whitfield township in Kingston, Jamaica, suggested that fathers spent considerably more time holding and playing with infants (2.95 hours in dual-earner families and 2.60 hours in single-earner families) than in basic caregiving activities (1.08 hours in dual-earner families and .83 hours in single-earner families in feeding infants; less time in cleaning and washing infants). Mothers also spent more time in holding and playing with infants (3.53 hours in dual-earner families and 3.70 hours in single-earner families) than in specified caregiving activities (2.00 hours in dual-earner families and 2.56 hours in single-earner families in feeding infants) (Roopnarine et al. 1995). Mothers spent more time in holding and playing with infants than fathers. These levels of investment in play with young children were also recorded in the caregiving patterns of families in Georgetown, Guyana; 64 percent of men who were living with a spouse and had older children played with them, and 40 percent took children for walks and to places of amusement (Wilson and Kposowa 1994). Unfortunately, the modes of play were not mentioned in these studies. In other traditional societies (e.g., Malaysia, Brazil), mothers did not differ from fathers in amount of play with children (Benetti and Roopnarine 2006; Hossain et al. 2008).

In a study of low birth weight and appropriate birth weight Jamaican children, observations were made of mother–child play during a brief laboratory play session. The low birth weight infants were assigned to a control group and an experimental group that received home visits (one hour weekly visits from birth to eight weeks that focused on cognitive stimulation) and demonstrations of play techniques (for half an hour each week from seven months to 24 months) geared toward facilitating children's cognitive skills (Wachs et al. 2007). Overall, there were low levels of social and symbolic play between mothers and infants over the course of the study. Likewise, vocalizations and object stimulation were low at initial assessment and at 24 months. The low birth weight infants receiving intervention did not differ significantly from the low birth weight infants who did not receive intervention on any of the play measures at 24 months. Mothers with higher levels of verbal intelligence provided more support for play during the initial assessment than did mothers with lower verbal intelligence. Interestingly, children spent most of their time away from objects or engaging in simple object manipulations despite significant differences in developmental quotient (as measured by the Griffiths Mental Developmental Scales) between the low and appropriate birth weight infants (Wachs et al. 2007).

Additional insights into mother–child play in Caribbean countries can be gleaned from data on The Roving Caregivers Programme (RCP), a home-based early stimulation program implemented in Jamaica, Grenada, Dominica, St. Lucia, and St. Vincent and the Grenadines. Basically, the program provides demonstrations of play stimulation to mothers and other caregivers through the use of puppetry and literacy activities to improve parent–child relationships and early cognitive and social skills in infants and toddlers (Impact Study of the Roving Caregivers Programme Research Findings 2008; Roopnarine 2013). Observations of mother–child play in families who received and did not receive the intervention in St. Lucia indicated that mothers in both groups engaged in parallel or independent activities. Control group parents encouraged their children to play more independently whereas mothers in the intervention group employed more control during play situations and stressed the educational versus the enjoyment aspects of play. Unlike the findings on symbolic play in Jamaican infants noted above, the St. Lucian children engaged in imaginative play themes that represented the activities of their mothers and fathers (Impact Study of the Roving Caregivers Programme Research Findings 2008).

Children's play

Children's perceptions of play

Children's ideas of what constitutes play can assist in better defining and determining the value of play. In one of the few in-depth, narrative case studies to document children's attempts to define play, Long (2013) found that Jamaican 5-year-olds described their indoor play as fun and outdoor play as fun, free, natural, and happy—seemingly reflecting the perceptions of parents and teachers that play should be conducted outdoors. When pressed for a more precise definition, they emphasized the functional aspects of play, to be with friends, and to have unfettered freedom (Long 2013).

Children's games

Table 4.1 displays a sample of children's games that are played in home, school, and community settings. Teachers may encourage participation in games during school recreation periods. Cricket and different spinning top games are played across the Caribbean. Wari is played in eastern Caribbean countries. Games such as skip and gig offer children opportunities to engage in solitary play in the yard or playground; wari, cricket, and brown girl in the ring encourage high levels of cooperation and invite the use of problem-solving strategies. For the most part, these games involve few objects and thus are accessible to children from different socioeconomic backgrounds.

Play in early childhood settings

Assessments (using the Early Childhood Environment Rating Scale, ECERS) conducted on the quality of early childhood settings in the Bahamas, Dominica, Grenada, St. Lucia, St. Vincent and the Grenadines, and Montserrat showed that the quality of play materials, space, and equipment were inadequate in early childhood centers across countries (Charles and Williams 2006). Similarly, a 15-nation study coordinated by the High Scope Foundation found that a significant number of young children

Table 4.1 Children's games in the Caribbean

Country	Game	Brief description
Believed to have originated in Jamaica, but played in Guyana and Trinidad and Tobago as well.	Brown Girl in the Ring	This is a singing game played by children across the Caribbean. A ring is formed and a boy or girl goes in the middle and starts to skip to the song. The child in the middle does a dance and picks a partner who is invited to join him/her.
Barbados, Antigua, and St. Lucia	Wari	Brought by slaves from Africa, the game is played with a rectangular board with two rows of six cup-like depressions with larger cups on both ends of the board. The game is played with beads which are moved from hole to hole across the board to the larger cups on the ends.
Guyana, Jamaica, Trinidad and Tobago, St. Kitts and Nevis, St. Lucia, and other English-speaking countries	Cricket	Inherited from British colonialism, cricket is modified significantly for young children. Usually there is a batsman, a bowler, a wicketkeeper and fielders—but I have observed 2–3 children playing the game in yards. The object is to make the most runs during your turn or your team's turn at bat. The bowler and fielders try to minimize the number of runs by the batting side.
Guyana, Jamaica, Trinidad and Tobago	Skip	Jump rope played by a single individual.
Jamaica	Gig	Carved wooden top with a nail serving as a tip. A string is wrapped around the tip and it is released in a whip-like manner.

(22 percent) between 3 and 5 years of age in Trinidad and Tobago spent their time waiting or were not actively engaged in meaningful activities (Logie 2013).

Today, play has evolved as a meaningful component of the early childhood curriculum in a number of countries. Follow-up data from the Trinidad and Tobago High Scope Mid-Term study revealed an increase in child-initiated activities from 29 percent in 1994–1995 to 67 percent in 2003–2004—indicating greater freedom for children to engage in play-related pursuits (Logie 2013). Play and discovery-based learning are key elements of the Guyanese curriculum, and it is a shared aspiration of the preschool systems in Trinidad and Tobago. Table 4.2 presents teachers' assessment of Indo Caribbean children's play and play-related activities in preschool settings in Guyana and Trinidad and Tobago. As displayed, teachers viewed children's play and play-related activities in both countries to be in the mid- to the low mid-range, with children in Trinidad and Tobago receiving higher ratings in all domains of functioning assessed than those in Guyana (Roopnarine 2010). The moderately low levels of play and social participation could be attributed to the greater emphasis on academic activities and seat-work in early childhood settings in both countries, while the country differences

Table 4.2 Teachers' assessments of children's play and play-related activities in preschools in Guyana and Trinidad and Tobago

Play activity*	Guyana mean (SD)		Trinidad and Tobago mean (SD)		Country difference	Gender difference
	Girls	Boys	Girls	Boys		
Symbolic Play and Imitation	2.04(1.08)	1.82(1.03)	2.90(.99)	2.80(1.09)	***	
Creative Imagination	2.03(.97)	1.79(.88)	1.96(1.16)	2.64(1.06)	***	**
Artistic Expression	2.00(1.07)	1.67(.71)	2.67(.94)	2.61(1.01)	***	
Social Interaction	2.49(1.21)	2.23(1.10)	2.78(1.01)	2.75(1.09)	***	
Cooperative Activities	2.51(1.16)	2.26(1.16)	2.90(1.01)	2.74(1.03)	***	

Notes: *Measured on a 5-point Likert-type scale; **$p<.05$, ***$p<.001$.

could be due to between-country discrepancies in socioeconomic conditions of the children sampled and variations in early educational philosophy.

Play and gender differences

Data suggest that Caribbean children are furnished with sex-typed toys (Leo-Rhynie 1995), that parents engage in different socialization strategies with boys and girls (Leo-Rhynie and Brown 2013), and that teachers have different behavioral expectations for boys and girls (Leo-Rhynie et al. 2009). Along these lines, boys in Trinidad and Dominica play more roughly and boisterously and are discouraged from play considered too "sissy" and "feminine." Additionally, Dominican boys preferred to play with trucks, wheelbarrows, and cars, while girls showed a preference for dolls and educational toys (Impact Study of the Roving Caregivers Programme Research Findings 2008). These traditional play preferences are similar to those expressed in other societies (Williams and Best 1990). They are indicative of the highly gendered roles of men and women that persist in Caribbean societies and of the preference of parents to furnish children with so-called "gender-appropriate" toys because of concerns about the masculinity of boys.

Play and childhood development

A persuasive argument regarding the benefits of play for growth and development in Caribbean children can be made from data obtained in well-designed intervention studies (quasi-experimental longitudinal design, differences-in-differences methodology) that involved early stimulation and followed children over a number of years. Beginning with the Roving Caregivers Programme in Jamaica, children who received play intervention and other services showed far less decline in cognitive functioning prior to entry into basic schools than did control children (Roopnarine 2013). A more extensive follow-up study of children in St. Lucia showed that children who entered the Roving Caregivers Programme between six and 18 months of age realized gains in fine motor skills and visual reception compared to control group children. With the exception of speech development, in which older children benefitted more, the effects were more pronounced for children who entered the program at an early age (Impact Study of the Roving Caregivers Programme Research Findings 2008). Families who enrolled in the program were more likely to engage in stimulation exercises with children compared to those who did not.

Perhaps the most impressive findings on the long-term impact of early play stimulation were shown in a Jamaican study of stunted children (stunting or linear growth retardation reflects the nutritional status of children). The children (aged 9–24 months) were either assigned to a supplement group (one kg milk-based formula per week), a stimulation group (weekly play sessions), a group with both types of intervention, or a group with no intervention. The cognitive scores of children were then compared to a group of non-stunted children at two years after entry into the program at ages 7–8, 11–12, and again at ages 17–18 years. Whereas the first three assessments did not reveal significant gains in test scores in the stunted children regardless of group assignment, the effects of play stimulation were superior to nutritional supplementation at ages 17–18 years (effect sizes of .4 to .6). Unfortunately, differences remained between stunted children who received play stimulation and non-stunted children (Walker et al. 2005).

Implications for early childhood education

Several influential bodies and government initiatives (e.g., Trinidad and Tobago) have advocated for more child-centered, play-based education and early childhood teacher training (Leo-Rhynie and Brown 2013). In the developing nations of the Caribbean, play-based early education that encourages children to explore and construct their own understanding of the object and social world is a critical first step toward human capital development and instilling principles of democratic thinking. There is also a clear call to redefine early childhood teacher training to address issues of democracy in the classroom (Leo-Rhynie and Brown 2013). These steps will require the strong will of Caribbean societies to invest more in the early childhood infrastructure systems in the face of difficult economic conditions.

References

Anderson, P. (2007). *The changing roles of fathers in the context of Jamaican family life.* Kingston, Jamaica: Planning Institute of Jamaica and the University of the West Indies.

Barrow, C. and Ince, M. (2008). Early childhood in the Caribbean. Working Papers in Early Childhood Development. The Hague, the Netherlands: Bernard van Leer Foundation.

Benetti, S. P. and Roopnarine, J. L. (2006). Paternal involvement with school-aged children in Brazilian families: Association with childhood competence. *Sex Roles, 55,* 669–678.

Bock, J. (2002). Evolutionary demography and intrahousehold time allocation in the Okavango Delta, Botswana. *American Journal of Human Biology, 14*, 206–221.

Brown, J. (2003). Parental resistance to child rights in Jamaica. In C. Barrow (Ed.), *Children's rights: Caribbean realities*. Kingston: Ian Randle Publishers.

Brown, J. and Johnson, S. (2008). Child rearing and child participation in Jamaican families. *International Journal of Early Years Education, 16*(1), 31–40.

Charles, L. (2004). Unpublished project proposal. Mobile Caregivers programme, Grenada.

Charles, L. and Williams, S. (2006). Early childhood care and education in the Caribbean Region (CARICOM States). Background Paper for the Education for All: Global Monitoring Report 2007. Paris: UNESCO.

Harding, F. A. (2013). A nation's important plank of social infrastructure: The development of early childhood education in Guyana. In C. Logie and J. L. Roopnarine (Eds.), *Issues and perspectives in early childhood development and early education in the Caribbean countries* (pp. 172–188). La Romaine, Trinidad and Tobago: Caribbean Publishers.

Hossain, Z., Roopnarine, J. L., Isamel, R., Menon, S. and Sombuling, A. (2008). Fathers' and mothers' reports of involvement in caring for infants in Kadazan families in Sabah, Malaysia. *Fathering, 5*, 58–78.

Impact Study of the Roving Caregivers Programme Research Findings (2008). Caribbean Child Support Initiative, Bridgetown, Barbados.

Kaplan, H., Hill, K., Lancaster, J. and Hurtado, M. (2000). A theory of human life history evolution: Diet, intelligence, and longevity. *Evolutionary Anthropology, 9*(4), 156–185.

Krishnakumar, A., Narine, L., Roopnarine, J. L. and Logie, C. (2014). The relationship between neighbourhood effects and child prosocial and antisocial behaviours in Trinidad and Tobago: The intervening role of parental control. *Journal of Abnormal Child Psychology*.

Landman, J., Grantham-McGregor, S. M. and Desai, P. (1983). Child rearing practices in Kingston, Jamaica. *Child: Care Health and Development, 9*, 57–71.

Leo-Rhynie, E. (1995). Girls' toys, boys' toys: Forming gender identity. *Caribbean Journal of Education, 17*, 248–264.

Leo-Rhynie, E. (1997). Class, race, and gender issues in child rearing in the Caribbean. In J. L. Roopnarine and J. Brown (Eds.), *Caribbean families: Diversity among ethnic groups* (pp. 25–55). Norwood, NJ: Ablex.

Leo-Rhynie, E. and Brown, J. (2013). Child rearing practices in the Caribbean in the early childhood years. In C. Logie and J. L. Roopnarine (Eds.), *Issues and perspectives in early childhood development and early education in Caribbean countries* (pp. 30–62). La Romaine, Trinidad and Tobago: Caribbean Publishers.

Leo-Rhynie, E., Minott, C., Gift, S., McBean, M., Scott, A-K. and Wilson, K. (2009). Competencies of children in Guyana, rural Jamaica and St. Vincent and the Grenadines making the transition from pre- to primary school with special emphasis on gender differences. Dudley Grant Memorial Trust for Caribbean Child Support Initiative of the Bernard van Leer Foundation.

LeVine, R. (2004). Challenging expert knowledge: Findings from an African study of infant care and development. In U. Gielen and J. L. Roopnarine (Eds.), *Childhood and adolescence in cross-cultural perspective* (pp. 149–165). Westport, CT: Praeger.

Logie, C. (2013). Pedagogical dilemmas and issues affecting early childhood teaching and learning: Reflections and experiences from Trinidad and Tobago. In C. Logie and J. L. Roopnarine (Eds.), *Issues and perspectives in early childhood development and education in Caribbean* countries (pp. 114–142). La Romaine, Trinidad and Tobago: Caribbean Publishers.

Long, C. (2013). A case study of Jamaican children's play. Unpublished manuscript.

Morelli, G. A., Rogoff, B. and Angelillo, C. (2003). Cultural variation in young children's access to work or involvement in specialised child-focused activities. *International Journal of Behavioral Development, 27*, 264–274.

Parmar, P., Harkness, S. and Super, C. (2004). Asian and European American parents' ethnotheories of play and learning: Effects on preschool children's home routines and social behavior. *International Journal of Behavioral Development, 28*, 97–104.

Pungello, E. P., Kainz, K., Burchinal, M. et al. (2010). Early educational intervention, early cumulative risk, and the early home environment as predictors of young adult outcomes within a high-risk sample. *Child Development, 81*, 410–426.

Roopnarine, J. L. (2010). Assessments of children's development in Guyana and Trinidad and Tobago. Unpublished manuscript.

Roopnarine, J. L. (2011). Cultural variations in beliefs about play, parent–child play, and children's play: Meaning for childhood development. In A. Pellegrini (Ed.), *Oxford handbook of the development of play* (pp. 19–37). Oxford: Oxford University Press.

Roopnarine, J. L. (2013). The Roving Caregivers programme: A home-based early childhood intervention programme with roots in Jamaica. In C. Logie and J. L. Roopnarine (Eds.), *Issues and perspectives in early childhood education in the Caribbean* (pp. 213–241). La Romaine, Trinidad and Tobago: Caribbean Publishers.

Roopnarine, J. L., Brown, J., Snell-White, P., Riegraf, N. B., Crossley, D., Hossain, Z. and Webb, W. (1995). Father involvement in child care and household work in common-law dual-earner and single-earner families. *Journal of Applied Developmental Psychology, 16*, 35–52.

Roopnarine, J. L. and Jin, B. (2012). Indo Caribbean immigrant beliefs about play and its impact on early academic performance. *American Journal of Play, 4*, 441–463.

Roopnarine, J. L., Krishnakumar, A., Narine, L., Logie, C. and Lape, M. (2013a). Relationships between parenting practices and preschoolers' social skills in African, Indo, and mixed-ethnic families in Trinidad and Tobago: The mediating role of ethnic socialisation. *Journal of Cross-cultural Psychology.*

Roopnarine, J. L., Yang, Y., Krishnakumar, A. and Davidson, K. L. (2013b). Parenting practices in Guyana and Trinidad and Tobago. *Interamerican Journal of Psychology, 47*(2) 313–328.

Samms-Vaughan, M. (2006). Children caught in the crossfire. Grace Kennedy Foundation Lecture.

Sigel, I. and McGillicuddy-DeLisi, A. (2002). Parental beliefs as cognitions: The dynamic belief systems mode. In M. Bornstein (Ed.), *Handbook of parenting* (2nd ed., Vol. 3, pp. 485–508). Mahwah, NJ: Erlbaum.

Super, C. and Harkness, S. (1997). The cultural structuring of child development. In J. Berry, P. Dasen, and T. S. Saraswathi, (Eds.), *Handbook of cross-cultural psychology: Basic processes and human development* (pp. 1–39). Needham, MA: Allyn & Bacon.

Wachs, T. D., Chang, S. M., Walker, S. P. and Gardner, J. M. M. (2007). Relation of birth weight, maternal intelligence and mother–child interactions to cognitive and play competence of Jamaican two-year old children. *Intelligence, 35,* 605–622.

Walker, S. P., Chang, S. M., Powell, C. A. and Grantham-McGregor, S. (2005). Effects of early childhood psychosocial stimulation and nutritional supplementation on cognition and education in growth-retarded Jamaican children: prospective cohort study. *The Lancet, 366*(9499), 1804–1807.

Whiting, B. B. and Whiting, J. W. (1975). *Children of six cultures: A psycho-cultural analysis.* Cambridge, MA: Harvard University Press.

Williams, J. E. and Best, D. L. (1990). *Measuring sex stereotypes: A multinational study* (rev. ed.). Newbury Park, CA: Sage.

Wilson, C. M. and Kposowa, A. J. (1994). Paternal involvement with children: Evidence from Guyana. *International Journal of Sociology of the Family, 24,* 23–42.

Wilson, L. C., Wilson, C. M. and Berkeley-Caines, L. (2003). Age, gender and socioeconomic differences in parental socialisation preferences in Guyana. *Journal of Comparative Family Studies, 34,* 213–227.

5 The ecology of play among young children of Mexican origin seasonal farmworkers

Smita Mathur

A migrant father called out to all four of his sons (ages ranging from 5–11 years) and said to them: "This good lady from school wants to see you play, so you all run around these trees as fast as you can for as long as she wants to watch you." The father then went into the trailer while their mother watched from the small window. The sons meanwhile ran around the trees under their father's authoritarian instruction and their mother's watchful eye.

Introduction

There are approximately three million seasonal migrant farmworkers in the US (National Center for Farmworker Health 2012), of which about 68 percent were born in Mexico. Farmworkers from Mexico regularly come to the US to harvest various crops. Typically, they spend 36 weeks per year engaged in farm work and return to Mexico during the slow months. Because of the politics surrounding US immigration, the move between the US and Mexico has become more difficult and increasingly dangerous. As a result, many farmworkers have established long-term residence in more permanent households in the US. Although their stay in the US has become more permanent, the seasonal migrant household continues to live in social and linguistic isolation (Martínez 1997; DiCerbo 2001; Green 2003; Alba and Silberman 2009; Academy for Educational Development 2009). The long, hard, and uncertain work days, inadequate healthcare, hazardous and overcrowded housing facilities, constant exposure to toxic pesticides and fertilizers, and the need for forced early retirement from the farm labor force all keep this community on the outer edges of the American dream (Harrington 1987; Grieshop 1997; Kearney 2000; Driessen et al. 2010).

In spite of the tremendous odds that are stacked against them, the typical migrant household maintains its child-centered focus as parents instill a deep value for education and citizenship in their children (Fagnoni 1999; Crosnoe and Kalil 2010; Mathur and Parameswaran 2012; Schofield et al. 2012). Elders painstakingly pass on their strong work ethic and cultural worldview to their children. Migrant families value family life, revere the wisdom in the older generation, and maintain deep religious and spiritual values. They strive to learn Standard English in an effort to seek better opportunities for employment and education, especially for their children (Gibson and Hidalgo 2009; Hossain and Shipman 2009; Howes et al. 2008).

Since 1965, the US Federal Government has allocated funds for the early education of children of migrant and seasonal farmworker families through the Migrant Seasonal Head Start Initiative (MSHS). Today, the MSHS operates 450 centers in 39 states. Young children of migrant workers are schooled in the context of high stakes testing, influx of teaching and learning technology in the early years, teacher accountability, and uncertain funding for early education. Within this climate, the play-based curriculum is under scrutiny and transformation. Whereas the value of play in childhood development remains unquestioned (Johnson et al. 2005; Ginsburg 2007; Oliver and Klugman 2007), the execution of play-based learning anchored in children's cultural backgrounds is still to take deeper and stable roots for children of migrants in the US (Eggers-Pierola 2002; Fisher et al. 2008). This chapter describes the context and content of play of children of Mexican migrant farmworkers. It considers parental knowledge, attitudes, and practices related to the play of young children. The descriptions that follow are based on extensive fieldwork conducted by the author on children of migrant workers who attended nationally accredited migrant Head Start programs in Central and South Florida.

Migrant families and children: conceptual framework

Migrant seasonal farmworker families in the US mostly hail from Mexico, and many are first- or second-generation immigrants in the US. Migrant families move three to four times a year in search of agriculture-based employment. Consequently, children of migrant farmworkers find themselves changing schools three to four times a year. Migrant children in US schools are typically described using a deficit model which highlights their poverty, compromised housing situation, mobile lifestyle, limited proficiency in Standard English, low levels of parental education, social isolation, and often their uncertain legal status in the US (López et al. 2001; Laosa and Ainsworth 2007; Mathur and Parameswaran 2011; Mathur and Parameswaran 2012). The deficit model sets an expectation of academic failure and charts a pathway for early school drop-out. These issues, while real, overshadow the strengths embedded within the child's family and cultural practices that can mitigate against the negative impact of the child's ecological environment.

Research on early childhood education and development of young migrant children is sorely lacking (Gibson and Bejinez 2002; Portes and Rivas 2011). Systematic inquiry on play of migrant children has not found focus yet and the research on play in other underrepresented and immigrant groups in the US (see Chapter 7 by Jung and Chapter 8 by Buchanan and Cooney, in this volume) cannot adequately inform the complex needs of migrant families and their children. A perspective that has some utility in examining socialization patterns in migrant families focuses on funds of knowledge (Purcell-Gates 2013). Not unlike eco-cultural frameworks (Whiting and Whiting 1975), funds of knowledge comprise ways in which culture-specific information is transmitted among members of the migrant culture. Families' funds of knowledge include information on the development and sustenance of relationships within cultural systems, the consequences of individual and collective actions, and cultural artifacts. There is a close camaraderie among community members that has its roots in cultures and communities of origin in Mexico. This complex ecology has rich, culturally-anchored funds of knowledge (Genzuk 1999; López et al. 2010) that manifest in daily household activities, celebrations, and other social and business transactions. Children have a front seat in observing these social and cultural transactions and draw upon them to engage the social and object world through play (Göncü 1999).

In the main, funds of knowledge can and do serve as familiar, reliable, trustworthy scaffolds during play and manifest themselves as children enter play frames (González et al. 2005; Hammer et al. 2012). Tapping into the family's funds of knowledge to design play-based activities creates culturally congruent learning environments (Genzuk 1999; Vesely and Ginsberg 2011), makes play environments familiar, and establishes a learning environment that moves a child from strength to strength and may accelerate learning. Thus, funds of knowledge serve not only as an impetus for play but also as a scaffold during play. They assist young migrant children in their move from performance to potential or competency level (Paradise and Rogoff 2009; Silva et al. 2010; Newton and Jenvey 2011). This conceptual perspective informs the ethnographic work outlined in this chapter.

Ecology of play and schooling

Play in schools is influenced by a host of factors. The geographical location of schools, availability of culturally responsive and qualified teachers, the rhythms of a school's schedules tied to seasons and crops, and even governmental policies related to immigration and education—all have a direct impact on the quality and quantity of play-based experiences available to the migrant child. Schools for migrant children are often located close to the fields where migrant parents work in rural and remote areas. Highly qualified teachers with adequate professional and academic preparation are difficult to find in these remote and rural locations. Therefore schools tend to hire teachers from the context in which the school is embedded. Teachers of migrant children usually are former migrant farmworkers, have limited proficiency in written and spoken English, and their professional and academic preparation is largely unrecognized in the US. Many have significant work experience from their country of origin which goes unrecognized in North America and gives rise to deep disappointment, a sense of helplessness, and sometimes even anger. Although the teachers are academically underprepared by US standards and many of them are former migrant workers, their similarity in background characteristics to the children and families they serve enables them to forge strong partnerships with the migrant families. Teachers are culturally-competent, linguistically compatible, and in sync with the strengths and challenges faced by the migrant children and families. They understand and embrace the strong relationships and social ties in and among the home, school, and community.

Of course, there are other challenges within the migrant communities that threaten home-school relationships. The 2007–2008 survey by the National Agricultural Workers concluded that 48 percent of farmworkers in the US are not legally authorized to work in America. With their legal status in limbo, parents live in fear of job loss and deportation. In many cases, parents work out contingency plans with local advocacy groups and churches for their US citizen children, should they or other family members face deportations. Teachers and school administrators are made aware of the plans. When parents are arrested in and around school premises, teachers and school personnel are compelled to take on the unique role of ensuring children's physical and psychological safety. Advocacy for migrant children and families is a key role of teachers of migrant children. Interestingly, in advocating for the migrant families, the schools tend to be very guarded and often distrusting in their interactions with those considered as "outsiders" such as researchers from local universities and individuals from government programs. Not surprisingly, any meaningful partnership with migrant schools and communities first requires building social capital and trust.

Because of the nature of migrant life, school attendance is tied to availability of work in the fields. In Florida, children typically start attending schools in November as the need to plant and harvest strawberries and blueberries peaks. The number of students starts to dwindle by the end of April and early May as families move north to states like Georgia, Michigan, and even New York. Typically, most schools close from June to October and are forced to lay off most of the teachers. Teachers of migrant children not only find themselves working in underserved rural communities but are forced to apply for unemployment benefits for a substantial part of the year. The predictable and constant job loss and dependence on government programs like food stamps and unemployment benefits create a challenging work context for teachers of migrant children. Most teachers take up seasonal employment at local stores. One has to wonder what effect this relentless horizontal professional mobility has on teacher motivation, retention, and competency and in turn, their ability to implement and execute play-based curriculum to meet the school readiness needs of young migrant children.

Play at home

Beliefs about play

Migrant parents view play as a natural, innate activity of childhood and do not think deeply about the value or outcome of play for childhood growth and development. The association between play and learning is rarely considered important. Thus, migrant parents who have great value for education itself do not see play as a way to promote education. They often express frustration and displeasure when they discover that children are allowed to play at preschool for a large portion of the day and would clearly prefer a traditional, structured, teacher-directed preschool experience for their children.

Migrant parents see play, work, and learning as loosely connected, if a link exists at all. Play needs to be curtailed lest children squander their childhood playing games.

Parental input during play is minimal, and when parents do get involved in play with children, it is usually to redirect children from play to other work or learning-related activities. Migrant parents are not able to articulate how play is linked to early childhood education and have therefore not thought about how they or teachers can maximize their child's learning through play. Learning, according to parents, happens in structured teacher-directed environments that call upon the child to obey, comply, and focus on teacher-designed tasks. In their minds, teacher-dominated schooling leads to the acquisition of skills that lead to stable employment and citizenship. Because migrant Mexican parents respect teachers and hold them in high regard, confronting, contradicting, and questioning a teacher's motivations is considered disrespectful. As a result, migrant parents are often reluctant to overtly and strongly express their frustration with play-based curricula in schools.

Psychological support for play

Adults in the migrant communities are generally watchful and nurturing towards young children. They maintain child-centered home environments and make sure that young children are taken care of by designated older siblings as care-givers in their absence. Play among young migrant Mexican children exemplifies the culture's value for interdependence and serves to strengthen a sense of responsibility toward younger siblings, parents, and extended family members. While parents and other adults do not see a direct role for themselves in children's play, they do remain watchful and consistently communicate a more psychologically nurturing message of "I am here for you" as opposed to using direct instruction to shape children's play. While at first glance it appears that parents assume a hands-off approach to children's play, they employ different strategies in providing psychological support for children's play at home. They watch children play and verbally intervene by shouting out comments such as "slow down," "take care," "not so fast," and "I am watching you" that are meant to support and comfort their children. Most of the time young children do not pay much credence to the content of the verbal exchanges, as they seldom slow down or change their play in any way. During these exchanges, there is a sense of psychological presence and approval by the parents that is supportive of the children. It likely contributes to emotional safety and reflects the child-centeredness seen in homes of migrant families. While their busy schedules do not permit much time to intervene or structure children's play, they do expect obedience and require compliance.

Play at home differs from play at school

Play of migrant children at home differs considerably from play in school settings. Play at home is characterized by minimal adult supervision, multi-age play groups, and occurs mostly during outdoor unstructured play environments with few toys. Interestingly, the frequency of verbal exchanges and use of Standard English is higher at home as compared to school. Likewise, play is more complex at home, reflecting higher frequencies of games with rules, pretend play, exploration, examination, and manipulation than at school. Play that promotes learning literacy skills, music, and rhythmic movement was minimal and rarely observed in the home settings. At home, migrant children are assigned chores from their early years. Taking care of younger siblings is a firm expectation and children are assigned non-negotiable childcare responsibilities that supersede play and learning. The number of responsibilities around the home increases incrementally until the child is ready to assist in income-generating farm work. Migrant families thus see a clear separation between times to play, work, and learn. As one family member remarked: "I say when it is time to play [then] play and when it is time to learn, and then learn."

Play and childcare responsibilities

Within and around the home environment, childcare-related responsibilities and play are intertwined for the young migrant child. As migrant children engage in play, they are acutely aware of the responsibilities assigned to them. Because parents and other adults spend most of their day in the fields, the role of childcare and supervision falls on older siblings and neighbors. Children are assigned the responsibility of taking care of one or two other children during the day and that responsibility takes precedence over any other activity. The children are socialized to take this responsibility very seriously and each one knows clearly who is assigned the responsibility to care for which children. If during play, a child is hurt, needs a bathroom break, a drink, or a change of clothes, the assigned "child caregiver" is approached and s/he immediately takes charge. Play halts until the need is addressed or resolved. Seeking adult assistance is rarely an option even when parents are physically present at home. Migrant children develop proficiency in self-care and emotional regulation early on and are very adept at solving their own problems.

Play and the natural environment

Young migrant children are very knowledgeable about their natural environment. They are aware of the characteristics of animals, bugs, plants, and different types of soil. This learning happens over time as the children teach themselves through observation, exploration, inquiry, and problem solving stimulated by their curiosity of the natural environment. Other natural phenomena like reading weather, classifying fruits like oranges, blueberries and strawberries by size, color, taste, and their value in the market are all funds of knowledge within a migrant community that is seamlessly transferred to children. It is true that at this young age this information is not clearly organized and categorized; however, over time young migrant children assimilate vast amounts of information related to nature. Such knowledge can be harnessed and used to stage many other learning experiences through play in the preschool environment that would help migrant children learn new skills.

Sibling play

Left to their own devices under the loose supervision of older siblings for extended periods of time each day, the play of young migrant children often imitates the play of older children. Based on our current understanding of the developmental milestones associated with learning cognitive and social skills, there is an expectation that children aged 4–5 years old are challenged by formal structured games with rules and that their play is usually guided by informal rules and play frames. Play is initiated by older children in the group and the composition of the playgroups changes frequently as the play proceeds. Children move in and out of playgroups if they are called upon to attend to a younger sibling or assist a parent. The boundaries of playgroups are fluid and not age-specific.

Play materials

As noted already, among migrant families play is essentially viewed as an outdoor activity. Indoor space is seen as a place for domestic activities—to cook, eat, sleep, and store things. Structured toys like dolls, play food, doll houses, tricycles, dressing-up clothes, puzzles, table toys, computers, and reading materials are used frequently in more structured play environments in schools but are largely absent in the home environment. Toys are expensive and so are purchased mostly during Christmas as gifts but then are quickly stored away out of the reach of young children. Toys decorate sections of the homes but are not readily available to children for play. As migrant families move frequently and moving bulky items is challenging, larger toys such as tricycles, and doll furniture are often left behind.

Play within classrooms

Within the micro-play environments, migrant children show unique strengths that need to be underscored and incorporated into play-based activities and curricula. Strengths that are evident in the play of young migrant children are: strong social skills and positive emotional regulation exemplified by low incidence of disruptive behavior and discipline issues in school; above-average attention span/on-task behavior; and gender neutrality in play of very young children, especially at home. Young migrant children show on-task behaviors that exceed the expected range of 12–20 minutes in a single play frame (Figure 5.1). If there are disruptions in the play, the children have the ability to regroup and commence play where they left off.

This ability to regulate their emotions and stay on-task can be used to stimulate cognitive processing and to learn school-readiness skills. It also allows the children to engage in lengthy reciprocal pair and small group interactions at a young age. Preschool-aged migrant children show remarkable ability to successfully play in pairs which requires significant reciprocity and sharing. The ability to stay on task and collaborate is more evident during structured indoor play in school as opposed to outdoor

Figure 5.1   Child demonstrates on-task behavior.

free play and perhaps reflects the cultural emphasis on group solidarity within the migrant culture.

A surprising observation on the play of young migrant children relates to the gender neutrality in play. Young migrant boys and girls do not show significant differences in the time they spend in various play-based activities inside the classroom such as art, music, pretend play, or computer-mediated play. Gender neutrality is also evident during outdoor free play both in schools and at home (Figure 5.2). This observation goes against the general expectation that during the preschool years there is a marked gender difference in the play of young children. Because migrant parents do similar work in the fields, the young migrant child may not have many opportunities to observe gender-specific roles. Moreover, the lack of direct parent involvement in children's play, limited gender-specific toys at home; and strong in-service training for migrant teachers may also contribute to gender neutrality in the play of very young migrant children. This emerging evidence on gender neutrality in the play of young migrant children requires further investigation. Migrant children eventually learn gender-specific expectations and commit themselves to gender-based roles. The onset of gender-specific play takes root in early elementary school.

A third of play time in school is spent in waiting, watching, wandering aimlessly, or cruising around the play space without a specific purpose; and oftentimes the learning generated by play is not aligned with school-readiness skills. However, this assertion requires deeper reflection. The early childhood centers for migrant children are nationally accredited and follow various constructivist-based models such as the High Scope curriculum; and teachers of migrant children undergo intensive in-service training. Interviews with teachers clearly show that they know about best practices in early

Figure 5.2   Emerging evidence of gender neutrality in play.

childhood. Nonetheless, although articulate about appropriate practices related to classroom management, curriculum development, and child development, teachers' knowledge about these issues do not translate into daily practices with children. The mismatch between teachers' knowledge of best practices and their actual behaviors in the classroom and with children indicates that there is a low buy-in by migrant teachers of the value of the play-based curriculum. They learn what is expected of them but translating it into action is difficult because it goes against their cultural norms. This low buy-in from the teachers and staff suggests a greater need to develop culturally-responsive play-based curriculum for children in the migrant community.

Nevertheless, teachers' cultural competence is clearly reflected in their classroom management skills that closely resemble the parenting styles used by migrant parents. Close observation of the daily events in a typical early childhood classroom that is dominated by children of migrant workers reveals that the number of aggressive or disruptive behaviors in the classroom that required any form of redirection is very low. The teachers typically are excellent in decoding children's behaviors and communicating their expectations in culture-specific ways that lead to smooth functioning of the classroom. Unfortunately, the training sessions provided to teachers are mostly aligned to practices that are accepted in mainstream US classrooms. These practices often do not resonate with the teachers and their cultural understanding of child development and teaching. Thus, they seldom execute what they learned during in-service and pre-service training. Clearly, the traditional center-based play in schools needs to be reviewed closely. Centers need to be inspired by the funds of knowledge and cultural tools available to the migrant children and families for the realization of maximum cognitive and social benefits to children.

In the classroom, verbal communication during play is infrequent and usually in Spanish across play settings. More often than not, children's play is conducted in silent camaraderie. For Mexican migrant children, where the main goal is to learn and practice Standard English, playing in silence is likely to impede language and literacy development. Upon further exploration, it becomes evident that the teachers of the migrant children, while culturally competent, often lack fluency and understanding of English. Thus, teachers are unable to model or facilitate language and literacy learning to the children through play activities.

Future directions

Whereas the connection between children's play and immigration policies, border security, educational reform, and federal budget cuts may not be obvious at first, it is relevant when considering the context of children's play in migrant communities. Fear and uncertainty guide parental behavior. Fear of deportation, fear generated by economically impoverished lives, fear of falling sick and not being able to afford medical care, fear of unemployment, and fear for the lives and well-being of family members who live uncertain lives in Mexico, surround a migrant family in the US. Teachers of migrant children know these realities all too well. These stressors have potential spillover effects on the lives of migrant children and their innate tendency to play.

Focusing resources and efforts on in-service teacher preparation, while simultaneously preserving their cultural competency, is the key to the education of young migrant children. Intensive in-service training and support to earn college degrees in early childhood education will not only equip the teachers with the knowledge they need to design and appropriately participate in children's play, but it will also allow them to draw on their cultural knowledge to implement play-related activities in early childhood settings. While this is an easy concept to embrace, it is hard to execute. Helping teachers of migrant children earn a four-year degree in early childhood education can take from 6–10 years, even when financial assistance, tutoring and other academic scaffolds are available. Appropriate teacher preparation will go a long way in increasing verbal communication during play and minimizing the time children spend waiting, gazing, or cruising around without purpose.

References

Academy for Educational Development (2009). *The invisible children of migrant and seasonal farmworkers in the United States: An examination of existing pre-K partnerships*. Academy for Educational Development.

Alba, R. and Silberman, R. (2009). The children of immigrants and host-society educational systems: Mexicans in the United States and North Africans in France. *Teachers College Record, 111*(6), 1444–1475.

Almasi, J. F. (2002). Border crossing dilemmas: What cultural currency is accepted at the toll booth? *Race, Ethnicity & Education, 5*(3): 317–325.

Crosnoe, R. and Kalil, A. (2010). Educational progress and parenting among Mexican immigrant mothers of young children, *Journal of Marriage and Family, 72*(4), 976–990.

DiCerbo, P. A. (2001). Why migrant education matters. *NCBE Issue Brief, 8*, 1–7.

Driessen, R., Leyendecker, B., Scholmerich, A. and Harwood, R. (2010). Everyday experiences of 18–36 month-old children from migrant families: The influence of host culture and migrant experience, *Early Child Development and Care, 180*(9), 1143–1163.

Eggers-Pierola, C. (2002). *Connections and commitments: A Latino-based framework for early childhood educators.* Homepage of Center for Children and Families: Education Development Center Inc. Online. Available at: http://ltd.edc.org/sites/ltd.edc.org/files/Connections_and_Commitments.pdf (accessed 11 March 2014).

Facts about Farmworkers. (2012). National Center for Farmworker Health (NCFH). Buda, Texas.

Fagnoni, C. M. (1999). *Migrant children: Education and HHS need to improve the exchange of participant information.* Washington, DC: General Accounting Office.

Fisher, K. R., Hirsh-Pasek, K., Golinkoff, R. M. and Gryfe, S. G. (2008). Conceptual split? Parents' and experts' perceptions of play in the 21st century. *Journal of Applied Developmental Psychology, 29*(4), 305–316.

Genzuk, M. (1999). Tapping into community funds of knowledge. In *Effective strategies for English language acquisition: Curriculum for the professional development of teachers, grades kindergarten through eight* (pp. 9–21). Los Angeles: Annenberg Metropolitan Project/ARCO Foundation.

Gibson, M. A. and Bejinez, L. F. (2002). Dropout prevention: How migrant education supports Mexican youth. *Journal of Latinos & Education, 1*(3), 155.

Gibson, M. A., Bejínez, L. F., Hidalgo, N. and Rolón, C. (2004). Belonging and school participation: Lessons from a migrant student club. In M. A. Gibson, P. Gándara and J. P. Koyama (Eds.), *School connections: U.S. Mexican youth, peers, and school achievement* (pp. 129–149). New York: Teachers College Press.

Gibson, M. A. and ERIC Clearinghouse on Rural Education and Small Schools (2003). Improving graduation outcomes for migrant students. *ERIC Digest.*

Gibson, M. A. and Hidalgo, N. D. (2009). Bridges to success in high school for migrant youth. *Teachers College Record, 111*(3), 683–711.

Ginsburg, K. R. (2007). The importance of play in promoting healthy child development and maintaining strong parent–child bond. *Pediatrics, 119*(1), 182–191.

Göncü, A. (1999). *Children's engagement in the world: Sociocultural perspectives.* New York: Cambridge University Press.

González, N., Moll, L. C. and Amanti, C. (2005). *Funds of knowledge: Theorizing practices in households, communities, and classrooms.* Mahwah, NJ: Lawrence Erlbaum Associates.

Green, P. E. (2003). The undocumented: Educating the children of migrant workers in America. *Bilingual Research Journal, 27*(1), 51–71.

Grieshop, J. I. (1997). Transnational and transformational: Mixtec immigration and health beliefs. *Human Organization, 56*(4), 400–407.

Hammer, C. S., Blair, C., Lopez, L., Leong, D., Bedrova, E. and Society for Research on Educational Effectiveness (2012). *Tools of the mind: Promoting the school readiness of ELLs.* Washington, DC: Society for Research on Educational Effectiveness.

Handley, M. A. and Grieshop, J. (2007). Globalized migration and transnational epidemiology. *International Journal of Epidemiology*, *36*(6), 1205–1206.

Harrington, S. (1987). Children on the road. *Instructor*, *97*(4), 36–39.

Hossain, Z. and Shipman, V. (2009). Mexican immigrant fathers' and mothers' engagement with school-age children. *Hispanic Journal of Behavioral Sciences*, *31*(4), 468–491.

Howes, C., Wishard Guerra, A. G. and Zucker, E. (2008). Migrating from Mexico and sharing pretend with peers in the United States. *Merrill-Palmer Quarterly: Journal of Developmental Psychology*, *54*(2), 256–288.

Johnson, J. E., Christie, J. F. and Wardle, F. (2005). *Play, development, and early education*. Boston/London: Pearson/Allyn and Bacon.

Kearney, M. (2000). Transnational Oaxacan indigenous identity: The case of Mixtecs and Zapotecs. *Identities*, *7*(2), 173–195.

Laosa, L. M. and Ainsworth, P. (2007). Is public pre-K preparing Hispanic children to succeed in school? *Preschool Policy Brief, Issue 13*, National Institute for Early Education Research. New Bruniswick: Rutgers University Graduate School of Education.

López, A., Correa-Chávez, M., Rogoff, B. and Gutiérrez, K. (2010). Attention to instruction directed to another by U.S. Mexican-heritage children of varying cultural backgrounds. *Developmental Psychology*, *46*(3), 593–601.

López, G. R., Scribner, J. D. and Mahitivanichcha, K. (2001). Redefining parental involvement: Lessons from high-performing migrant-impacted schools. *American Educational Research Journal*, *38*, 253–288.

Martínez, Y. G. (1997). Migrant farmworker families, cultural capital and schooling: An anthropological analysis of implications for interventions. Doctoral dissertation. University of South Florida, Tampa, Florida.

Mathur, S. and Parameswaran, G. (2011). Educating the young migrant child: Professional development for teachers of young children of seasonal farmworkers. *Journal of Multiculturalism in Education*, *7*(3), 1–16.

Mathur, S. and Parameswaran, G. (2012). School readiness for young migrant children: The challenge and the outlook. *ISRN Education*, 2012, Article ID 847502. doi: 10.5402/2012/847502

Newton, E. and Jenvey, V. (2011). Play and theory of mind: Associations with social competence in young children, *Early Child Development and Care*, *181*(6), 761–773.

Oliver, S. J. and Klugman, E. (2007). Building a play research agenda: what do we know about play? What new questions do we need to ask?, *Exchange*, *173*, 14–24.

Paradise, R. and Rogoff, B. (2009). Side by side: Learning by observing and pitching in. *Ethos*, *37*(1), 102–138.

Portes, A. and Rivas, A. (2011). The adaptation of migrant children. *Future of Children*, *21*(1), 219–246.

Purcell-Gates, V. (2013). Literacy worlds of children of migrant farmworker communities participating in a Migrant Head Start Program. *Research in the Teaching of English*, *48*(1), 68–97.

Schofield, T., Beaumont, K., Widaman, K., Jochem, R., Robins, R. and Conger, R. (2012). Parent and child fluency in a common language: Implications for the parent–child relationship and later academic success in Mexican American families. *Journal of Family Psychology, 26*(6), 869–879.

Silva, K. G., Correa-Chávez, M. and Rogoff, B. (2010). Mexican-heritage children's attention and learning from interactions directed to others. *Child Development, 81*(3), 898–912.

Vesely, C. K. and Ginsberg, M. R. (2011). Strategies and practices for working with immigrant families in early education programs. *Young Children, 66*(1), 84–89.

Whiting, J. W. M. and Whiting, B. B. (1975). *Children of six cultures: A psycho-cultural analysis.* Cambridge, MA: Harvard University Press.

6　The play behavior of African American children: the need for a cultural prism

Janice E. Hale and Erika L. Bocknek

> The first day I played in the sand,
> the sand got in my eye;
> The second day I played in the sand,
> the sand made me cry.
> I went over to my Grandma's house,
> and asked her for some cake.
>
> She turned me 'round and 'round,
> and 'round and said,
> "Give that po' gal some cake!
> Oh, give that gal some cake; oh, give
> that gal some cake!"
> She turned me 'round and 'round
> and 'round and said
> "Give that po' gal some cake!"
>
> (Traditional African American folk song)

Introduction

Before discussing the current literature on the play behavior of African American children, we feel it is important to acknowledge the unique beginnings of this play: the slave plantations of the pre-Civil War United States. It is a testimony to both the resilience of the children and the resilience of play itself that despite the sometimes horrific and always dehumanizing conditions of the plantations and that "peculiar institution" of slavery, the children of slaves did, in fact, play. The richness and complexity of this play, known mostly through the interviews of former slaves conducted by the Works Progress Administration (WPA) during the 1930s, can be looked at using some of the same categories of analysis currently used to examine children's play in general.

Play in socio-historical context

Types of play

The children of slaves engaged in the same forms of play that we associate with typical childhoods. They played with dolls, balls, jump ropes and engaged in such activities as hopscotch and ring games (Mintz 2004). Some of their play and games were their own creations but the children also participated in such traditional games as "skeeting" and "smut" (Wiggins 1980). One of the most popular games, particularly for the boys, was marbles (Wiggins 1980). And, like the children of today who have access to open spaces, the slave children occupied themselves by wandering through the woods and across fields, sometimes hunting for small animals or fishing and sometimes gathering what fruit and nuts they could find (Mintz 2004).

Playthings

As one might imagine, the children of slaves did not have access to store-bought or fancy toys. Most of what they played with had to be created, either by themselves or by a parent. Balls were fashioned out of discarded yarn, dolls built out of sticks and rags, and dress-up clothes created out of flowers and leaves (Chudacoff 2007). The marbles they used were made out of bits of clay (Mintz 2004).

Peer play

The playmates for the slave children included members of their own families, other slave children living on the plantation, and in some cases, slave children living on neighboring plantations (Figure 6.1).

An interesting aspect of the peer play among the slave children was the "apparent absence of any games that required the elimination of players" (Wiggins 1980: 29). This practice seemed to reflect the value the slave community placed on cooperation and community. As an example of the "no elimination" principle, a former slave remembered that in playing one particular game that might have been similar to the current game of dodgeball, "they would get six on one side of the house and six on de other. When somebody got hit we would just start the game over again" (p. 29).

One of the more intriguing facts about the play of slave children is that playing with the white children of the plantation (and slave) owner was not that unusual (King 2005). It was often the case that the "white children of the plantation earnestly sought the friendship of the slave children their own age and thoroughly enjoyed the opportunity to frolic in the quarters" (Wiggins 1980: 30).

Although the play of slave children with white children had moments that suggested equality (Wiggins 1980), the reality of the situation was never far from the play and at times was part of the play: "In fact many interracial games reenacted the relationship between masters and slaves, reinforcing the plantation hierarchy and accentuating the divide between the white and black children. When the game was wagon, slave children served as mules" (Mintz 2004: 105).

Figure 6.1 Slave children at play.

The relationship between the slave children and the white children seemed to change when the black playmate reached adolescence and the age at which regular plantation work could be expected. As one former slave recalled, "I alwas' played aid de white chilluns tip I wiz big enough to be put to wuk" (King 2005: 33). And as another former slave told the interviewers, "I discovered the difference between myself and my master's white children. They began to order me about, and were told to do so by my master and mistress" (p. 33).

Representative play

The slave children engaged in what is typically thought of as make-believe, imitative, or role-play. They played out parts of their lives that were important to them and would often assume the roles of the leading characters of the story (Wiggins 1980). They often engaged in play related to the three events that were central to their experience: church activities, funerals, and slave auctions. They also enjoyed playing dress-up and imitating the important people in their lives, as evidenced by the words of a former slave: "sumtimes we wud dress up in mammies dresses, an' play oak we wis find ladies.

Sum times we wud break down er bush and hol' it over our heds and lak dat wis er parasol" (Chudacoff 2007: 55).

As is often the case with children's play, the dramas they portrayed within play followed the rules of the larger society that existed outside of their play. For example, when staging a mock funeral, "These children appeared to know enough about funerals to use the appropriately coloured shroud and black ribbon denoting the sorrowful occasion. They also seemed to know that social etiquette in the plantation South forbade the mixing of black and white mourners" (King 2005: 30).

Of course, this representative play would often reflect the reality of the harsh and difficult conditions within which the slave children lived. There were descriptions of how the slave children brought the experience of whippings and slave auctions into their play (Marten 1998). There was an example of slave children and white children imitating the use of carriages pulled by animals and the black children were "given" the role of the animals (King 2005). As Wiggins wrote, "Notwithstanding those occasional friendships, a caste system frequently operated with the 'play world' of the slave and white children just as it did in the everyday affairs of the plantation community" (1980: 31).

The purposes and consequences of play

Although children do not necessarily play with the intention of doing anything more than entertaining themselves and enjoying a particular moment in time, play may have effects that go beyond simple enjoyment. This could have been the case for the play of slave children as well. Play may have been practice and preparation for their future lives as adults in that, "Many games prepared children for adult roles, such as cooking and caring for babies . . . Role-playing games . . . acted out baptisms, funerals, and weddings" (Mintz 2004: 107). Play was perhaps the way in which "cultural traits were preserved from one generation to the next" and it was "often the medium through which they learned the values and mores of the adult world" (Wiggins 1980: 22, 34).

Play may also have been a way in which slave children made sense of, coped with, and at times resisted the dehumanizing situations in which they were held captive. As Mintz writes:

> Children were not simply slavery's victims; they were also active agents, who managed to resist slavery's dehumanising pressures . . . black children [reenacted] what they saw around them in order to understand and cope with slavery's stresses. Other forms of play instilled a sense of self-worth that was vital in resisting slavery's humiliations. Play taught enslaved children that they were equal or even superior to their white counterparts.
>
> (2004: 107)

It is possible that slave children were able to build within their play what Erik Erikson (1972) called "microcosms." Microspheres, according to Erikson, are spaces in one's life where you can exert some control over your experience. Wiggins (1980) made the point that, certainly, much of the life of a slave child was not in his or her control. It may have been the case that

> play was one activity where slaves could realise a certain degree of dignity and could affirm and sustain their unique existence. They could withstand bondage much more easily when allowed to participate with fellow slaves in a variety of different play activities.
>
> (Wiggins 1980: 36)

This, then, was the beginnings of the play of African American children. With this as the backdrop, the purpose of this chapter is to examine a sample of the current literature on the play of African American children. Following this review, we offer a critique of the ways in which the play has been studied and present some suggestions for future research.

The play of African American children today

Although the research into the play of Black children has been limited, there have been a number of studies that illustrate the type of inquiry that can occur. Weinberger and Starkey (1994), for example, examined the free play behavior of African American children in Head Start classrooms from the perspective of Smilansky's (1968) assertion that disadvantaged children show lower levels of pretend play (Figure 6.2). The authors found that most of the play behaviors observed did fall into the functional play category, the lowest level of play, according to Smilansky, but the children also engaged in a significant amount of pretend play, Smilansky's highest level of play.

In another study looking at pretend play, Karnik and Tudge (2010) were interested in seeing if there were any differences in preschool-aged children's pretend play based on racial, socioeconomic, or gender differences. They conducted an ethnographic study in which the children were observed in their natural environments, i.e., not simply in a preschool classroom of some sort. A general finding of the study was that the children evidenced relatively low levels of pretend play. Where there were differences in the amount of pretend play observed, the variation was based on socioeconomic status and not race; the middle-class children, be they Black or White, produced more pretend play than the working-class children, again whether they were Black or White. This was particularly true for the girls.

Several key studies (e.g., Bulotsky-Shearer et al. 2012) have demonstrated the role of play in promoting resilience among Black children. These studies are most likely to focus on low-income, Black preschool children and describe the promotion of early learning and school readiness through peer play interactions, interactions that can take place both at home and in the classroom.

There have been a number of other studies examining the salience of early play experiences in promoting the classroom competencies of African American children. Fantuzzo et al. (2004), for example, looked at the relationship of the peer play that

Figure 6.2   African American child engaging in solitary play.

occurred in the classroom to competencies in the realms of emotional regulation, autonomy, and language. They found that the children who evidenced higher amounts of peer play interactions also showed higher levels of self-determination and receptive vocabulary skills, while also demonstrating lower levels of aggression and shyness. Conversely, those children who engaged in fewer peer play interactions or interactions of a more disruptive or disjointed nature, evidenced more negative outcomes in terms of emotion regulation.

In another study focused on peer play, Fishbein et al. (2009) looked at preschool children's choices of playmates based on race, sex, and physical attractiveness. In terms of playmate preferences based on race, the authors found moderate support for the following results: the White children, both boys and girls, rated children within their own race as favorite playmates. For the African American children, the results were slightly different. Black boys indicated the same within-race preferences as the White children (i.e., choosing Black children as their favorite playmates) but Black girls chose both White and Black children as playmates. One possible reason for this difference, according to the authors, is that Black girls may conform more to the pressures to fit into the White society than Black boys do.

There have also been studies looking at how the parents of young African American children think about play and the degree to which they value it in the lives of their children. As the research for her dissertation, Muhammad (2009) examined this question by interviewing the mothers of children attending a Head Start preschool program. Her conclusions were that, in general, these mothers held relatively positive views about the importance of play and believed that play could have a positive impact on their children's cognitive development and readiness for kindergarten. Fogle and Mendez (2006) also looked at the play beliefs of African American mothers and found that there was a positive relationship between valuing children's play and higher ratings of children's peer play. The valuing of an academic focus by the mothers (as opposed to a play focus) correlated more highly with disruptive and disconnected peer play.

In general, these representative studies have viewed the play experience of African American children through the same lenses used to think about play of children in general. We think that this may be a weakness of the existing literature and in the remainder of the chapter we offer a different lens, a cultural prism, that we think can be a more appropriate and powerful way of looking at the play of African American children.

Conceptualizing a cultural prism

While the literature describing the play among Black children might be sparse, there is a robust literature describing the risks for Black children in regard to learning outcomes as well as a multitude of outcomes across cognitive, social, and emotional domains of development (Campbell and Ramey 1995; McLoyd et al. 1985). This is important to note given the emphasis on play as a source of resilience and its potential for improving learning and developmental outcomes.

To analyse both the academic challenges faced by African American children and the characteristics of their play, we need a perspective we are calling a cultural prism. We are suggesting that this cultural prism could be a rich lens through which to view the play of African American children and the educational challenges that many of them face.

W. E. DuBois ([1903] 1961: 3) said: "The Negro is a sort of seventh son, born with a veil, and gifted with second-sight in this American world." It is our position that the scholar/educator who is proficient in using the cultural prism must be gifted with a number of "DuBoisian sights," all of which are necessary to fully understand the play of African American children and the difficulties they experience in school since they are at the highest risk for the lowest academic achievement and a constellation of associated risks (Campbell and Ramey 1995; Hale 2001). The scholar or professional who uses the cultural prism must be proficient in each of the following areas and must be able to move seamlessly between each of the dimensions.

First sight

This is an understanding of African and African American history and culture as a context for behavior. Any scholar who seeks to interpret the educational profile of

African American children must be grounded in the history and culture of African and African American people. All of the ramifications of racism are included in this category.

A study by Soileau (2002) is an example of analyzing the play of African American children through the first sight of the cultural prism—an understanding of African and African American history and culture as a context for behavior—with an emphasis on culture. This is a study of a select body of African American schoolyard games and how they were shared, changed, preserved or adapted into new play modes as racial integration provided a new set of social interactions. Soileau examined certain elements of boys' cultural expressions: "playing the dozens," telling jokes in mixed racial and gender settings, and entertaining and overseeing a community church's baby-sitting group. She also examined girls' cultural expressions: playing jump-rope rhyming games, ring games and preserving schoolyard play space. She also analyzed the influences on play from television situation comedies, movies, videos, popular music, and the martial arts.

Soileau suggested that play is a form of experimentation in learning to control one's environment, whereas games involve rules, opponents, winning and losing. It is her opinion that both are important learning mechanisms for African American urban children, especially in the face of schools that are unable to meet their needs. Children with low economic opportunities must often deal with prejudice, poverty, drugs, and sometimes chaotic family situations that derive from those conditions. Soileau further opines that the play and games of African American children can serve as coping mechanisms in a stressful world. She argues that obscenities, racial jokes, brutal teasing, and aggressive physical games all serve this function for young African American male children in particular.

Soileau's work is highlighted as an example of the cultural prism because she brings the perspective of a folklorist and anthropologist to the study of African American children's play. Her years of listening to young people have convinced her that great numbers of children, from as young as 4 through high school age, possess a substantial body of folklore that is highly imaginative and which is transmitted from child to child in subtle and sophisticated ways.

There needs to be more ethnographic studies of the play of Black children to determine the manner in which the Black milieu shapes the play behavior and expressive styles of Black children. If it is true that one's culture shapes one's cognition (see Fogle and Mendez 2006), then research in early childhood should specifically describe that process. There have been studies which have adopted an ethno-theoretical approach to the study of children's play in other cultures including Asian American children (Parmar et al. 2004) and Italian children (Chessa et al. 2013). These studies could serve as models for the kind of ethnographic research advocated, focusing on the play culture of African American children.

Second sight

This is an understanding of the socioeconomic exigencies of African American life. This dimension incorporates social class considerations in interpreting play and the achievement patterns of African American children. This dimension is essential because African American people have emerged from and been relegated to the lower social class in America in disproportionate numbers. This dimension also encompasses the need to create the science to accurately assess social class as it relates to school achievement.

Third sight

This is an understanding of African American child development, learning, behavioral, and cultural styles. This dimension requires a grounding in empirical research related to African American child development, a body of literature that is not typically included in mainstream child development and early education texts. One example of how the elements of African American child development relate to learning can be examined is the text, *Black Children*, written by the first author (Hale 1986).

The importance of this third sight emphasizes the need to broaden our conception of play to encompass Black children's expressive styles that include a range of behaviors, tastes, and preferences that we might not ordinarily include as part of play behavior. Movement, dance, music, environmental arts, folklore, and magico-spiritual beliefs have all been important to aspects of African American culture and therefore have influenced the play and development of African American children. An understanding of Black folklore, for example, might facilitate the interpretation of fantasy play among Black children.

Fourth sight

This is an analysis of statistics related to achievement patterns of African American children. It is important that the concept of the cultural prism be applied to the interpretation of statistics related to children's play, developmental profiles, and school achievement. For example, reporting data simply by ethnic or racial group may not tell the whole story. As the studies by Karnik and Tudge (2010) and Fishbein et al. (2009) demonstrate, there may be within-group differences that are important to understand. In both those studies, the play of African American girls was different than that of African American boys. It is often the case that the data may exist describing differences between ethnic groups and differences between genders but as the first author learned in her personal experience consulting with school districts, accessing the data that compared African American boys with African American girls was a challenge.

Fifth sight

This is an ability to identify discrepancies in educational practice that affect African American children. Discrepancies in educational practice include both instructional practices in addition to administrative decisions. Research demonstrates that racism impacts the care and education of even the youngest children and likely impacts the development of social competence and play (Caughy et al. 2004). In some cases it is necessary to identify the "educational malpractice" that is perpetuated against African American children. In Hale (2001), the first author provides examples of such malpractice that took place as her son made his way through an expensive, private school.

Play, culture, and the achievement gap

For more than 30 years, desegregation has been the focal point for educational reform efforts designed to benefit African American children, despite the fact that in most urban areas with large African American populations, there has been a declining pool of white children with whom African American children might be integrated. Other efforts at improving the academic achievement of African American children have involved such compensatory education programs as Head Start. These programs have demonstrated varying degrees of success. Central to an examination of these efforts is the question of whether or not we can bring about an improvement in educational outcomes for African American children without recognizing their unique culture. The study of the play behavior of African American children can provide a window into that culture.

Boykin (1994), for example, posits a kind of "soulfulness" that characterizes African American life. African American children are exposed to a high degree of stimulation from the creative arts. They are surrounded by artifacts of the visual arts, such as posters, paintings, and graffiti; from the audio arts in the form of electronic and radio recordings; television and films from the video arts; and creative hairstyles, hats, and scarves from the fashion arts. There is also a general orientation toward adorning the body that grows out of the African heritage.

The performance styles that permeate the African American community—and are expressed through play behaviors—are further evidence of this affinity for the creative arts. African American children learn from an early age the significance of perfecting the role of performer. This expressiveness is seen in the behavior of African American preachers, athletes, singers, and dancers and is cultivated in individuals throughout the African American community.

The Afro-cultural themes described by Boykin are African in origin and have been maintained and transmitted across generations in communities and families of African descent throughout the world. Boykin (1994: 5) suggests that these themes will find some level of expression in the lives of many African American children. These themes have a "special developmental potency for many African American children, particularly those of low-income background who are more likely to be more distant from mainstream values and practices." The recognition of the importance of these cultural themes is crucial to our understanding of the resilience of young African American children and to the development of educational programs best designed to meet their needs. These themes become the central points of children's identity formation, relationship development, and early coping strategies.

Everything we do in the study of play behavior should be directed toward fighting for educational excellence for African American children. Closing the achievement gap is one step toward that goal. As Franklin (1994) has noted, our ultimate goal must be to prepare African American children for their leadership roles among African people throughout the world. Educational mastery and excellence are the primary objectives toward that end. The study of the play behavior of children of the African diaspora is the first step in that process.

References

Boykin, A. (1994). A talent development approach to school reform. In *American Educational Research Association*, April. New York, NY: AERA.

Bulotsky-Shearer, R., Manz, P., Mendez, J., McWayne, C., Sekino, Y. and Fantuzzo, J. (2012). Peer play interactions and readiness to learn: A protective influence for African-American preschool children from low-income households. *Child Development Perspectives*, 6(3), 225–231.

Campbell, F. and Ramey C. (1995). Cognitive and school outcomes for high-risk African American students at middle adolescence: Positive effects of early intervention. *American Educational Research Journal*, 32(4), 743–772.

Caughy, M., O'Campo, P. and Muntaner, C. (2004). Experiences of racism among African American parents and the mental health of their preschool-aged children. *American Journal of Public Health*, 94(12), 2118–2124.

Chessa, D., Lis, A., Di Riso, D., Delvecchio, E., Mazzeschi, C., Russ, S. and Dillon, J. (2013). A cross-cultural comparison of pretend play in U.S. and Italian children. *Journal of Cross-Cultural Psychology*, 44(4), 640–656.

Chudacoff, H. (2007). *Children at play: An American history*. New York, NY: New York University Press.

DuBois, W. ([1903] 1961). *The souls of Black folk*. Greenwich, CT: Fawcett Publications.

Erikson, E. (1972). Play and actuality. In M. W. Piers (Ed.), *Play and development*. New York, NY: W. W. Norton and Company.

Fantuzzo, J., Sekino, Y. and Cohen, H. (2004). An examination of the contribution of interactive peer play to salient classroom competencies for urban Head Start children. *Psychology in the Schools*, 41(3), 323–336.

Fishbein, H., Malone, D. and Stegelin, D. (2009). Playmate preferences of preschool children based on race, sex, and perceived physical attractiveness. In D. Kuschner (Ed.), *From children to Red Hatters: Diverse images and issues of play. Play and Culture Studies*, Volume 8. Lanham, MD: University Press of America.

Fogle, L. and Mendez, J. (2006). Assessing the play beliefs of African American mothers with preschool children. *Early Childhood Research Quarterly*, 21, 507–518.

Franklin, V. (1994). Foreword. In J. Hale, *Unbank the fire: Visions for the education of African American children*. Baltimore, MD: The Johns Hopkins University Press.

Hale, J. (1986). *Black children: Their roots, culture and learning styles* (rev. ed.). Baltimore, MD: The Johns Hopkins University Press.

Hale, J. (2001). *Learning while black: Creating educational excellence for African American children*. Baltimore, MD: The Johns Hopkins University Press.

Karnik, R. and Tudge, J. (2010). The reality of pretend play: Ethnic, socioeconomic, and gender variations in young children's involvement. In E. E. Nwokah (Ed.), *Play as engagement and communication. Play and Culture Studies*, Volume 10. Lanham, MD: University Press of America.

King, W. (2005). *African American childhood: Historical perspective from slavery to civil rights*. New York: Palgrave Macmillan.

Marten, J. (1998). *The children's Civil War*. Chapel Hill, NC: The University of North Carolina Press.

McLoyd, V., Ray, S. and Etter-Lewis, G. (1985). Being and becoming: The interface of language and family role knowledge in the pretend play of young African American girls. In L. Galda and A. D. Pellegrini (Eds.), *Play language, and stories: The development of children's literate behavior*. Norwood, NJ: Ablex.

Mintz, S. (2004). *Huck's raft: A history of American childhood*. Cambridge, MA: Belknap Press.

Muhammad, Y. (2009). Low-income African American parents' views about the value of play for their preschool age children. Electronic Theses, Treatises and Dissertations. Paper 2202. http://diginole.lib.fsu.edu/etd/2202

Parmar, P. Harkness, S. and Super, C. (2004). Asian and Euro-American parents' ethnotheories of play and learning: Effects on preschool children's home routines and school behavior. *International Journal of Behavioral Development, 28*(2), 97–104.

Smilansky, S. (1968). *The effects of socio-dramatic play on disadvantaged preschool children*. New York, NY: Wiley.

Soileau, J. P. (2002). African American children's folklore: A study in games and play. (Order No. 3057548, University of Louisiana at Lafayette). ProQuest Dissertations and Theses. Available at: http://search.proquest.com/docview/276271202?accountid= 2909. (276271202).

Weinberger, L. and Starkey, P. (1994). Pretend play by African American children in Head Start. *Early Childhood Research Quarterly, 9*, 327–343.

Wiggins, D. (1980). The play of slave children in the plantation communities of the old South, 1820–1860. *Journal of Sport History, 7*(2), 21–39.

7   Play and Asian American children

Eunjoo Jung

It is late afternoon, and children are back from school. "Mom, can I play now?" "You know what mommy will say, you can play when you are finished with your homework." Parents would sit with their children to help them with their work or do academic activities together before allowing them to go play. When children were free to play, some children would build objects using blocks and others would assemble puzzles. Some would play video games, read books, watch television, play educational games, or use technological devices. If space allowed, some would run around and play ball outdoors with their friends and socialize.

Introduction

As these scenes suggest, while play is an important element of children's cognitive, socio-emotional, and academic achievements (Johnson et al. 2005), play is frequently viewed by some Asian American parents as primarily a social or entertaining activity (Tudge et al. 1998) and of less importance in children's education. Asian Americans in this context refer to "adults (ages 18 and older) living in the United States, whether US citizens or not US citizens and regardless of immigration status" (Pew Research Center 2013: 9). There are about 18.2 million Asian Americans in the US, and they constitute nearly 6 percent of the total American population (US Census Bureau 2011). More than 22 Asian subgroups are identified as Asian Americans. Among those, Chinese, Filipino, Indian, Japanese, Korean, and Vietnamese make up the six largest American Asian subgroups (Pew Research Center 2013). While the importance and significance of children's play in childhood development may be shared across different Asian American families, play and play-like activities vary widely both within and between cultural groups (Larson and Verma 1999; Huntsinger et al. 2011). Hence the relationship between play and Asian American culture in dynamic and reciprocal terms warrants consideration.

This chapter provides a description of some defining features of parents' views of play and early education in some Asian American cultural groups. Conceptual considerations that may apply to understanding play in Asian American children are presented. It then discusses the literature and my own research on the play activities of

Asian American children, the implications of play and play-like activities for early childhood education and future directions in implementing play in early childhood curricula for Asian American children. I rely mostly on my personal observations and a handful of research studies with limited sample sizes of particular subgroups of children. Thus, I am cautious in drawing general conclusions about all Asian American children within this chapter. Nonetheless, there are certain issues regarding children's play and parental views about growth and development that may cut across Asian American cultural groups.

Views on play and early education

Play and play-like activities are part of the daily lives of preschool and school-aged children worldwide (Johnson et al. 2005; Singer et al. 2009; Pellegrini 2011). The influence family members, teachers, and others have on the play of Asian American children is dynamic and culturally situated (Roopnarine et al. 1994; Sy et al. 2007; Roopnarine 2010). Across cultural groups, parents have differing roles in children's development and school success, and there are different approaches to children's education (Chao 1996; Smith 2010). How Asian American children function and are perceived in the American educational system may depend on the activities that their parents engage in with them (Farver et al. 2000; Kuschner 2007; Cote and Bornstein 2009). To understand play of Asian American children, considerations of parents' views on play, work, and early academic activities and their roles in children's education and acculturation are necessary.

Parental views on play and work

Asian American parents may agree in theory that play is important in children's cognitive development and social skills. Yet, in reality, many of them place a stronger value on hard work than on play (Farver et al. 2000; Ng et al. 2007). While European American parents in general tend to view play as an important vehicle for early development, Asian American parents tend to see less developmental value in it (Parmar et al. 2004). In particular, Asian American parents from Chinese, Korean, Pakistani, Nepalese, and Indian backgrounds believe that starting academic training and learning-related activities early in life is critical for children's success and development (Parmar et al. 2004). Some Asian American parents may even regard play as the antithesis to work and a waste of time. The word "play" often denotes laziness, idling, doing nothing, amusement, and "a way to escape boredom" (Farver et al. 1995: 11).

These views have substantial implications for children's play and non-play activities (academic activities) and are reflected in parental practices at home and in children's daily routines, activities, and social interactions in some Asian American families (Parmar et al. 2004). European American mothers generally embrace a play-based curriculum and the inclusion of educational play in daily routines (Parmar et al. 2004). By comparison, Asian American mothers (Korean Americans in the study) desire more emphasis on academic skills, contents learning, and school readiness (Farver et al. 1995).

Because of the latter beliefs, teacher–parent disagreements about the nature of early childhood programs are not uncommon (Farver and Lee-Shin 2000). In the next few sections, I focus on two issues—beliefs about parenthood and the acculturation process—to provide some insights into play in Asian American families with young children.

Beliefs about parenthood

In general, Asians are known to believe strongly in hard work and effort rather than in innate ability, talent, and competence (Wu 2008; Cote and Bronstein 2009). A survey of a nationally-representative sample of 3511 Asian Americans (Pew Research Center 2013) which is based on a detailed analysis of US Census Bureau and government data (US Census Bureau 2011: 134) shows that "Asian Americans express a stronger belief in the value of hard work than does the broader American public." That belief relates to Asian parents' views on their responsibilities as parents. Asian parents tend to think they are responsible for and should have significant influence on their children's education and future careers (Pew Research Center 2013). Most Asian American parents in the stated survey (57–78 percent) thought that being a good parent is one of the most important things in their lives, regardless of whether they were born in or outside of the United States. They tend to intervene more and push their children harder to succeed in life.

A popular belief among Asian American parents is that the responsibility of a good parent is to educate their children well (Wu 2008; Raghavan et al. 2010). For many Asian American families, their children's innate abilities can be improved with hard work, more effort, and good parenting (Figure 7.1). In that sense, play is often seen as

Figure 7.1 An Asian American child practices English language skills by writing an interactive diary with his mom.

peripheral to childhood development. Perhaps, as Wu (2008) indicated, even among Chinese American families who reside in the United States, parenting beliefs and practices are still deeply rooted in and influenced by traditions in the natal cultures. The view among many Asian American parents is that "you can play and take rest once your work is completed" (Shiakou and Belsky 2013). Rather than allowing children to have free play or decision-making in play activities, Asian American parents tend to control, lead and preplan play activities (Lowinger and Heide 2001). The goal is to connect play with some kind of educational purpose that will translate into academic activities.

The family's acculturation and play

When they become more assimilated and acculturated to the United States, Asian American mothers (Koreans parents in the study) are more open to and encouraging of children's play and creativity. These parents are also more involved in parent–child play at home than those who are less integrated into American society as a whole (Berry 1997; Farver and Lee-Shin 2000). It is noteworthy that when the children of Korean American parents display behavioral traits that would be considered individualistic (e.g., assertiveness, independence), they are viewed as difficult by classroom teachers. Often these behaviors are interpreted as discrepant from the "prototypical" Asian American child who is presumed to be shy, obedient, quiet, focused on academic skills, and dependent. The manner in which these stereotypical behaviors and traits of Asian American children influence how teachers and caregivers structure play activities for children is largely speculative at this point. Because Asian American children move between two or more cultural worlds, it is likely that their play participation is more nuanced with children who are more fully integrated into American society, displaying better abilities to blend play practices from the natal culture with those in the larger cultural community.

Conceptual considerations

Play is a generic process that occurs in all cultures observed to date but varies a good deal in manifestation and mode (Gaskins 2002; Cote and Bornstein 2009). The cultural specificity concept as espoused in the developmental niche framework (Harkness and Super 1992) provides a useful lens for understanding the play activities of Asian American children and families. Parental ethno-theories, environmental and social settings of daily life, childcare practices and routines all have significant influences on children's development. A child's culturally structured developmental niche shapes his/her experiences, opportunities, and time for learning and growth over the course of development (Super and Harkness 1999). Although Asian Americans embrace early childhood practices in the United States, they tend to hold on to different ethno-theories about childhood development. As a result, the developmental niches of home and school may be incongruous in many ways (Parmar et al. 2004). Play patterns in Asian American children may demonstrate this duality (Hoffman 1988).

Play of Asian American children

To understand the play activities and practices of Asian American children, I first discuss some play forms in early childhood program settings and homes. I then present an analysis of play behaviors and academic activities at home.

Among various play forms, pretend play is highly valued as contributing to social and cognitive development in North American children (Lillard and Witherington 2004; Ma and Lillard 2006). Although studies on play patterns, especially social pretend play of Asian American children in early childhood program settings, are sparse, a few studies that include my own work provide some insights into modes of play participation among Asian American children.

Play characteristics

Asian American parents may share similar views on parenthood and the value of hard work (Wu 2008), but their attitudes toward play and early education differ within and between cultural groups. Although they might differ in their home play patterns from European Americans, most Asian American children follow the routines provided by the American school system. Hence, many of these children participate in the play activities that reflect cultural practices within the United States and the natal culture. For instance, in the Korean American community, children sometimes participate in traditional play such as Yut, Jegichagi (Korean shuttlecock game), marble games, slap-match games, and kite-flying. They are also involved with many toys and games and educational- and technology-enhanced play activities that are prevalent in the United States. As such, alphabet drills and "quiet desk work" are said to be increasingly prevalent among Asian Americans.

In terms of actual play and social interactions, Asian American preschool children show different patterns of involvement than European American children. Specifically, Asian American children's social behaviors, interactions and play tend to be observed more during outdoor play activities than indoor play activities (Farver et al. 1995). Asian American children's play appears highly structured and involves object-mediated (more functional play activities) rather than pretend or imaginative play. Overall, they tend to engage in low frequencies of pretend play (Farver et al. 1995). Differences in social interactions and play behaviors between Asian American and European American children appear to be a manifestation of children's culture-specific socialization practices and the adaptation and acculturation processes of immigrant families in the United States (Farver et al. 1995). At the same time, the children's own interactive styles, social interactions with peers, and levels of creativity are significantly related to levels of children's pretend play. This may indicate that children's individual characteristics as well as cultural socialization factors interact with each other, with the possibility of individual factors surpassing cultural ones in determining levels of pretend play (Farver and Lee-Shin 1997; Farver et al. 2000; Kostelnik et al. 2009).

Teacher–child play

European American and Asian American teachers display notable differences in the ways they organize their classrooms, lessons, and environments (Farver et al. 1995; Zhou et al. 2006). European American teachers tend to provide classroom environments that allow children to think independently, solve problems, and be actively involved in learning activities (Farver et al. 1995). These teachers also offer more opportunities for children to engage in social interactions and play, and children are more frequently involved in collaborative activities with their teachers compared to Asian American children (Farver et al. 1995). According to Farver et al., Korean American teachers in Korean American preschools organize their classrooms and lessons in ways that encourage the development of academic skills, task perseverance, and less active involvement in learning. Collaborative activities between teachers and children are infrequently initiated or observed in Korean American preschools. The Korean American teachers who participated in the study were born in the United States and trained in American colleges; however, their teaching styles and academically-oriented curricula reflected traditional Korean values, expectations, and educational goals for children (Farver et al. 1995). Overall, Asian American children tend to have more opportunities for constructive and functional play activities with, and by, Asian American teachers.

Parent–child play

The way in which parents spend time with their children influences their children's functioning (Bornstein et al. 1996; Parmar et al. 2004). Parental practices at home in regards to the use of time and the supply of toy materials have been used to gauge the involvement of Asian immigrant and European American parents in their children's daily activities. Parents in both groups spend similar amounts of time in play activities with their children; but Asian American parents do more constructive play than pretend play. Although Asian American parents acknowledged the importance of play, they generally did not practice play with their children at home. Asian American parents spent much more time on pre-academic activities such as learning letters and numbers, playing math games, and working with computers. In comparison to Asian American parents, European American parents engaged in more pretend play with their children (Farver et al. 1995; Parmar et al. 2008).

Technology and educational play

One aspect of Asian American children's play worthy of attention is the prevalence of educational play and use of technological devices (Haugland 1999; Zimmerman et al. 2007). Activities involving technology have the possibility of isolating individuals while taking away valuable time from family activities (Cordes and Miller 2000). The introduction of various technologies including computers, the internet, and cell phones, increased urbanization, and limited places for outdoor activities have led more children to play indoors. Many of the play forms that Asian American parents experienced in their childhoods are being replaced by constructive and symbolic play and materials including involvement with technological devices (Zhang and Prosser 2012). Because of the strong emphasis on education, a large number of Asian American families embrace electronic toys, lap ware, computer toys, computer games, video games, and educational play using computers, smart toys including robots and digital images, and internet activities for their children (Haugland and Wright 1997; Zhang and Prosser 2012). While children are not advised to use technological devices to practice didactic materials, to use electronic books, and engage in drill and practice worksheets (Levin and Rosenquest 2001), many of them are exposed to this type of technology-enhanced early learning at home and in early childhood program settings.

Play and activities at home

Using large data sets from the Early Childhood Longitudinal Study-Kindergarten Class (ECLS-K) on early childhood education and children (National Center for Education Statistics 2009), I examined parents' views about play and their activities with children, use of educational materials, television viewing, and play behaviors in Asian American and European American families and children. Although a comparison of more groups (African Americans, Hispanics, etc.) would have provided more information, I limited my analysis to the two aforementioned groups to highlight the similarities and differences between Asian American and European American families. I also focused on socio-economic differences within the groups because play and activity patterns in households have been shown to be related to economic status (Tudge et al. 1998).

Parental views

Table 7.1 displays data on the values that Asian American families (n = 979) and European American families (n = 10,256) place on play at the beginning of kindergarten. Asian American parents had higher regard for counting numbers and knowing letters and lower regard for sharing behaviors with others, drawing, and being calm and communicating well with others than did European American parents. The educational expectations of Asian American parents for their children were much higher than those of European American parents (Yamamoto and Holloway 2010). As noted earlier, Asian American parents strongly value hard work and academic success (Wu 2008), and they also want their children to build socio-emotional and communicative competencies through interactions with others (Farver et al. 2000).

Activities during kindergarten year

Table 7.2 summarizes some of the data related to the educational activities of Asian American (n = 1059) and European American children (n = 10,885) in the spring

Table 7.1 Mean scores on the values parents rate at the beginning of kindergarten

Categories	Means	
	Asian Americans (n = 979)	European Americans (n = 10,256)
Counting numbers	3.81	3.55
Sharing behaviors with others	4.09	4.33
Drawing	3.86	3.91
Being calm	3.94	4.04
Knowing letters	3.85	3.72
Communicating well with others	4.07	4.33
*Degree expected of child	4.41	3.90

Note: Each item without * was measured on a 5-point scale: 1 (not important), 2 (not very important), 3 (somewhat important), 4 (very important), 5 (essential). The item with * was measured on a 6-point scale: 1 (less than high school), 2 (high school), 3 (two or more years of college), 4 (four years of college), 5 (master's degree), 6 (PhD, MD, or other higher degree).

Table 7.2 Mean scores on the educational activities in the kindergarten year

Categories	Means	
	Asian Americans (n = 1059)	European Americans (n = 10,885)
Attended sport events	1.67	1.51
Participated in athletic events	1.68	1.40
Participated in organized clubs	1.90	1.82
Presence of a home computer for child's use	1.35	1.32
Use of computer to learn skills	.25	.38
Use of computer to learn drawing	.29	.44
Use of computer for internet	.70	.90
*Child's actual use of a home computer	1.14	1.41
*Reading outside of school	3.06	2.93

Note: Each item without * was measured on a yes (= 1) or no (= 0) scale. The item with * was measured on a 4-point scale: 1 (not at all), 2 (once or twice a week), 3 (3 to 6 times a week), 4 (every day).

semester of kindergarten. The mean rankings indicate a preference for academic reading and structured activities for Asian American children and play-related activities for European American children. Asian American children read more outside of school and attended and participated more in athletic events and organized clubs than did European American children. Overall, the presence of a home computer for the child's

Table 7.3 Mean scores of kindergarten children's television viewing by socioeconomic backgrounds

	SES categories	Means	
		Asian Americans (N = 1059)	European Americans (N = 10,885)
Weekday television viewing	First quintile	13.97	2.52
	Second quintile	7.89	2.17
	Third quintile	4.76	1.98
	Fourth quintile	2.40	2.13
	Fifth quintile	1.91	2.28
	Total	5.31	2.18
Weekend television viewing	First quintile	3.66	5.22
	Second quintile	4.54	4.93
	Third quintile	4.71	4.68
	Fourth quintile	4.13	4.36
	Fifth quintile	3.78	3.94
	Total	4.08	4.47

Note: Each item was measured on a number of hours that the child watches television. The first quintile represents the lowest fifth of the data (1–20%) and the fifth quintile represents the highest fifth of the data (81–100%).

use was slightly higher for Asian American than European American children. However, Asian American children made less use of computers to learn skills, to draw, or to go on the internet than European American children. In Asian American families, parents tried to equip their children with computers, but they were not used fully for learning-related activities.

As shown in Table 7.3, the Asian American children from lower SES backgrounds relied more on television viewing than did children from European American families. For instance, the week-day television viewing of children from less advantaged economic backgrounds was almost five times that of economically privileged children from European American families. Television viewing during the weekend was higher for European American children across all SES backgrounds than among Asian American children. The roles of television viewing during weekdays and computer use in the lives of culturally and linguistically diverse Asian American children may be areas of interest for future research.

Activities of the first graders

As shown in Table 7.4, Asian American first-grade children (n = 837) continued to participate more frequently in athletic events and organized clubs than European

Table 7.4 Mean scores on the activities of the first graders

Categories	Means	
	Asian Americans (n = 837)	European Americans (n = 9249)
Participated in athletic events	1.56	1.30
Participated in organized clubs	1.77	1.61
*Tell stories	2.61	2.76
*Sing songs together	2.38	2.82
*Help with art	2.14	2.31
*Make children do chores	2.82	3.28
*Play games	2.49	2.64
*Teach about nature	1.90	2.24
*Build things together	1.97	2.08
*Do sports together	2.42	2.71
*Read to children	2.98	3.20
*Use computer for educational purpose	1.32	1.48
**Child doing homework	4.21	3.87
**Helping children with homework	3.67	3.55
***Degree expected of child	4.34	3.87
****Reading materials in household	67.01	130.83

Note: Each item without * was measured on a yes (= 1) or no (= 0) scale. The item with * was measured on a 4-point scale: 1 (not at all), 2 (once or twice a week), 3 (3 to 6 times a week), 4 (everyday). The item with ** was measured on a 5-point scale: 1 (never), 2 (less than once a week), 3 (1 to 2 times a week), 4 (3 to 4 times a week), 5 (5 or more times a week). The item with *** was measured on a 6-point scale: 1 (less than high school), 2 (high school), 3 (two or more years of college), 4 (four years of college), 5 (master's degree), 6 (PhD, MD, or other higher degree). The item with **** was measured on the number of books the child has.

American children (n = 9249). Asian American parents had higher aspirations for their first-grade children, and they were more involved in helping children with homework than European American parents. European American parents were more apt to tell stories, sing songs together, help with art, make children do chores, play games, teach about nature, build things, do sports together, and read to children than Asian American parents did. Moreover, European American families made more use of computers for educational purposes than did Asian American families. There were about twice as many reading materials in European American than in Asian American households, regardless of socioeconomic status. In short, Asian American children were involved in more academic-related activities and structured activities than were many European American children.

Implications for early childhood education

Play varies widely both within and between cultures (Roopnarine et al. 1994; Roopnarine 2010). It seems that although Asian American children learn to play in the American culture, they retain some play forms and approaches from their countries of origin. Despite making adjustments toward cultural practices of socialization and early education in the United States, children's play behaviors may continue to serve as a means by which Asian American children learn about their culture and themselves (Roopnarine et al. 1994). As studies have shown, individual characteristics may be more important in children's behavior and in parents' attitudes toward play than cultural background, or culture would play a more important role in children's play behavior than individual differences would (Roopnarine et al. 1994; Kostelnik et al. 2009). Nevertheless, Asian American children and parents might be expected to show certain patterns of play or behavior based upon their expected cultural norms.

When discrepancies exist between natal culture and new cultural community norms, children's behaviors may or may not be accepted well by teachers and others (Farver et al. 1995; Johnson et al. 2005). Asian American children appear to be viewed by different standards and stereotypes, and when children do not meet these standards or deviate from the expected norms, they may be regarded as being difficult (Farver et al. 1995). In the United States, certain modes of play, such as social pretend play and constructive play, are emphasized (Lillard and Witherington 2004; Ma and Lillard 2006), and it needs to be asked whether it is fair to emphasize the importance of the same modes of play for all ethnic groups, including Asian Americans. Asian American children may not engage in high levels of pretend play, but they are more likely involved in functional play, constructive play, play with academic-related activities and objects, and structured activities (Figure 7.2).

To implement and support play in early childhood curricula for Asian American children, the roles of parents, schools, teachers, and society in understanding and guiding Asian American children as they grow up in the United States appear to be of tremendous importance. To meet the future educational needs of Asian American children, early childhood teacher education programs should include practices that consider the challenges and distinct characteristics of Asian American children and families. Understanding the characteristics of these children, the value of various forms of play as an activity that is rich with social and cognitive properties may need to be shared by teachers and schools with the Asian American community, families, and children. Moreover, teacher education programs need to emphasize play as a crucial element of early childhood curricula, especially through field experiences and in courses that pertain to educational practices working with Asian American children (Jung and Han 2013).

For those children who are living in a dual cultural world, trust and interaction among teachers, children, and their families are critical to Asian American children's school adjustment, readiness, and success (Jung and Han 2013). This calls for educators to establish a positive relationship not only with their students, but also with parents; this is particularly true for families from minority backgrounds in general who may not be proficient in English language skills, including the Asian American population (Jung and Zhang in press). Initially, Asian American children may find it difficult to build friendships

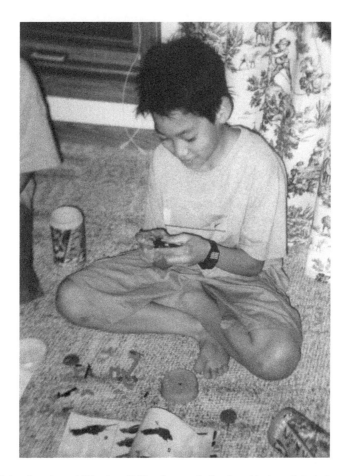

Figure 7.2   Asian American children's activities frequently involve object-mediated play.

with children from different ethnic groups in the US and may prefer to remain quiet and focus on desk work. It is incumbent upon early childhood professionals to reach out to these children through collaborative play activities in order for them to make connections with children from diverse ethnic backgrounds.

References

Berry, J. W. (1997). Immigration, acculturation, and adaptation. *Applied Psychology*, *46*(1), 5–34.

Bornstein, M. H., Haynes, O. M., O'Reilly, A. W. and Painter, K. M. (1996). Solitary and collaborative pretense play in early childhood: Sources of individual variation in the development of representational competence. *Child Development*, *67*(6), 2910–2929.

Chao, R. (1996). Chinese and European mothers' beliefs about the role of parenting in children's school success. *Journal of Cross-Cultural Psychology*, *27*, 403–423.

Cordes, C. and Miller, E. (2000). *Fool's gold: A critical look at computers in childhood.* Available at: http://www.allianceforchildhood.org/fools_gold (accessed 28 May 2013).

Cote, L. R. and Bornstein, M. H. (2009). Child and mother play in three U.S. cultural groups: Comparisons and associations. *Journal of Family Psychology, 23*(3), 355–363.

Farver, J. M., Kim, Y. and Lee-Shin, Y. (1995). Cultural differences in Korean- and European-American preschoolers' social interaction and play behaviours. *Child Development, 66*, 1088–1099.

Farver, J. M., Kim, Y. and Lee-Shin, Y. (2000). Within cultural differences: Examining individual differences in Korean American and European American preschoolers' social pretend play. *Journal of Cross-Cultural Psychology, 31*, 583–602.

Farver, J. M. and Lee-Shin, Y. (1997). Social pretend play in Korean- and Anglo-American preschoolers. *Child Development, 68*, 544–556.

Farver, J. M. and Lee-Shin, Y. (2000). Acculturation and Korean American children's social and play behavior. *Social Development, 9*(3), 316–336.

Gaskins, S. (2002). Children's daily activities in a Mayan village: A culturally grounded description. *Journal of Cross-Cultural Research, 34*, 375–389.

Harkness, S. and Super, C. M. (1992). From parents' cultural belief systems to behaviour. In L. Eldering and P. Leseman (Eds.), *Effective early intervention: Cross-cultural Perspectives* (pp. 67–90). New York: Falmer Press.

Haugland, S. W. (1999). What role should technology play in young children's learning? *Young Children, 54*(9), 26–30.

Haugland, S. and Wright, J. (1997). *Young children and technology: A world of discovery.* Boston: Allyn and Bacon.

Hoffman, L. (1988). Cross-cultural differences in child rearing goals. In R. Levine, P. Miller, and M. Maxwell (Eds.), *Parenting behaviors in diverse societies: New directions for child development.* San Francisco: Jossey-Bass.

Huntsinger, C. S., Jose, P. E., Balsink, K. D. and Luo, Z. (2011). Cultural differences in Chinese American and European American children's drawing skills over time. *Early Childhood Research Quarterly, 26*, 134–145.

Johnson, J. E., Christie, J. F. and Wardle, F. (2005). *Play, development and early education.* Boston: Allyn and Bacon.

Jung, E. and Han, H. S. (2013). Teacher outreach efforts and reading achievement in kindergarten. *Journal of Research in Childhood Education, 27*(1), 93–110.

Jung, E. and Zhang, Y. (in press). Parental involvement, children's aspirations, and achievement in new immigrant families. *The Journal of Educational Research.*

Kostelnik, M. J., Whiren, A. P., Soderman, A. K. and Gregory, K. (2009). *Guiding children's social development: Theory to practice* (6th ed.), Albany, New York: Delmar.

Kuschner, D. (2007). Children's play in the journal, *Young children*: An analysis of how it is portrayed and why it is valued. In D. J. Sluss and O. S. Jarrett (Eds.), *Investigating play in the 21st century: play and cultural studies* (vol. 7, pp. 55–67). Lanham, MD: University Press of America.

Larson, R. and Verma, S. (1999). How children and adolescents around the world spend time: Work, play, and developmental opportunities. *Psychological Bulletin, 125*(6), 701–736.

Levin, D. and Rosenquest, B. (2001). The increasing role of electronic toys in the lives of infants and toddlers: Should we be concerned? *Contemporary Issues in Early Childhood*, *2*(2), 242–247.

Lillard, A. S. and Witherington, D. C. (2004). Mothers' behaviour modifications during pretense and their possible signal value for toddlers. *Developmental Psychology*, *40*, 95–113.

Lowinger, R. J. and Heide, K. (2001). Parental overprotection in Asian American children: A psychodynamic clinical perspective. *Psychotherapy: Theory, Research, Practice, Training*, *38*(3), 319–330.

Ma, L. and Lillard, A. S. (2006). What is the real cheese? Young children's ability to discriminate between real and pretend acts. *Child Development*, *77*(6), 1762–1777.

National Center for Education Statistics (2009). *Combined user's manual for the ECLS-K eighth-grade and K–8 full sample data files and electronic codebooks*. Available at: http://nces.ed.gov/ecls/data/ECLSK_K8_Manual_part1.pdf.

Ng, F. F-Y., Eva, M. and Lam, S. (2007). European American and Chinese parents' responses to children's success and failure: Implications for children's responses. *Developmental Psychology*, *43*(5), 1239–1255.

Parmar, P., Harkness, S. and Super, C. M. (2004). American and Asian parents' ethnotheories of play and learning: Effects on home routines and children's behaviour in school. *International Journal of Behavioral Development*, *28*(2), 97–104.

Parmar, P., Harkness, S. and Super, C. M. (2008). Teacher or playmate? Asian immigrant and Euro-American parents' participation in their young children's daily activities. *Social Behavior and Personality*, *36*(2), 163–176.

Pellegrini, A. D. (2011). Play. In P. D. Zelazo (Ed.), *Oxford handbook of developmental psychology*. New York: Oxford University Press.

Pew Research Center. (2013). The rise of Asian Americans. Available at: http://www.pewsocialtrends.org/files/2013/04/AsianAmericans-new-full-report-04-2013.pdf (accessed 31 Dec. 2013).

Raghavan, C. S., Harkness, S. and Super, C. M. (2010). Parental ethnotheories in the context of immigration: Asian Indian immigrant and Euro-American mothers and daughters in an American town. *Journal of Cross-Cultural Psychology*, *41*(4), 617–632.

Roopnarine, J. L. (2010). Cultural variations in beliefs about play, parent-child play, and children's play: Meaning for childhood development. In A. Pellegrini (Ed.), *Oxford encyclopedia on play*. Oxford: Oxford University Press.

Roopnarine, J. L., Johnson, J. and Hooper, F. (1994). *Children's play in diverse cultures*. Albany, NY: State University of New York Press.

Shiakou, M. and Belsky, J. (2013). Exploring parent attitudes toward children's play and learning in Cyprus. *Journal of Research in Childhood Education*, *27*(1), 17–30.

Singer, D. G., Jerome, L., Singer, H. D. and Raeka, D. (2009). Children's pastime and play in sixteen nations: Is free-play declining? *American Journal of Play*, *1*, 218–232.

Smith, P. K. (2010). *Understanding children's worlds: Child and play*. Chichester: Wiley-Blackwell.

Super, C. M. and Harkness, S. (1999). The environment as culture in developmental research. In T. Wachs and S. Friedman (Eds.), *Measurement of the environment in developmental research* (pp. 279–323). Washington, DC: American Psychological Association.

Sy, S. R., Rowley, S. J. and Schulenberg, J. E. (2007). Predictors of parent involvement across contexts in Asian American and European American families. *Journal of Comparative Family Studies*, *38*(1), 1–29.

Tudge, J., Haogan, D., Lee, S., Meltsas, M., Tammeveski, P., Kulakova, N., Snezhkova, I. and Putnam, S. (1998). Cultural heterogeneity: Parental values and beliefs and their preschoolers' activities in the United States, Korea, Russia, and Estonia. In A. Göncü (Ed.), *Children's engagement in the world: A sociocultural perspective*. Cambridge: Cambridge University Press.

US Census Bureau. (2011). *Facts for features*. Available at: http://www.census.gov/newsroom/releases/pdf/cb13ff-09_asian.pdf (accessed 21 Apr. 2013).

Wu, E. C. (2008). Parental influence on children's talent development: A case study with three Chinese American families. *Journal for the Education of the Gifted, 32*(1), 100–129.

Yamamoto, Y. and Holloway, S. (2010). Parental expectations and children's academic performance in sociocultural context. *Educational Psychological Review*, 22, 189–214.

Zhang, S. and Prosser, M. H. (2012). Globalisation, Asian modernity, values, and Chinese society. *China Media Research*, 8(2), 18–25.

Zhou, Z., Peverly, S. T. and Xin, T. (2006). Knowing and teaching fractions: A cross-cultural study of American and Chinese mathematics teachers. *Contemporary Educational Psychology*, *31*, 438–457.

Zimmerman, F. J., Christakis, D. A. and Meltzoff, A. N. (2007). Associations between media viewing and language development in children under 2 years. *Journal of Pediatrics*, *151*(4): 364–368.

8 Traditional Native American children's play: the nature-culture connection

Michelle Buchanan and Margaret Cooney

A number of us boys would get on our ponies and go out to an open space where we had plenty of room. There we would take turns in riding up and down in front of the rest of the group while they looked on. Pretending that we were riding in front of an enemy, we would lean away over on the side of the pony out of sight of our supposed enemy. Just our knee would be over the pony's back, but our head and body would be out of sight . . . after considerable practice, we would be able to stay in this position at full speed with just our heel over the pony's back. Only a foot would be visible to the enemy, so there was not much to shoot at.

(Standing Bear 1931: 36)

Introduction

In this chapter, we bring historical accounts of American Indian childhood together with contemporary voices to provide a perspective of childhood and play in traditional Native American cultures. We emphasize "a perspective" in that there is no such thing as "the Native American" or "the play of Native American children" in general. Joseph Bruchac (2003), a contemporary Native author, suggests that anyone who writes about Native Americans must begin with qualifying remarks because "seeing all Indians as being alike is as foolish as not being able to see them at all" (Bruchac 2003: 8). Special attention is given to the Eastern Shoshone people of the Wind River reservation in Wyoming and in particular, an honored chief of the Shoshone people, Chief Washakie. In this chapter, we draw on stories of traditional Indian childhoods, including that of Chief Washakie, and autobiographies and biographies of a select few of his contemporaries.

There are over 560 federally recognized Native American tribes with different cultures, languages, social and political structures and spiritual traditions. Despite this great diversity, all Native tribes shared a profoundly similar post-colonial history and series of events that played out repeatedly throughout the history of European occupation and settlement of the continent. Bruchac describes these experiences as follows: (1) the first Europeans were welcomed; (2) that welcome was repaid by aggression and ingratitude; (3) the Indian people were forced into resistance; (4) superior white weaponry and European diseases overcame Native resistance; (5) the Indian nation was devastated and the people were forced into slavery or driven off their land by one means or another; (6) reservations were established, often on the poorest soil and in the most inaccessible locations; (7) Indian children were taken from their families and placed in boarding schools or adopted by Whites; and (8) the survival of Indian languages and traditions became threatened (Bruchac 2003: 11).

These post-European contact experiences caused disruption in tribal lifestyles and cultures that shape any significant human behavior such as childhood play. In this chapter, historical context is used as a lens for viewing play in Native American culture from pre-colonial to post-colonial and contemporary time periods. The historical documents, interviews and stories that we draw upon represent Intermountain, West and Plains tribes, many of which were buffalo-based and warrior societies. These were societies that prepared children for hunting, domestic life, the keeping of spiritual traditions, the protection of people and property, intertribal conflict and the resistance of immigrant occupation. Children's play, then, can be seen as a reflection of the habitat, customs and occupations of these tribes historically and contemporarily. Both Native America and Native American cultures and lifestyles have changed dramatically over time, as has children's play.

Contemporary Native Americans are reclaiming their original languages and traditional cultures for their children and future generations. Because connection to nature was central to every aspect of the culture and spiritual life of Native Americans, we suggest that reclaiming traditional cultures can benefit all children in a society now experiencing what Richard Louv (2005) has called the "nature-deficit disorder" or a loss of intimate contact with nature. We conclude this chapter by suggesting that the present society has much to learn about the traditional and nature-based play of Native children and that knowledge may help us all in finding ways to bring our children back to nature through play.

Children's play, Vygotsky and play as a cultural activity

For the purposes of this chapter we adopt Gray's (2009) five characteristics of play in writing about the play of Native American children. Play is a child activity that is: (1) self-chosen and self-directed; (2) intrinsically motivated; (3) structured by mental rules or a structure that derives from rules that players hold in mind; (4) imaginative; and (5) produced in an active, alert, but non-stressed state of mind. Descriptions of children's play from historical documents and interviews that are discussed in this chapter are congruent with these five characteristics that collectively define children's play.

Following Vygotsky (1978), play and playthings are seen as cultural artifacts through which children acquire the tools and meanings of culture. Vygotsky proposed a sociocultural theory that conceptualized development as a process of socialization into established cultural meanings. For young children, the motivation for play, or the need being satisfied, is the ability to perform activities, through imagination, that are not available to children in real life (i.e., cooking over a fire, hunting for game, war-fare, performing ceremonies). Play is considered a "leading activity" for children in that it becomes a means for developing imagination and abstract thinking as well as socialization into cultural meanings. Play becomes a "world of instruction" where children take on different roles and perform certain actions to both create and resolve problems during the play activity (e.g., wounding a buffalo and then escaping the wrath of the angry wounded buffalo as described later in this chapter).

Understanding children's play as a cultural activity requires giving consideration to social, economic and physical contexts that determine which activities are available to children and have survival value. Children's play varies from community to community, and a cultural approach to examining play includes an understanding of the opportunities children have for play, the community values regarding children's play, and the ways in which those values are conveyed socially and through the provision of time, space, and playthings for play. Children's play is presented in this chapter as an activity that satisfies personal desires, is determined by the availability of time, space, and materials, and is a process of socialization into the culture. In descriptions of the traditional play of Native children, attention is directed at the types of activities or play available to children, children's engagement in that play, and the ways in which play has supported certain cultural and survival values.

In the next section we provide a brief introduction to the group of Native Americans that are a focal point of discussion in this chapter. We also discuss the tribal cultural meanings related to children that set the stage for talking about traditional Native children's play as a meaningful life activity.

Chief Washakie and the Eastern Shoshone Indians

For almost 60 years, Washakie was the primary chief of the eastern band of Shoshone Indians from 1843 to his death in 1900. The Eastern Shoshones are a band of the Northern Shoshone tribe, also known as Snakes, a division of the widely distributed Shoshonian family. The Northern Shoshones ranged over the greater part of western Wyoming, southwestern Montana, central and southern Idaho, northern Utah and Nevada. In 1868, the Eastern Shoshone people were granted reservation land in the Warm Valley region of Wyoming, now known as the Wind River region of west central Wyoming. Traditional post-colonial Eastern Shoshone people were nomadic, moving with the seasons and the wildlife that sustained them (particularly the buffalo).

Washakie was born at the turn of the eighteenth century to a Shoshone mother and a Flathead/Salish father. Historians estimate the year of his birth to be 1798. During the years before his death in 1900, he witnessed the transition from pre-colonial traditional Native life through the commencement of the emigration era, western expansion and reservation life. He rose to leadership as a venerated warrior in defense of his people and a diplomat who negotiated the Bridger Treaty in 1868. In this treaty, Chief Washakie was able to secure nearly four million acres for his people on what is now known as the Wind River reservation—the only tribal chief to secure land of his people's choosing from the government (Hebard 1930).

In negotiating treaties with the government, Washakie demanded schools, teachers, physicians, and skilled craftsmen because he understood that his people would need these resources to survive and he recognized the need for his people to be educated in order to be successful in maintaining their land and heritage in a new world.

Children are sacred

In his book, *Our Stories Remember: American Indian History, Culture and Values Through Storytelling*, Joseph Bruchac (2003) writes about shared values among many Native tribes and cites the prominent world-view of the circularity of existence. In this view of life as a circle, the human life cycle can be seen as an evolution through four phases—childhood, youth, adulthood and the elder years—with the elder approaching the same place on the circle as the child. Both children and elders are seen as sacred by many Native peoples because both are closer to the Creator than the generations in between. Black Elk talks of how little children see things that their elders are not able to see and, as such, make important contributions to the people. Black Elk explained that the cottonwood tree is sacred to the Sioux people because its leaves are a template for the tipi. Young children who used cottonwood leaves to make toy houses made this discovery. Here, Black Elk explains how young children, in their play, brought this insight to the people: "This too is an example of how much grown men may learn from very little children, for the hearts of little children are pure, and, therefore, the Great Spirit may show to them many things which older people miss" (Brown 1987: 74–75).

In a circular world-view, no individual is more important than his or her people and people are no more important than the beings with which they share the Earth. In her biography of Chief Washakie, Urbaneck wrote of how these spiritual values were expressed in the raising of children:

> When a baby began to crawl, he was left to burn his fingers at the lodge fire and to adjust himself early to the facts of nature. He was not restricted by, nor came to resent the "no, no" commands of his elders. He explored the world and took the consequences. Children's rights were respected and what was theirs – such as sticks, balls, dolls, small bows and dull arrows – could not be taken from them without their consent.
>
> (Urbaneck 1971: 15)

Traditional Native childhood play

Childhood activities for Plains Indians, including play, reflected the nomadic, buffalo-based lifestyle and nature-based spirituality of the tribes and those activities varied with the seasons and seasonal habitat of the tribe. By all accounts, child play was a valued activity and children had many opportunities for play and were active players through all seasons. Playthings consisted of natural materials that were often crafted and provided by adults, and adults at times participated in children's play. Children's play had cultural and survival value because children developed and practiced skills they would need as adults.

Though winters were long and extremely cold in the mountains and on the plains, children were active players. They played sliding games on the ice. They would run to a stream and try to slide all the way across it without falling. Sledding was also popular with sleds being made out of ribs of buffalo lashed together with strong strips of rawhide. The thick wool of the buffalo's head served as a seat in the middle of the sled. Girls played marble games with colorful stones that were rounded and polished by their older relatives and given to them as playthings. Marble games were played on the ice, with two groups of girls sitting opposite each other about 50 feet apart, and a block of wood, $2 \times 2 \times 4$ inches, central between them. One side began by shooting all the marbles at the block trying to dislodge it. If they succeeded, they got another chance; if not, the marbles went to the other side. The winning side won a prize, such as an ornament or bracelet. Girls also played a sliding game with sticks called "Pa-slo-han-pi." The girls used long slender, ornate sticks or wands that were tipped with the polished horn of elk or buffalo. The wands, made by fathers or grandfathers, are described as a labor of love, requiring hours of whittling and polishing and were highly prized by the girls. The girls threw the sticks on the ice to see whose stick would go the furthest and the sticks were said to slide surprisingly long distances (Standing Bear 1931).

Both Schultz (1913) in his biography, *Sinopah the Indian Boy*, and Eastman (1902), in *Indian Boyhood*, describe spinning tops as being a popular winter game. Tops were heart-shaped and made of polished wood, bone or horn and were whipped with a long throng of buckskin. Each boy would whip his top until it hummed and then one would become the leader and whip his top and the rest would follow through an obstacle course around the ice and through bars of snow. The tops must spin all the way through and the top that held out the longest was the winner.

During summer months, young boys spent their days playing and practicing the skills they would need to become hunters, warriors and chiefs. Urbaneck explains that endurance was the basic purpose of this training and footraces were the staple of many kinds of play. In one game, boys would choose a fast runner to be a "deer" and, given a brief head start, the "wolves" would chase after him, down creeks, across prairies and up and over hills. Pinaquanah (Smells Sweet), the young Chief Washakie, was known to chase butterflies while his playmates rested, knowing that he would need to work harder than others to be the "deer." When pausing to rest, the boys would watch, listen to, and study the habits of birds and animals. In the evening, fathers would ask questions about what they had learned, such as what was the shape of a deer's track and how old were the tracks (Urbaneck 1971).

In 1931, Luther Standing Bear, a Lakota Indian of the Western Sioux nation, published a book entitled, *My Indian Boyhood*. Standing Bear provides a detailed account of his childhood during the latter days of the traditional Sioux nation. In a chapter on games, Standing Bear describes similar childhood games as those written about by Urbaneck in her biography of Chief Washakie. A favorite chase game was Wounded

Buffalo, a group game wherein one boy who could run the fastest played the buffalo. He would carry a long stick with a large piece of cactus attached to the end of the stick. The cactus was covered with long thorns or stickers on all sides and was the size of a plate. In the center of the cactus was painted a red circle to symbolize a wounded buffalo and the boy playing the buffalo acted like an angry wounded buffalo in every way. The other boys were hunters and gathered around the wounded buffalo shooting arrows at the red spot on the cactus. The boy whose arrow hit the red spot then became the target for the charging buffalo that ran after the boy "clothed only in breechcloth to land a thorny sting on his bare anatomy" (Standing Bear 1931: 136). Standing Bear also describes a variety of ball games similar to the soccer, football or hockey games of today.

Bows and arrows were essential playthings and boys played many games to hone their skills with the bow and arrow. Being a successful hunter required both accuracy and speed in shooting at moving objects. In one game, a leader shot an arrow and others in the game would try to shoot their arrows as close as possible to the arrow of the leader. This game taught players to measure distance as the arrow coming closest to the leader's arrow was the winner. Because shooting had to be done on the run in all kinds of weather, boys would practice shooting at a buffalo chip on the ground and then another shooter would send it rolling so that they could "shoot on the run." On windy days, players would shoot at right angles to the wind to make hitting the target even more difficult. Shooting at objects tossed into the air was another favorite game. It was said that Pinaquanah, the young Chief Washakie, could hit a buffalo chip tossed into the air with a second arrow before it hit the ground (Urbaneck 1971).

Boys often divided into two groups to play war games. They painted their faces and bodies with red iron ore or clay and black with charcoal. They would throw balls of mud on ends of sticks at each other. Eastman describes these wrestling games or battles that involved groups of boys:

> Wrestling was indulged in by us all. It may seem odd, but wrestling was done by a great many boys at once ... It was really a battle, in which each one chose his opponent. The rule was that if a boy sat down, he was let alone, but as long as he remained standing, he was open to attack. No one struck with the hand, but all manner of tripping with legs and feet and butting with the knees was allowed ... only the young athlete could really enjoy it.
>
> (Eastman 1902: 66–67)

As they grew older, children's war games became more complex and intense and often involved great skill in riding ponies and shooting.

Luther Standing Bear (1931) describes the deep and intimate relationship young boys developed with their ponies in play. The play may begin with the boy learning to tame and mount a pony for the first time. The boys would drive the ponies into deep water and swim and play with them. This was relatively safe for the boys because horses cannot kick hard under water. When the horse was no longer afraid of the boy, the boy would mount and, with much practice, learn to keep his seat as the horse raced, turned or stopped suddenly.

In several accounts of the early life of traditional Native Plains Indians, adults play a role in supporting children's play, as was the case when fathers polished stones for marbles or fashioned decorative sticks for their daughters' games. In a boyhood story of Sinopah, who would grow to become a Blackfoot chief, Chief Pitamakan (Running Eagle), James Schultz (1913) described how adults encouraged the use of skill and perseverance in play. Making clay toys was a pastime of Blackfoot children and that play was taught by elders, often grandparents. Certain clay found by riverbanks was used in this activity and was referred to as "image earth." Schultz describes a time when Sinopah's grandfather, Red Crane, taught Sinopah and his playmates to process and mould clay to represent animals. For young children this process was hard work, requiring much effort in pounding and kneading the clay for long periods of time. If children became impatient and rushed to sculpt before properly processing the clay, the clay figures they made would begin to fall apart as they dried. The story goes that Sinopah, after preparing the clay as his grandfather requested, struggled to mold a buffalo:

> Grandfather Red Crane sat beside him, smoking his long pipe and saying not a word. Very often Sinopah would sigh, stop work, and look beseechingly up, and getting no offer of help, make another trial. And so it went on for a long time. Quite often the old man muttered some words, but the boy did not hear. He was praying; praying to the sun: "O great one! O you maker of the day and ruler of the world!" he kept saying: "Give this boy of ours an enduring heart. Give him a brave heart. Give him the will to strive and keep striving for that which he wants."
>
> (Schultz 1913: 61–62)

After watching Sinopah work with little success, Red Crane took the clay and rolled it so that it was much larger at one end than the other, pointing out that the buffalo is very tall in front and quite low in the hindquarters. He then fashioned his high hump and big head out of the large end of the clay. He worked the piece with his fingers until he created a lifelike body of a buffalo. He used sticks for legs and covered the legs with clay so that they resembled the legs of a living animal. Observing this, Sinopah took a lump of clay and attempted to make his own. The first one that Sinopah made roughly resembled a buffalo. He made one model after another until the last one was a very fair likeness of the animal (Schultz 1913).

There are also written accounts of adults creating play spaces for children in much the same way that we provide play spaces for young children at home, in classrooms and in the outdoors today. Schultz, in his biography of Sinopah, describes how Sinopah's mother and the mothers of his playmates worked late into the evening for weeks to create a child-size lodge, complete with lodge poles, tanned elk hide, robes and blankets for bedding, parfleches (hides) stuffed with dried meat and berries and pemmican. The lodge was finished with a fire pit in the center and a kettle for fetching water at the door. The lodge was placed a safe distance from camp and both boys and girls were free to play as they wished in their "own" play space. Schultz recounts:

> Never were there happier children . . . sitting there in their own little lodge and eating their first meal in it. They at once began to plan their play for the next day, and at sundown were happy to go with their mothers, leaving the big cottonwood trees to guard their treasures during the night.
>
> (Schultz 1913: 42)

Play that was considered by adults to be irreverent, took on a more subversive nature and took place in secret spaces. Eastman (1902), in *Indian Boyhood*, describes a play called "medicine dance" where children imitated sacred dances and ceremonies of the adults. Pine boughs were used to build a medicine lodge and players took on the role of members, initiates, doorkeepers and medicine or holy men. The ceremony commenced with drumming, singing and dancing by members. Certain boys imitated medicine men, painting and decorating their bodies and carrying bags and charms. Initiates were brought in by doorkeepers, cast down "dead" with medicine and then revived and brought back to life. They were then able to take their places in the lodge with the others. The ceremony ended with dancing and a feast.

The traditional Native tribes referenced in this chapter were hunter–gatherers living a nomadic lifestyle moving with the seasons and living in a symbiotic relationship with the elements and creatures that sustained their lives and livelihoods. The foundation of these Native cultures was a nature-based spirituality and children's play was nature-based. As the lifestyle, language, culture and spiritual traditions of Native peoples were eroded under pressure to assimilate into the dominant Anglo culture during the nineteenth and twentieth centuries, the nature-based play of traditional Native children lost its relevance. Not only did daily nature-based experiences become limited and less available to children, the play itself began to lose survival value. As such, traditional play became less available and less valuable as a developmental process for young children.

Native children's play in the twenty-first century

Visiting early childhood programs on the Wind River reservation today, you would see young children playing in much the same ways that children of any ethnic group play. You would see familiar curricula, similar playthings, usual classroom centers, outdoor play grounds and steel mechanical play equipment. You would see adults using play as a context for teaching children the skills and knowledge considered important for success in school. One exception would be the Cultural Immersion Preschool Program where young children are being taught their Native language, cultural values and spiritual traditions. Native elders are important teachers in these programs and classrooms are filled with cultural artifacts such as tipis, drums, beads and other craft materials. Here storytelling and a collection of Wind River children's stories are central to the curriculum. Noticeably absent from typical early childhood programs, including the

Immersion program, are large natural spaces for play in the wild with natural materials. We suggest that the provision of natural spaces for play and a return to nature-based play may be critical to the effort of teaching traditional cultural and spiritual values.

Nature-based play, nature-deficit disorder

For traditional Native people, nature-based play was more than an activity occurring in nature. It was a means of learning about and becoming an inseparable part of the natural world. It was part of a nature-based spiritual tradition. This play in nature may be seen as a way for children to practice skills that they would use in everyday adult life, but, equally important, it was also a way to inculcate spiritual values, most notably values related to people's connection to the earth and natural world. It is difficult for those of us who live in a transient society with little attachment to the land we live on to imagine how central a connection to ancestral land is to the spiritual life of Native people.

Native American culture provides a unique contribution to society at large with the understanding that contact with nature can be a spiritual experience and one that leads to reverence and a desire to preserve the natural world. During a conference in Denver in 1968, elders from a number of Native tribes throughout the country addressed the question, "Can the Red Man Help the White Man?" The purpose of the gathering was to discuss the extent to which the wisdom, philosophy and intuition of the Native American could be used to help solve the social ills of the present. When the topic turned to Native culture and the education of young children, elders maintained that Indians have long felt that there is something lacking in the education of White children, and that something is an intuitive feeling about nature and life. As one elder stated: "White men would never say that animals are their brothers, the earth is their mother, or that beans, corn and squash are three sisters. The Indian says it and means it" (Morey 1970: xii).

There are many today who express concerns about our children's loss of free play in nature in favor of adult-planned and adult-supervised activities and play mediated through technology. Native American parents and teachers join many others in our society in voicing concerns about children favoring media and video games over tribal stories and outdoor play. In his book, *Last Child in the Woods: Saving Our Children from Nature-Deficit Disorder*, Richard Louv (2005) makes the case that within the last two decades the way children understand nature has changed radically. Children today are much more aware of global threats to the environment (i.e., global warming, pollution, destruction of the rain forests) but their physical contact and intimacy with nature are fading. Children no longer talk about wandering alone in the woods, lying in a grassy meadow watching clouds float by, or exploring a mountain stream. Nature has become more abstract than a reality. Louv describes a recent television advertisement that depicts a four-wheel drive SUV racing along a mountain stream while two children sit in the back seat watching a movie on a flip-down video screen, oblivious to the landscape around them.

There is a growing body of research that links our physical, mental and spiritual health to our connection with nature. Louv's work, and that of many others across all disciplines, have inspired the rise of the global Children and Nature Movement, which in the United States is sometimes referred to as the No Child Left Inside movement. In the words of Richard Louv, "the more high tech we become, the more nature we need!" (2012: 24). We need both nature and technology in order to develop a hybrid mind that is equally trained through natural and virtual experience. Louv suggests that we need a balance in our ability to use technology to process intellectual data and natural environments to sharpen the senses and enhance our ability to learn and feel. Research on the connection between nature and mental acuity, creativity, physical and spiritual health is in its infancy. There is some evidence that time spent in natural environments stimulates the senses, and increases our ability to pay attention, think clearly and be more creative (Berman et al. 2008). Though there is still much to be done to understand how the nature connection benefits our children, we do have the benefit of the wisdom of those who once thrived in a deeply natural lifestyle:

> No people have better use of their five senses than the children of the wilderness. We could smell as well as hear and see. We could feel and taste as well as we could see and hear. Nowhere has the memory been more fully developed than in the wild life . . . we were close students of nature. We studied the habits of animals just as you study your books.
>
> (Eastman 1902: 8)

References

Berman, M. G., Jonides, J. and Kaplan, S. (2008). The cognitive benefits of interacting with nature. *Psychological Science, 19*(12), 1207–1212.

Brown, J. (1987). *The sacred pipe: Black Elk's account of the seven rites of the Oglala Sioux.* New York: Penguin Books.

Bruchac, J. (2003). *Our stories remember: American Indian history, culture and values through storytelling.* Golden, CO: Fulcrum Publishing.

Eastman, C. A. (1902). *Indian boyhood.* New York: McClure, Phillips & Co.

Gray, P. (2009). Play as a foundation for hunter–gatherer social existence. *American Journal of Play, 4*(1), 476–522.

Hebard, G. R. (1930). *Washakie: Chief of the Shoshones.* Cleveland, OH: A. H. Clark Co. Lincoln, NE: University of Nebraska Press Bison Books Edition (1995).

Louv, R. (2005). *Last child in the woods: Saving our children from nature-deficit disorder.* Chapel Hill, NC: Algonquin Books of Chapel Hill.

Louv, R. (2012). *The nature principle: Reconnecting with life in a virtual age.* Chapel Hill, NC: Algonquin Books of Chapel Hill.

Morey, S. M. (1970). Introduction. In S. M. Morey (Ed.), *Can the red man help the white man?: A Denver conference with the Indian elders.* New York: Myrin Institute Books.

Schultz, J. W. (1913). *Sinopah the Indian boy.* New York: The Riverside Press Cambridge.

Standing Bear, L. (1931). *My Indian boyhood*. Lincoln, NE: University of Nebraska Press.

Urbaneck, M. (1971). *Chief Washakie of the Shoshones*. Boulder, CO: Johnson Publishing Company.

Vygotsky, L. S. (1978). The role of play in development. In M. Cole, V. John-Steiner, S. Scribner, and E. Souberman (Eds.), *Mind in society: The development of higher psychological processes* (pp. 92–104). Cambridge, MA: Harvard University Press.

Part II

Africa

9 Take me to the (dry) river: children's play in Turkana pastoralist communities of Kenya

John Teria Ng'asike

The dry river courses provide play areas for Turkana children. These children are returning home from school. However, playing at the river bed is always fantasy. They use the dry sand to construct homesteads and animal kraals. The socio-dramatic play activities include milking, taking care of the kids of goats and camels. The milk is stored in gourds and the remaining is given to children and members of the family to drink as an evening meal.

Introduction

In the Turkana pastoralist communities, children play independently as adults tend to assume a passive role in play with children. Infants and toddlers play within proximity of their mothers or grandparents, but by themselves. Older children play away from the homesteads at the dry river courses or on pathways to the river (Figure 9.1). Adults rarely construct objects for children's play or set aside areas for children to play, though they do not interfere with areas children decide to use as play areas. Children use the natural environment to create their sociodramatic play activities based on their cultural everyday life experiences. This chapter explores the play of children of the nomadic Turkana pastoralist people of Kenya. Because children's play consists of episodes of cultural imagination, Turkana children's play activities are used to call attention to early childhood education policies and pedagogies in Africa. The vignette of Turkana children's play above illustrates an example of such play episodes discussed in this chapter.

Conceptual and cultural context

This chapter describes data from a qualitative ethnographic study of Turkana children in and out of school in a Turkana pastoralist community of Kenya (Ng'asike 2013). The study sought to honor indigenous epistemologies and draws upon decolonizing methodologies (Malinowski 1922; Maanen 1988; Wolcott, 1988; Thomas 1993; Smith 1999;

Figure 9.1   The dry river courses provide play areas for Turkana children.

McCabe 2004; Mutua and Swadener 2004; Kawagley 2006). Analysis and interpretation of the observations are situated in sociocultural activity theory (Leontiev 1977). The focus is on the relationship between Turkana children's everyday sociocultural practices of their pastoralist lifestyles and play and early education practices. Taking note of research information from indigenous groups in Canada, the United States, and other communities, including those in Africa (Aikenhead and Jegede 1999; Aikenhead, 2001; Kawagley 2006), I argue that nomadic pastoralist communities in Kenya require similar early childhood development and education research data to stimulate discourses about play, curriculum content and culturally responsive pedagogies in early childhood education.

Contemporary Turkana nomadic communities of Kenya have undergone significant changes due to western religious influences, exposure to educational activities, and the impact of urbanization. However, the Turkana communities by and large continue to maintain their culture, leading traditional lifestyles of livestock herding, wild fruit gathering, and wild life hunting for survival. In urban settlements, the Turkana live by selling firewood, charcoal, wood carvings, basketry and livestock products such as hides, milk, meat, and fat. Turkana children attend the surrounding pre-primary and primary schools operating in both rural and peri-urban centers. They spend half of the day in school, and the rest of the day playing and herding livestock at the river courses.

Theoretical implications and related research on children's play in Africa

Vygotsky (1978), and later Wertsch (1991), conceptualized play as a cultural activity in which children internalize and appropriate the skills of the adult world. According to Vygotsky's theory, pretend play enables children to recreate real-life events through imaginary situations of the play environment. The imaginary situations allow children freedom from the constraints of the real world that surrounds them, and stimulate them to try on social roles and skills that they have not yet mastered. As children engage in imaginary play with objects such as balls of camel dung, cooking utensils or stones, the objects are not only used as materials for play but are assigned meanings as well, enabling children to engage in higher-order mental processes based on signs and language as mental tools. As suggested by Leontiev (1977) and elaborated by Göncü et al. (1999) and Hennig and Kirova (2012), play is used by children to understand their culture and to learn individual skills. At play, children nurture their cultural heritage and history of their society. Based on the work of Rogoff (2003), individual development is conceptualized as occurring through participation in the sociocultural activities of one's community. Rogoff and her colleagues (Rogoff et al. 2003) concur with Vygotsky (1978) that young children learn spontaneously and incidentally by attending, observing, imitating, creating, co-constructing, and participating in self-driven activities or in play-guided activity by peers or adults. These learning mechanisms have been classified as intent participation which children use to gain knowledge from their natural environment. Lave and Wenger (1991) developed the notion of a "community of practice" to explain how learning takes place through social interaction between groups of learners. Learning as a group allows for cooperation, sharing, and collaboration, all of which makes it easier for learners to acquire new knowledge. Lave and Wenger (1991) emphasize that learning as a community of practice is situated, context-based, cultural and depends on children's experience and prior knowledge.

Turkana pastoralist parents' socialization practices and children's play

The phrase "children go outside and play" is popular among Turkana mothers as well as men. This happens especially when children are perceived to be idling around adults. When ordered to go out and play by their parents, children run away and disappear into their playing areas. Culturally, the presence of the child around the mother indicates incompetence and developmental dysfunction. Playing at a distance from parents is regarded as an opportunity to learn with others and be challenged to develop normatively. Mothers do not send their children out to play just because they want to be free to perform household chores. They are aware that the child must be separate from them and be out there to learn the skills needed to become competent and responsible children and, later on, skilled adults. African cultural beliefs assume that children are agents and actors of their own developmental learning and interaction with the environment (Nsamenang 2011a; Nsamenang and Tchombe 2011). African parents appear not to be involved directly and actively in raising their children but are present to monitor children's activities passively using remote control mechanisms (Nsamenang 2011b). Observations of African socialization practices suggest that parental values create participative spaces that permit children to emerge or mature by themselves moving from one set of developmental tasks to the next (Marfo and Biersteker 2011; Nsamenang 2011b; Nsamenang and Tchombe 2011). This may be true for other cultures also as demonstrated by Hewes (2006: 2) when she observed that "Young children learn the most important things not by being told but by constructing knowledge for themselves during interaction with the physical world and with other children and the way they do this is by playing." Similarly, Gonzalez-Mena observed that:

> In some cultural communities children learn by simply being present as adults go about their jobs and household activities. Adults do not create learning situations to teach their children. Rather, children have the responsibility to learn culturally valued behaviours and practices by observing and being around adults during the course of the day.
>
> (2008: 111)

In most African cultures, child rearing is the responsibility of the family and the community, as reflected in the phrase "it takes a village to raise the child" (Swadener et al. 2000). African socialization practices use siblings and peers as major support systems for children's play in order to free children from parental supervision and adult control (Marfo and Biersteker 2011; Nsamenang 2011b; Nsamenang and Tchombe 2011). African children receive reinforcement to play from the adults who are themselves playful or play actors. For example, Turkana adults perform dances during celebrations, sing and perform pretend activities such as bull fighting, warrior dances, fighting demonstrations, wedding songs and other community entertainment activities, with children observing close by. When sitting under a shade tree, Turkana elders play with pebbles, camel dung balls or seeds, using four rows of 10–12 holes on the ground matched parallel to each other (this game in Turkana is called Peya Arei, meaning one and two). As the men play, children play by their side.

Sutton-Smith, in his (1997) book *The Ambiguity of Play*, provides a repertoire of types of play that are similar to those performed in Turkana culture by both adults and children. Examples of such play themes identified by Sutton-Smith include: (1) mind or subjective play (dreams, daydreams, fantasy, imagination); (2) solitary play (hobbies, collections, building models, constructions, art projects, bird watching, cooking); (3) playful behaviors (playing tricks, playing around, playing up to someone, playing a part, playing upon); (4) informal social play (joking, parties, dancing, dinner play, speech play); (5) vicarious audience play (warrior, hunting); (6) performance play (playing music, being a play actor, playing the game for the game's sake, playing the fishes); (7) celebrations and festivals (birthdays, Christmas, weddings); (8) contests (games and sports, athletics, gambling, drinking, bullfights, cockfights, physical skill, animal contests, arm wrestling, gymnastics); and (9) risky or deep play (caving, hang gliding, rafting, jumping, mountain climbing, kite skiing). Many of the play themes are cultural but have similarities across cultures. Turkana children play independently or are always present next to adults playing close by or are observing adults work and play. They record the events and activities of the adults which they reproduce in their play. In the next section, I describe play among Turkana pastoralist families and their children.

The physical setting and Turkana children's play activities

The context of play and playmates

Rivers in Turkana are seasonal and most of the time they remain dry in periods of prolonged droughts. For many days, rivers in Turkana will be dry with white sand dunes. However, rivers in Turkana continue to be sources of water even in the dry season. During the dry season, the community digs water wells on the river beds. Depending on the length and severity of the drought, the water wells can be as deep as 10 meters. During the time of my research, it was the rainy season and river beds had water running downstream. The river beds were a hive of activities. Children drew drinking water as they played at the river beds. Other children were swimming and fishing at the water ponds by the river banks. At other times, girls would fetch water and carry it in buckets on their heads to the dormitory to use for bathing at night (Figure 9.2).

Adults, children and livestock were busy at the wet river bed. School children were drawing water while having fun on the wet sand on the river bed as it was conducive for construction activities. Children played in small groups and sometimes a child would play alone or two or five children played together. Girls and boys played together, especially among preschool-age children. These children were neighbors, siblings, classmates or schoolmates. Preschool-aged children played with the assistance of older children or played by their side.

Children's play and work activities

In pastoralist lifestyle, children combine herding with play activities and sometimes when children get immersed in play, livestock herding is forgotten. This may lead to livestock straying and failing to return home. The children are strictly disciplined for neglecting livestock at the expense of play. As children become older, play is no longer acceptable and family chores take priority. Children play as long as they have no household chores to attend to. Although nomadic children are able to combine household chores with play, family work remains a priority.

At the time of my fieldwork, children engaged in both realistic and imaginative play activities, including livestock herding, fishing by the river ponds, swimming, or hunting frogs, birds, insects, lizards and all sorts of animals found on the trees at the river banks. Other children were climbing trees, swinging and jumping from the tree branches to the sand. Swings were made from improvised strings obtained from the tree branches. Figure 9.3 shows how Turkana children use the trees at the river bed to play with and as well as explore nature.

Figure 9.2 Children's play combines with cultural activities for survival like drawing water and digging water well.

By the homes other children hung around their mothers and relatives. These children helped in the small business activities that supported the family's income. They ran errands for the family and assisted their parents in selling groceries, charcoal, goat's and camel's milk, and firewood, and engaged in other family socioeconomic activities. When the children were not involved in running errands, they would start to creatively construct a play activity with strings tied on their legs or would draw a structure on the ground to start a jumping or hopping activity. For the most part, these children were playing undisturbed as their parents continued to engage in family chores. But occasionally a child would be asked to help bring up some change or help sell groceries.

Away from the homesteads, the dry river beds provided a stimulating play environment for children after school. One interesting play episode involved children playing herding activity with dry camel dung. The care of camels involves specific tasks on the part of adults. In the evening, the young camels are locked in a separate sleeping area away from the adult camels (if the calves sleep with their mothers, by morning, they would have nursed several times depleting the available milk supply). In the morning, the mothers are released from the kraal and are allowed brief contact with

Figure 9.3 Children use the natural environment for play.

their calves before they are milked for breakfast. The herders then drive the camels to the pastures where adults and calves graze separately but converge at home in the evenings where the calves are allowed to suckle their mothers briefly before the milking for the evening meal is done.

Using the black balls of dry camel dung collected from the animal resting grounds or from the pathways to the river, children's imaginative play activities of camel herding were creatively and precisely carried out the way adults do them in reality. For example, after converting the dung into camels, they are taken to the rivers to be given water, are branded to give a family or clan identity, and are slaughtered for meat. Further, the children pretended that they owned camels, naming, herding and counting their stock. When they wanted to milk the camel, they would call it by name to calm it down. Children treated a sick camel with herbs obtained from a local medicinal tree.

During other episodes children's imaginative play also represented real-life situations, irrespective of the ages of the children. Another elaborate play activity involved a child (aged 3–4 years) playing alone away from the family home. The child was imitating a woman carrying out household chores. Before starting to play, the child had collected several objects for her sociodramatic play. These included household utensils, firewood, baby toys and baby clothes, pieces of blankets for the child to sleep and sit on, foodstuff, a grinding stone and grains to grind, water and cooking pots. She prepared her play space and started cooking, grinding her grains while her baby slept close to her. This child was imitating her mother or a woman at work in practical life experiences in the culture of her ethnic community.

I found the child completely immersed in her household play and all by herself. It was fascinating watching her creativity and the manner in which she was in control of her environment. Safety was not an issue even though the child was by herself. Close by there was a small round hut and outside a woman, whom I suspected to be the mother of the little girl, was busy doing her household chores completely unconcerned with the little girl's play activity. The mother and the child were busy performing separate activities. The mother's absence in the child's play presented interesting questions regarding parental socialization practices of children in Turkana culture. How was the mother able to monitor and ensure the safety and security of her child from a distance?

Adults' views on play

It is difficult to say what Turkana people culturally think about children's play. Generally Turkana people accept play as an activity for children. However, adults (men in particular) find children's play mythical and sometimes wonder how children can imitate adults' roles with accurate precision. For example, I came across two men who were passing by but were intrigued by the play activities of the children. The two men stood by to watch what the children were doing during the play episode. The children were playing herding and milking at the homestead. They imitated the roles of men bringing livestock home and women preparing to milk the stock. The men were amazed at the accuracy of the play imaginations of children. However, the men just laughed it off and left, wondering how the children were able to imagine and replicate the adults' activities in a very real way.

Like men, women do not seem to care what goes on in children's play. However, sometimes women are happy to have children play close by so that the children can alternate between play and running errands. Not unlike other cultural groups (e.g., Mayans or migrant farm workers, see Chapter 2 by Gaskins and Chapter 5 by Mathur, in this volume), when children are out playing, adults can continue to work, including engaging in conversations that are not supposed to reach children's ears. Play helps keep adults' secrets away from the children.

Early childhood education policies in Africa and implications for Turkana children's play learning

African countries are implementing universal early childhood education based on Western ideologies with policies driven and funded by the World Bank and related multinational agencies (Pence 2004; Biersteker et al. 2008; Garcia et al. 2008; Swadener et al. 2008). Even though early childhood policies across Africa proclaim that learning and instructional practices are based on holistic development and promoted through the use of play, policy implementations have always been very problematic, as play continues to be misinterpreted and given different meanings by teachers and non-governmental organizations (NGOs) working in early child-hood education (Pence 2004; Biersteker et al. 2008; Garcia et al. 2008; Marfo and Biersteker 2011). Even the little play that takes place in early childhood education settings is based on the Euro-American model (Samuelsson and Carlsson 2008). Western style schooling continues to be the foundation of African children's educa-tion (Krätli 2000, 2001; Dyer 2006; Nsamenang 2008, 2011b; Marfo and Biersteker 2011). African culture is only recognized as a token in the early childhood educa-tion curriculum.

Not surprisingly, questions are being raised regarding early childhood programs targeted for investment in Africa by the World Bank, multilateral institutions and other bilateral organizations. Do, for example, the philosophy and vision of early childhood programs come from within Africa or outside of Africa? Early childhood programs imposed on Africa are likely to lack African ways of bringing up children. Nsamenang (2008) proposes that research on African children and families should focus on: the physical and social settings of early childhood programs; the culturally regulated cus-toms and practices of child care and child rearing of African people; the psychology of caretakers, teachers and peer mentors working in early childhood in Africa; and the positive or negative elements of African culture that can be used to improve the African early childhood education system. Africa stands to transform its education only if African culture and pedagogy become the focus of policy, curriculum and instruction in early childhood education (Marfo and Biersteker 2011).

Pedagogical implications for Turkana children's early education

African children's play as culturally constructed has an immense value as pedagogy for formal learning in early childhood education (Kirova 2010; Marfo and Biersteker 2011; Hennig and Kirova 2012). African schools have the potential to transform education through play to reflect African vision and philosophy. Ethnographic studies of chil-dren across Africa (see, for example, Katz 1986, Reynolds, 1989; Marfo and Biersteker 2011) demonstrate that children's play and work are inseparable; children's play reflects adult roles of their every day cultural survival activities and happens without adult supervision. In addition, African children's play materials and play areas are con-structed by the children themselves. The challenge is how to incorporate African chil-dren's play activities in early childhood education settings in ways that the African cultural context value as knowledge. This requires that the pedagogy used in early childhood education truly acknowledges the existence of multiple world-views (Hennig and Kirova 2012), with African being one such view.

Researchers concerned with cultural diversity in early childhood education are in agreement that play is critical as a pedagogy for multicultural education. For example, a study of Mexican children's sociodramatic play activities showed that they are able through their play to demonstrate cultural elements, behaviors, beliefs, language and customs that reflect "funds of knowledge" of the cultures of their families (Riojas-Cortez 2001; see also Chapter 5 by Mathur, in this volume). Like the Turkana children, Mexican children display their cultural knowledge in their sociodramatic play activities. The implication is that play can be a mediating tool for children's learning and a vehicle that teachers can use to engage the interest of the children in curriculum activities in the classroom. The sociodramatic play of both Mexican and Turkana children reflect their cultural funds of knowledge consisting, for example, of family values, food, holidays, music, beliefs, gender roles, language and other aspects of their cultural heritage. Similar findings are reported for other African children (Lancy 1980). The sociodramatic play activities of Kpelle cultural life is referred to as "talking matter." Kpelle children dramatizing "talking matter" were observed performing as defendants, elders, judges and other cultural activities. In their pretend play, Kpelle children demonstrated a high level of wit, spontaneity, verbal agility, and the memory for proverbs. The Kpelle children showed astute understanding of linguistic and dramatization skills as they challenged and questioned one another in their play episodes (Lancy 1980). A similar trend was reported in the observations of children in Cape Town, South Africa, in which the children demonstrated their cultural understanding as shown in their drawings and rehearsals of local cultural practices when pretending to build a village in the sand dunes using scraps, leaves and household items (Reynolds 1989, cited by Marfo and Biersteker 2011).

Hennig and Kirova (2012) and Kirova (2010) established the value of using cultural artifacts from the natal culture in intercultural education involving Canadian and African refugee children who were learning English as a first language while struggling to maintain their home language. Hennig and Kirova described the behavior of refugee children at play as follows:

> In the play episode, Nansi was playing work – pretending to crush grains while singing. While this was an activity she had observed women in her home community doing, and perhaps had participated in, the song she was singing was a pure experimentation with her newly acquired English language. Thus, the consolidated learning from her environments – both her home and her school environments – was evidenced in this short play episode. This example demonstrates how the child reworked her knowledge of two sets of expectations (rules) and emerged from the activity with new knowledge.
>
> (2012: 11)

The narrative demonstrates how the inclusion of familiar cultural artifacts of African origin in the play area in an intercultural preschool classroom in Canada made a great difference to the African refugee children's approach to sociodramatic play. The familiar materials stimulated problem solving, creativity, trial and error in children's approaches to learning a new language, new songs and rehearsals of their cultural practices. At play, children displayed learning that is consistent with approaches such as constructivism, inquiry and exploration, and discovery that reflect Western styles of learning scientific concepts (Marfo and Biersteker 2011; Ng'asike 2013). Early childhood teachers should be cultural brokers who can support children's play in the community using funds of knowledge from the culture (Moll 1990; González et al. 2005) with the goal of bringing culture to the early childhood setting to enable children to learn in a context that is meaningful and intellectually engaging.

Conclusion

The narrative of Turkana children's play highlights the role of play as a social agent that children use to acquire the skills they need to develop as competent individuals who can fit into their culture and contribute to the growth and survival of their families. The function of play is as important as formal education to Turkana children and families. Through play, children develop without adult supervision but with the support of other children and the community. However, adults are not completely absent as they remain passively in the background as children play; they use distal monitoring mechanisms. Turkana children's play can inform educators' thinking about appropriate pedagogy in African early childhood education. This requires the need to appreciate and strengthen child-constructed play and to recognize the role of culture as the context of learning in early childhood education settings in Africa.

References

Aikenhead, G. S. (2001). Integrating Western and Aboriginal sciences: Cross-cultural science teaching. *Studies in Science Education, 26*, 1–52.

Aikenhead, G. S. and Jegede, O. J. (1999). Cross-cultural science education: A cognitive explanation of a cultural phenomenon. *Journal of Research in Science Teaching, 36*(3), 269–287.

Biersteker, L., Ngaruiya, S., Sebatan, E. and Gudyanga, S. (2008). Introducing preprimary classes in Africa: Opportunities and challenges. In G. Marito, P. Alan and L. E. Evans (Eds.), *Africa's future, Africa's challenge: Early childhood care and development in Sub-Saharan Africa* (pp. 227–248). Washington, DC: The World Bank.

Dyer, C. (Ed.) (2006). *The education of nomadic peoples: Current issues, future prospects.* New York: Berghahn Books.

Garcia, M., Pence, A. and Evans, L. J. (Eds.) (2008). *Africa's future, Africa's challenge: Early childhood care and development in Sub-Saharan Africa.* Washington, DC: The World Bank.

Gonzalez-Mena, J. (2008). *Diversity in early childhood care and education: Honoring differences* (5th ed.). New York: McGraw-Hill.

Göncü, A., Tuermer, U., Jain, J. and Johnson, D. (1999). Children's play as cultural activity. In A. Göncü (Ed.), *Children's engagement in the world: sociocultural perspectives* (pp. 148–170). Cambridge: Cambridge University Press.

González, N., Moll, L. C. and Amanti, C. (Eds.) (2005). *Funds of knowledge: Theorizing practices in households, communities and classrooms.* Mahwah, NJ: Lawrence Erlbaum Associates.

Hennig, K and Kirova, A. (2012). The role of cultural artifacts in play as tools to mediate learning in an intercultural preschool programme. *Contemporary Issues in Early Childhood, 13*(3). Available at: www.wwwords.co.uk/CIEC.

Hewes, J. (2006). *Let the children play: Nature's answer to early learning.* Edmonton, Canada: Canadian Council on Learning (CCL).

Katz, C. (1986). Children and the environment: Work, play and learning in rural Sudan. *Children's Environment Quarterly, 3*(4), 34–51.

Kawagley, A. O. (2006). *A Yupiaq worldview: A pathway to ecology and spirit* (2nd ed.). Long, Gove, IL: Waveland Press, Inc.

Kirova, A. (2010). Children's representations of cultural scripts in play: Facilitating transition from home to preschool in an intercultural early learning program for refugee children, *Diaspora, Indigenous, and Minority Education, 4*(2), 1–18. http://dx.doi.org/10.1080/15595691003635765

Krätli, S. (2001). *Educating nomadic herders out of poverty? Culture, education, and pastoral livelihood in Turkana and Karamoja.* Institute of Development Studies, University of Sussex, UK.

Krätli, S. (2000). *Education provision to nomadic pastoralists: Literature review.* Undertaken under World Bank contract 7528355.

Lancy, D. F. (1980). Work as play: The Kpelle case. In H. Schwartzman (Ed.), *Play and culture* (pp. 295–304). West Point, NY: Leisure Press.

Lave, J. and Wenger, E. (1991). *Situated learning: Legitimate peripheral participation.* Cambridge: Cambridge University Press.

Leontiev, A. N. (1977). Activity and consciousness. In R. Daglish, *Philosophy in the USSR, Problems of dialectical materialism.* Moscow: Progress Publishers. Available at: http://www.marxists.org/archive/leontev/works/1977/leon1977.htm

Maanen, J. V. (1988). *Tales of the field: On writing ethnography.* Chicago: University of Chicago Press.

Malinowski, B. (1922). Introduction. In *Argonauts of the Western Pacific: An account of native enterprise and adventure in the archipelagoes of Melanesian New Guinea* (pp. 1–25). London: Routledge & Kegan Paul.

Marfo, K. and Biersteker, L. (2011). Exploring culture, play, and early childhood education practice in African contexts. In S. Rogers (Ed.), *Rethinking play and pedagogy in early childhood education: Concepts, contexts and cultures* (pp. 73–86). London: Routledge.

McCabe, J. M. (2004). *Cattle bring us to our enemies: Turkana ecology, politics, and raiding in a disequilibrium system.* Ann Arbor, MI: University of Michigan Press.

Moll, L. C. (Ed.) (1990). *Vygotsky and education: Instructional implications and applications of socio-historical psychology.* New York: Cambridge University Press.

Mutua, K. and Swadener, B. B. (Eds.) (2004). *Decolonizing research in cross-cultural contexts: Critical personal narratives.* New York: State University of New York Press.

Ng'asike, J. T. (2013). Cultural practices of Turkana children and science curriculum and instruction in Kenyan early childhood education. In A. M. Jesinta, E. Emeke, E. Adenike and N. S. Kang'ethe (Eds.), *Early childhood education for holistic development of the child* (pp. 111–132). Nairobi: Catholic University of Eastern African (CUEA) Press.

Nsamenang, A. B. (2008). (Mis)Understanding ECD in Africa: The force of local and global motives. In G. Marito, P. Alan and L. E. Evans (Eds.), *Africa's future, Africa's challenge: Early childhood care and development in Sub-Saharan Africa* (pp. 135–146). Washington, DC: The World Bank.

Nsamenang A. B. (2011a). Developmental learning in African cultural circumstances. In B. Nsamenang and T. M. S. Tchombe (Eds.), *Handbook of African educational theories and practices: A generative teacher education curriculum* (pp. 5–19). Bamemda: Human Development Resource Centre (H.D.R.C.).

Nsamenang, A. B. (2011b). Toward a philosophy for Africa's education. In A. B. Nsamenang and T. M. S. Tchombe (Eds.), *Handbook of African educational theories and practices. A generative teacher education curriculum* (pp. 235–244). Bamemda: Human Development Resource Centre (H.D.R.C.).

Nsamenang, A. B. and Tchombe, T. M. S. (2011). Introduction: Generative pedagogy in the context of all cultures can contribute scientific knowledge of universal value. In A. B. Nsamenang and T. M. S. Tchombe (Eds.), *Handbook of African educational theories and practices: A generative teacher education curriculum* (pp. 5–19). Bamemda: Human Development Resource Centre (H.D.R.C.).

Pence, A. (2004). *ECD policy development and implementation in Africa.* Victoria, British Columbia: UNESCO.

Pence, A., Evans, J. L. and Garcia, A. M. (2008). Children in Sub-Saharan Africa. In G. Marito, P. Alan and L. E. Evans (Eds.), *Africa's future, Africa's challenge. Early childhood care and development in Sub-Saharan Africa* (pp. 1–9). Washington, DC: The World Bank.

Reynolds, P. (1989). *Childhood in crossroads: Cognition and society in South Africa.* Cape Town: David Philips.

Riojas-Cortez, M. (2001). Preschoolers' funds of knowledge displayed through sociodramatic play episodes in a bilingual classroom. *Early Childhood Education Journal, 29*(1), 35–40.

Rogoff, B. (2003). *The cultural nature of human development.* Oxford: Oxford University Press.

Rogoff, B., Paradise, R., Arauz, R. M., Correa-Chávez, M. and Angelillo, C. (2003). Firsthand learning through intent participation. *Annual Review of Psychology, 54*(1), 175–203.

Samuelsson I. P. and Carlsson. M. A. (2008). The playing learning child: Towards a pedagogy of early childhood. *Scandinavian Journal of Educational Research, 52*(6), 623–641.

Smith, L. T. (1999). *Decolonizing methodology: Research and indigenous peoples.* London and Dunedin, New Zealand: Zed Books Ltd and University of Otago Press.

Sutton-Smith, B. (1997). *The ambiguity of play.* Cambridge, MA: Harvard University Press.

Swadener, B. B., Kabiru, M. and Njenga, A. (2000). *Does the village still raise the child? A collaborative study of changing child rearing practices and early education in Kenya.* Albany, NY: State University New York Press.

Swadener, E., Wachira, P., Kabiru, M., and Njenga, A. (2008). Linking policy discourse to everyday life in Kenya: Impacts of neoliberal policies on early education and childrearing. In G. Marito, P. Alan, and L. E. Evans (Eds.), *Africa's future, Africa's challenge: Early childhood care and development in Sub-Saharan Africa* (pp. 407–422). Washington, DC: The World Bank.

Thomas, J. (1993). *Doing critical ethnography.* London: Sage.

Vygotsky, L. S. (1978). *Mind in society: The development of higher psychological processes.* Cambridge, MA: Harvard University Press.

Wertsch, J. V. (1991). *Voices of the mind: A sociocultural approach to mediated action.* Cambridge, MA: Harvard University Press.

Wolcott, H. F. (1988). Ethnographic research in education. In R. M. Jaegue (Ed.), *Complementary methods for research in education* (pp. 327–353). Washington, DC: American Educational Research Association.

Part III

Asia and the Pacific

10 Understanding Taiwanese children's play via constructing and reconstructing: a prospective vision

Pei-Yu Chang

Once you have finished your assignment, you can play.

Nope . . . you did it the wrong way. Look at me, see how I make it work and then you try the way I show you.

You have to share with Tong-Tong or you cannot play. We need to get along with each other harmoniously, no fighting!

I chose the school because children in this preschool are obedient and behave well, so that my child won't be a trouble to teachers and can get along with others quite well.

Don't send children to those public preschools because children play all day long without learning anything. When your child attends the first grade, you will be called for a meeting by the first grade teacher. It's better to send your child to some private preschools where children are taught math, Chinese phonics and characters, and English. By doing so, he is well prepared for elementary school.

Which preschool does your child attend? Are there English classes and some arts classes taught by art specialists?

Introduction

The first three scenarios listed above are quite often heard in conversations between parents and children or between teachers and children in Taiwan. The next three statements are frequently found in conversations among parents in Taiwan. Together these six statements represent Taiwanese parents' perceptions of the relationship between play and work, their beliefs about how children should learn and work with each other, their beliefs about the purpose of early learning, and their expectations of preschool curriculum.

Children's play tells us about the culture to which they belong. To understand Taiwanese children's play, we must explore teachers' and parents' beliefs about the purpose of early education and their expectations for children since their beliefs and expectations influence the choices they make for children. Parental beliefs and decisions about childhood development and early education, in turn, are closely related to children's rights, and to the contents and features of their play. To understand parental beliefs and actions in Taiwan, an examination of the multilayered contexts of Chinese culture and history is necessary. The current social environment, educational policy, and family structures profoundly influence children's play as well. This chapter examines the history of play in Taiwan and play trends today in both non-school and school settings. It views factors that directly or indirectly relate to Taiwanese children's play through the lens of Bronfenbrenner's (1979) ecological systems model of human development and Super and Harkness' (1986) concept of the developmental niche.

Conceptual frameworks

Ecological systems theory

Bronfenbrenner (1979) believed that a child develops within a complex system of relationships that are affected by the surrounding environment. He regards development as the product of the interaction of a growing individual and the changing environment. The environment is seen as a series of nested structures that include four layers, which are the microsystem, the mesosystem, the exosystem, and the macrosystem. The innermost layer of the environment, the microsystem, is where the activities of children take place. The mesosystem refers to the connections among various microsystems—such as the relationship between home and school, and the way parents work with teachers. The exosystem contains the social settings that do not directly involve children but still have profound influences on them, such as parents' workplace and friends. The macrosystem is the outermost level, which is not a specific context but includes the values, customs, attitudes, regulations, and laws of a particular culture. Examples of the influence or expressions of this outermost layer are Taiwanese school entrance examinations and the Chinese emphasis on filial piety.

The developmental niche

Super and Harkness (1986) posited that there are three systems that shape the lives of children. The first system includes the physical and social contexts in which children live—the size and content of households, the family structures, the institutions children attend, and their relationships with siblings, peers, parents, and teachers. The second system includes the customs, norms, and mores of a culture. For example, a culture determines the appropriateness of the care of children or the relationship between teachers and students. The third component refers to the inner psychology of the caregivers, such as their beliefs, understandings, expectations, and goals for caregiving.

Historical background: influences of Confucianism and cultural practices

Confucianism has had a profound influence on beliefs about play held by parents and teachers in Taiwan. Some of the elements of Confucianism that may have influenced adults' views on children, play, and education are discussed briefly next.

Emphasis on education

In traditional Chinese society, scholars were regarded as at the highest level of the occupational ladder and they were highly respected compared to individuals in other occupations (e.g., farmers, laborers, and merchants). Consequently, more education was viewed as the route to higher social status and economic advancement (Stevenson and Lee 1996; Liou 1996). To this day, people in Taiwan are strongly motivated to obtain higher degrees or diplomas (Kim 2007). As a result, academic success is valued highly in Taiwan (Wanless et al. 2011). For example, the Ministry of Education in Taiwan recently changed the traditional test-based examination to diverse entrance options to higher education, but parents are still cautious and remain very concerned about their children's test scores and school grades. Parents still feel the need to make sure that their children can get into a good college and eventually obtain a better position in society.

Hsu and Aldridge (1995) claimed that in Taiwan emphasizing academic learning begins when children are young. From the start, Chinese parents make great efforts to provide quality education for their young children (Lu and Huang 2012). Kim (2007) shared a similar viewpoint when noting that it is not uncommon to see parents emphasize education and give support for early learning. According to Hsu (2013), many junior high school students in Taiwan indicated that their parents put academic pressure on them, and that these pressures are felt more intensely than academic pressure from teachers. Since Taiwanese parents are acutely concerned about their children's academic achievement, they devote a substantial amount of family resources to help children succeed in school. Taiwanese parents are believed to possess the genes of "Tiger Mom." They fervently make inquiries about the scores and rankings of their own children and their children's classmates. They send their children to cramming or test preparation schools for extra learning; they want their children to have taken more than ten simulation tests before the real, formal examination (Chen 2011). Parents' emphasis on early academic learning influences the curriculum provided in the schools and, in turn, many private preschools provide a structured approach to the teaching of mathematics, Chinese phonics, and English. This is why there are so many academically oriented preschools in Taiwan, and the academic orientation tends to push play into the background.

The parental emphasis on education is also revealed in their efforts to arrange out-of-school learning opportunities for their children. Many parents send their children for extra learning and have them attend one after-school program after another.

Children are expected to be "talented babies" who will not fall behind the rest (Leu 2008). These programs offer classes in dancing, singing, learning to play musical instruments, and painting. Sports classes are popular as well. Recently, the phrase "soccer mom" was introduced by a business magazine to describe today's mom in Taiwan. Soccer moms are full-time mothers who are busy taking their children to different clubs or classes. Because of the strong emphasis on education, parents try their best to fill children's out-of-school life with many structured activities (e.g., attending cramming schools or practicing worksheets), which wind up taking priority over play. Children have less time to play, especially to engage in free play.

Chu (2004) found that Taiwanese children living in urban areas, though cultivated with essential education and very capable of learning, did not have time to play. As a result, their minds were poorly developed. In contrast, children living in suburban areas had access to nature and were happier. However, they lacked cultural stimulation and their access to technology was falling behind. She claimed that having children live in balance with both competitive abilities and happy lives should be society's overarching goal.

Work is valued over play

Hard work is valued over play. "Accomplishment comes from hard work and failure is derived from play" and "Hard work is worthy and play is useless" are old Chinese sayings (Lu and Hwang 2012). It is believed that good grades come from hard work and diligence. The Western belief of learning through play is in conflict with the mechanical way of learning held by Confucianism. Imagination or pretend play is never related to learning in society (Kim 2007). Play is not considered as important as work. Play has long been established as lying within the physical development domain that is separated from intellectual development in the culture. To many parents, working hard is the primary path to learning, with play perceived as recreational and not educational in its purpose (Cooney and Sha 1999). Parents arrange formal education for their children at an extremely young age so that children can engage in what parents perceive to be learning (Kim 2007). Leu (2008) claims that Taiwanese parents tend to believe that only goal-oriented activities can be counted as learning.

Learning is through repetitive rote and memorization

Based on Confucian philosophy, children learn through rote memorization without reasoning (Lu and Hwang 2012). Even in early childhood, this kind of approach to learning is encouraged. To make sure children have learned, adults check whether children can state what they have memorized. Some parents are happy to listen to their children memorize abstract values from classic literature. Today, memorizing sentences from the classics is still valued by adults because they think it functions as character education and that children will be capable of applying what is memorized to the conflicts they may encounter in later life. Consequently, quite a few preschools include the Chinese classics in the curriculum and schedule time for children to memorize sentences from the classics. Rote memorization is also believed to be useful in preparing children for the high stakes standardized testing they will face later. In these circumstances, play seldom has a role in children's learning.

To be a good member of society is highly valued

According to Hsu and Aldridge (1995), Taiwanese people are concerned with benevolence, tolerance, and consideration of others. Children are expected to be good people who get along well with others. This expectation is recognized whenever children play with others or when there are conflicts among peers during play. When children start their play, they are usually reminded to cooperate with the other children and not fight. Whenever there are conflicts, adults usually cast blame and ask children to get along well with each other. Hadley (2003), for instance, found that teachers tried to develop in children a sense of peer group membership and directed children to refrain from excluding their peers during free play. Following this directive, children have fewer learning opportunities to resolve social conflicts in play on their own and may become less competent and self-confident in handling social conflicts.

Obedience and goal-oriented learning

In Chinese culture, the older generation exercises discipline and control over the young (Park 1993). An investigation conducted by the Child Welfare League Foundation found that 40 percent of Taiwanese parents thought that children were their personal property and that they had the right to punish their children if they did something wrong (Hung 2006). Taiwanese parents tend to believe that they know what is good for their children and therefore make decisions for their children (Chen 2011). Traditionally, adults believe that a parent never does wrong (Hung 2006). Children are expected to follow the adult's lead (Hsu and Aldridge 1995). Children are regarded as debtors who come to the world to repay a debt to their parents (Chen 2011). Thus, children are expected to be obedient and accept demands from adults without questioning the reasons. In view of such expectations, children may be hesitant to express their own ideas as the following interaction with one of my college students illustrates. One day the student came to me to talk about her interests and decisions about her future plans. Soon after the talk, she sent me a message stating that she could not make her own decision because her father did not allow her to do what she wanted. She felt that her father never took her interests and ideas into consideration. This type of parenting may lead to situations where Chinese children tend to accept knowledge, view things uncritically, and avoid exploration (Kim 2007).

Hadley (2003) noted that kindergarten teachers in Taiwan draw on traditional Chinese Confucian values to develop children who will become good students and peers. Leu (2008) indicated that Taiwanese teachers expect children to be compliant, polite, and respect authority. Class activities are adult-directed; teachers are strict in order to prevent chaos and noise. The way for students to show respect to teachers is by sitting and listening quietly in class (Hadley 2003). The relationship between adults and children has an impact on the interactions between them in play. The play provided in school is usually more adult-structured without free exploration by children (Barclay 1989). This is fine with parents who think that children should learn from teachers. The mimetic approach is widely valued in Taiwan and parents are used to the didactic way of learning.

Chinese children's play during the old era

The earliest artwork representing children's play was made by Chou Fang in the Tang dynasty (780–804), which portrayed royal children's play while taking a bath or playing with nature (such as chasing butterflies or playing with lotuses). After that, other artists produced more paintings of children's play, and these representations still revealed that nature was one of the elements of children's play. Children played with different types of flowers (lotus, jujubes, or willow) and insects or animals (e.g., toads, crickets, butterflies, cats). Moreover, these paintings also demonstrated that children played with traditional toys like water boats, kites, leather balls, puppets, and shuttle-cocks. The paintings also depicted children participating in such sporting activities as horse riding, cart pulling, and shooting with bows and arrows. Some games with rules that children played, such as Chinese chess, top games, rope jumping, and hopscotch, were portrayed in the paintings (Cooney and Sha 1999).

The traditional play of Chinese children is usually associated with Chinese festivals. During the Chinese New Year, for example, children play with fireworks, lanterns, and traditional instruments (e.g., gongs, drums). As another example, in the Dragon Boat Festival, they pretend to be toads, which were used to cure diseases during that season (Chang 2001).

Taiwanese children's play during different societal stages after World War II

According to Yang and Tsai (2010), Taiwanese children's play has been affected by changes in the economy, life styles, and the universalization of education. Three stages of societal development can be identified in order to understand how children's play is related to the situation in society, the status of the economy, and the educational policies.

The agricultural society stage (1945–1960)

In 1945, Taiwan was freed from Japanese occupation. The entire society had felt the effects of the devastation of World War II. Families were short of daily essentials and only a few factories were producing toys. Widespread poverty prevented parents from purchasing any toys for their children. Children found materials to create their own toys: guava tree twigs were used to make tops or slingshots; small pebbles, leaves, and sticks were materials for make-believe play; and stones and longan fruit seeds were used as substitutes for marbles. In addition, children played with field snails, crickets, cicadas, frogs, clams, and anything that they were able to find and catch. In a way, their play began to resemble the more traditional play that was depicted in the old Chinese paintings.

Changes in family structure influenced children's play as well. There were now more children in each household so children's play partners were both siblings and children in the neighborhoods. Educational influences on children's play were also evident. During this period students who wanted to attend junior high schools were required to pass an entrance examination in middle childhood. In order to prepare children for the examination, cramming schools became popular. Children spent considerable time in cramming schools and doing household tasks, leaving little time for play. Because of the academic pressures, children who could actually enjoy play had to be in lower grades before the testing became serious and started to interfere with opportunities for play.

The industrial and commercial society stage (1960–1980)

During the industrial and commercial stage, Taiwan was expanding its economic exports. Under the strategic encouragement of the government, the toy export industry grew four hundred-fold. The toy markets were flourishing and parents' consumer power was stronger under the better economic situation. Children had various types of toys. Along with commercialized traditional toys (such as marbles, tops, and shuttlecocks), children played with blocks, Matchbox cars, hand-held game consoles, and small toy figurines from popular cartoons. In 1962, Taiwan saw its first television program, and a traditional Chinese puppet show was popular as were some cartoons. Children's toys included action figures from television programs, and children's play gradually began to be influenced by the media. Watching television used up more of children's time, with the result that there was less time for play.

Play was also influenced by government policy and the dynamics of the economy. Families had fewer children (between two and four) because the government instituted a population control strategy that was called "Two kids are just on, and one is not too few." Because the family structure changed, children's playmates were siblings or children in the neighborhood and they started to play in small groups. As families moved to urban areas, children had fewer opportunities for play in natural settings; most of their play was limited to indoor activities. As parents were more economically capable of supporting children's learning, not only in cramming schools but also in other extracurricular activities, children had noticeably less time for engaging in self-directed play.

The scientific and technological society stage (after 1980)

Taiwan earned the nickname "the Toy Kingdom" because of the large number of toys exported in the 1980s. The largest importing country was the United States, and so the toys made in Taiwan, and with which Taiwanese children also played, were influenced by American popular culture. At the same time, Taiwan had toys imported from mainland China and Japan. Among the imported toys were television-related games and playthings, stuffed animals, and indoor games. It was obvious that children's play activities were changing with the development of electronic toys and instruments. With the steady development of the economy and the increase in numbers of two-income families, children had fewer siblings and fewer interactions with family members and with the crime rate increasing, parents also began to restrict children's outside play. Children spent quite a bit of time staying at home and watching television. As in previous decades, children's pretend play behavior began to reveal the influences of increased television viewing (Hsu and Hsieh 2010). Parents were also anaesthetized by the slogan "the earlier, the better" used by businesses focusing on children. Parents sent their children to learn art, English, mental calculation, and chess. Children were weighed down with those extracurricular activities and had less time to play. Li (2006) states that the slogan "the earlier, the better" harms children's play.

In sum, during these three stages, children's play shifted from outdoors to indoors. Their toys changed from self-made objects to commercialized and technological products. Social play changed from large groups comprised of siblings and neighbors to smaller groups of siblings, and finally to playing primarily alone (Figure 10.1).

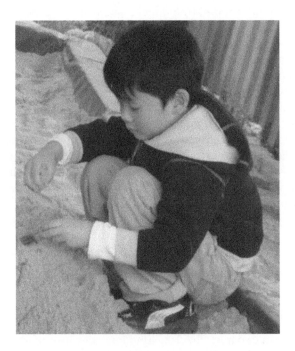

Figure 10.1 More and more play involves individual activity at home.

Children's play today in non-school contexts

Play opportunity provided in communities

With the development of child welfare, by 2012, most of the local governments in Taiwan had set up child resource centers. These centers were devised to provide multiple care services to parents with children younger than 3 years of age. The services include providing information about parenting, activities for parent and child interaction, recommendations for play equipment, and book and toy lending services. These services allow parents to become acquainted with other parents with children of similar ages, which could be a source of information for the parents and playmates for their children. These centers help parents learn to play with young children, and the lending services provide quality toys for the children to play with at home.

Public recreational space and child resource centers cannot meet all the needs of parents. Appropriate recreational spaces for young children in Taiwan are less than desirable. According to the Construction and Planning Agency, supervised by the Ministry of the Interior, about one in four counties and cities in Taiwan have less than one hectare space for every 10,000 children (Chu 2004). Chu states that the Director of the Children's Bureau focuses on protecting children's right to play by calling attention to the need to establish more recreational equipment and play spaces to cultivate healthy and happy new generations. Chu quotes Professor Chen from Taitung University, who asserts that in Hualien, the only recreational equipment suitable for young children is found at Sea World and in the play spaces provided in fast-food stores. She wonders whether we want our children's childhood memories to be only about Uncle Ronald McDonald.

Influences of social contexts on play

According to Lin (2010), the current birth rate in Taiwan is only half of what it was in the 1980s. More and more parents are having only one child; "only child" students now occupy many seats on the school campuses over the island. Because women are still regarded as the main caregivers in the family, working mothers are hesitant to have more children. The age at which parents have their first child has also increased. Research shows that the highest percentage of new mothers was in the 30–34-year-old age group and the highest percentage of new fathers was between the ages of 35 and 39. Simply put, there are more and more "older" daddies and mommies. The situation directly influences parent–child relationships and the play between adults and children. Some parents claim that they are too old to play with their little children. At the same time, having the first child at an older age prevents parents from having more children because they have concerns about children's development and health. This worry also relates to the "only child" circumstances and indirectly influences children's play.

Families with fewer children have difficulty finding playmates for their children. In the past few years, because of the convenience of the internet, some parents benefit from the chance to become acquainted with other parents through websites like

Figure 10.2   Organized play at public places is popular in Taiwan.

www.Babyhome.org or First Born (FB). Various community institutions provide art lessons, sports, or leisure activities (such as Baby Boss, Kidsburgh, or the Recreational Factory). Families visit these on weekends or go to the Recreational Factory, which is a parent–child restaurant (with furniture specifically designed for young kids and cheap toys or learning materials). The Recreational Factory is quite popular in Taiwan because parents like to take their children there to learn about the operation of a specific store or an industry; they can also join their children to make such things as crayons, cakes, or chocolates (Figure 10.2).

Taking children to these special sites provides them with different experiences each time, but children seldom have the same play partners unless a play arrangement involves a parent's friend. In other ways these recreational activities limit children; they remain indoors most of the time and usually do not have much freedom to explore. They are instead engaged in more structured and often rather passive activities. For instance, at Baby Boss, where different imaginative career options are provided, children choose an occupational role to imitate as employees; children put on the costumes (career uniforms) in order to make them feel that they are working in different jobs that are found in Taiwanese society. The entire play is scripted by a guide (e.g. an employee at Baby Boss) who leads the children to the completion of prescribed tasks. For instance, working as employees at Pizza Hut, children follow the direction of the guide in putting toppings on pizzas, sending pizzas to the ovens, cleaning up the environment, and finally getting a piece of pizza to eat.

Other recreational outlets children attend include those that provide children with sports activities such as skateboard lessons or art activities such as drawing classes; piano and dancing classes are also popular. These more structured classes are valued because parents believe that children seem to "learn" something from structured lessons. Joining these adult-sponsored and adult-controlled activities cuts into children's time for free play and decreases the opportunities for parent–child play. By contrast, a popular option for some families with young children is camping.

Parents enjoy weekend camping and take their children to camping sites for one-and-a-half day trips. Camping experiences allow children to have more free and natural play. Parents who can undertake this kind of arrangement are usually from higher socioeconomic backgrounds.

Play in school contexts

Play in the classroom

Though the belief of play as a learning vehicle for children is widely accepted, the actual practice of using free play as an educational instrument is still uncommon in Taiwanese early childhood programs. Pan (1992) claimed that valuing play as a learning tool for children is not common among Taiwanese kindergarten teachers. Barclay (1989) found that the activities provided in Taiwanese early childhood programs were mostly teacher-directed, and Hwang (2009) also indicated that the incidence of child-initiated play is low in Taiwanese preschools. Most curricula in Taiwanese early childhood programs are academic in nature. Schools that provide half-day or even whole-day English classes are popular. According to the research conducted by Hsin-Yi Early Childhood Education Foundation, 75 percent of private kindergartens in Taipei city teach reading, writing, and arithmetic. The situation stems from parental pressure for an academic focus in early childhood education (Chen 1988).

Leu (2008) found that preschool teachers in Taiwan still struggle with the tension between play-oriented learning and meeting the needs of parents. Early childhood educators know that parents are concerned about their youngsters being well prepared for elementary school and becoming competent in English. Most private directors of programs change the curriculum to meet parents' needs and expectations. Nevertheless, some preschools adopt a more child-centered or theme-based curricula, such as the Project or Steiner approach to early education. Children in these programs have more child-initiated play, but such schools are rare. More common are programs that have center-based learning; children at these schools do have more free exploration time and student-directed learning opportunities but this is not the same as play. As for outdoor play, preschool teachers put less effort into scaffolding here. The reason may be that keeping children safe is the priority. The other reason is that outdoor free play has long been regarded for physical purposes only and is not believed to be essential for learning.

Children's outdoor play at school

Keeping children safe during outdoor playground time is the priority of preschool teachers because parents today blame schools for any injuries. Few preschool teachers spend time planning outdoor activities. Creative or adventure playgrounds are not yet popular in Taiwan. As safety is a top priority, a current project is developing a checklist, the Preschool Playground Equipment Safety Checklist. This checklist is based on the national standard of Public Child Playground Equipment. Currently the scale has been evaluated and revised and is ready for preschool teachers' trial use.

Preliminary results show quite a few problems exist with regard to the outdoor playground equipment. For example, buffer distances are frequently not sufficient, the equipment is damaged, and the ground surfaces are not smooth. The most serious problem is that some producers of the equipment used shoddy workmanship or inferior materials. Preschool teachers are not able to report these problems and the government has not taken specific steps to correct the situation. Hopefully, the checklist in development will help early childhood educators learn to make judgments about safety and danger in the playground and seek corrective measures.

Changed role of play in curriculum guidelines

Due to the integration of preschools and kindergartens, a new tentative preschool curriculum guideline was announced by the Ministry of Education in 2012. Before 2012, the old standard of kindergarten education curriculum asserted that play was one of the curricular areas but did not specifically call for the integration of play throughout children's learning. In the new preschool curriculum guideline, play is emphasized as the way children learn. Children's explorations and free play are now emphasized. According to this guideline, early childhood educators are expected to work with children within a play-based curriculum. They have to focus on children's play and offer enough time for self-exploration and for imaginative and creative play. Teachers are encouraged to observe children's interests in order to provide activities that foster children's active learning. Teachers are also advised to avoid giving too many directives, regulations, and requests so as to protect children's interests in learning (Ministry of Education 2012).

Role of play in pre-service teacher training

The value of play is widely accepted globally. Early childhood educators play an important role in children's play life. It is essential for teachers to embrace the belief that children learn through play and catch the essence of playful learning. Being a good play facilitator requires an understanding and awareness of children's play and the ability to play with children. A prevailing belief is that play needs to be an essential part of teacher education. In Taiwan, more than 40 colleges are preparing early childhood educators, with only a few of them listing a course on play as a required part of the curriculum. It is unfortunate that pre-service training requirements do not stress play as an educative process. Without an emphasis on play in early childhood educator training, how can the belief in play as essential to children's learning and development ever be actualized adequately in preschool or kindergarten classrooms?

As frequently happens when teachers do not have the essence of play-based learning, play-related indoor and outdoor activities and materials are not fully integrated into the early childhood curriculum. Hwang (2009) warns us that the integration of play with curriculum should not be superficially coordinated through interconnections of different subject contents. Doing it correctly must be via the integration of children's abilities, interests, needs, and experiences during play, and through the children themselves in constructing a framework that is meaningful to them.

Conclusion and suggestions

Play is the text in cultural context (Schwartzman 1978). Understanding children's play requires tracing the features of culture and history and related social and institutional elements. Children's play is influenced by cultural, historical, economic, and educational factors (Chowdhury and Rivalland 2012). Among these factors, understanding contemporary educational policies as anchored in cultural traditions and belief systems is clearly essential to unearthing the seriousness of the problem of barriers to play in the lives of children in Taiwan. There is a need to improve play in both non-school and school settings. The following are some suggestions for changing the face of children's play in Taiwan.

Opening up dialogue among directors from different levels of education

The parents of preschool-aged children have concerns about their children's entrance into elementary school. The problem derives from the disconnect between the two systems. Teachers of these two systems have distinctly different educational philosophies. It seems that when children enter elementary school, they are expected to say goodbye to free exploration and play because didactic and mimetic approaches are more frequently used in their new school environment. In view of this, discussions among the directors at different education levels are needed. If practical dialogue could commence between the teachers at different levels, perhaps children would experience smoother transitions from one level to the next. Maybe more teachers and parents would then dare to accept child-initiated and playful learning without upsetting traditional values.

Strengthening teachers' and parents' competency of play application

Even when there is understanding and acceptance of the value and importance of play, this in itself does not provide teachers or parents with specific procedures on how play can be integrated into the curriculum. Li (2006) opined that play should be thoroughly understood by teachers through their realization of developmentally appropriate practice. It is crucial to help teachers experience the essence of play through concrete examples during the teacher training process. The training experiences should include learning to help parents understand how children learn through play and how to deliver the curriculum through children's play.

Continuing the social welfare services

Young children's welfare is taken seriously in Taiwan. Children and parents both benefit from community services. These services include helping parents acquire appropriate parenting beliefs, increase parent–child interactions, and enrich children's play resources. Children can have more intimacy with nature and learn more about Chinese culture when they play.

References

Barclay, L. K. (1989). Early childhood education in Taiwan. *Dimensions, 18*(1), 8–10.

Bronfenbrenner, U. (1979). *The ecology of human development.* Cambridge, MA: Harvard University Press.

Chang, P.-Y. (2001). Taiwanese kindergarteners' play and artistic representations: Differences between two classrooms and relationships to parents' and teachers' beliefs about education. Unpublished doctoral dissertation, The Pennsylvania State University, State College.

Chen, H.-C. (1988). A guide for early childhood education. In R. O. C. *Education Information Periodical, 13,* 215–235.

Chen, Y.-H. (2011). The Tiger Mom storm. *Common Wealth Parenting, 21,* 36–39 (in Chinese).

Chowdhury, N. N. and Rivalland, C. (2012). Value of play as an early learning instrument in Bangladesh context: A socio-cultural study. *Australasian Journal of Early Childhood, 37*(4), 115–122.

Chu, Z.-J. (2004). Children, what kind of the world I should give you? *Common Health, 72,* 178–190 (in Chinese).

Cooney, M. H. and Sha, J. (1999). Play in the day of Qiaoqiao: A Chinese perspective. *Child Study Journal, 29*(2), 97–111.

Hadley, K. G. (2003). Children's word play: Revisiting and accommodating Confucian values in a Taiwanese kindergarten classroom. *Sociology of Education, 76,* 193–208.

Hsin-Yi Early Childhood Education Foundation (1987). *An analysis of the investigation of kindergartens and day care centers in Taipei city.* Taipei, Taiwan: Hsin-Yi Early Childhood Development Center.

Hsu, F.-J. (2013). 12 year mandatory education is hardly to be successful without changing the way of teaching. *Commonwealth,* 276–284.

Hsu, S.-L. and Hsieh, Y. (2010). A study of young children's play in outdoor playground: Using a kindergarten class as an example. *Journal of Early Childhood Education, 21,* 1–29 (in Chinese).

Hsu, Y. and Aldridge, J. (1995). Developmentally appropriate practice and traditional Taiwanese culture. *Journal of Instructional Psychology, 22*(4), 320–323.

Hung, C.-L. (2006). The integrated curriculum design for early childhood education, children's rights and children's welfare. *International Journal of Learning, 13*(2), 67–71.

Hwang, Z.-C. (2009). When play meets early childhood curriculum. *Journal of Educational Research and Development, 5*(2), 27–54.

Kim, K. H. (2007). Exploring the interactions between Asian culture (Confucianism) and creativity. *Journal of Creative Behavior, 41*(1), 28–53.

Leu, J. C.-Y. (2008). Early childhood music education in Taiwan: An ecological systems perspective. *Arts Education Policy Review, 109*(3), 17–25.

Li, F.-S. (2006). Earlier learning and childhood play: A dilemma for current parents. *Journal of Child Care, 4,* 63–78 (in Chinese).

Lin, H.-F. (2010). The new trend of three-people family: The family changes. *Common Wealth, 137,* 110–115 (in Chinese).

Lin, Y.-Y. and Tsai, M. (1996). Culture and the kindergarten curriculum in Taiwan. *Early Child Development and Care, 123*, 157–165.

Liou, Y. F. (1996). Little reader of the classics. *Sinorama, 21*(1), 78–85.

Lu, M.-K. and Huang, Y.-M. (2012). Key competencies for Taiwanese young children: A framework of folks' childhood imagination. *Journal of Early Child & Care, 8*, 1–21 (in Chinese).

Ministry of Education (2012). *Tentative preschool curriculum standard.* Taipei: Ministry of Education (in Chinese).

Pan, H. L. W. (1992). Early childhood education in Taiwan. In G. A. A. Woodill, J. Bernhard and L. Prochner (Eds.), *International handbook of early childhood education* (pp. 471–479). New York: Garland.

Park, B.-C. (1993). An aspect of political socialization of student movement participants in Korea. *Youth and Society, 25*(2), 171–180.

Schwartzman, H. B. (1978). *Transformations: The anthropology of children's play.* New York: Plenum.

Stevenson, H. W. and Lee, S. (1996). The academic achievement of Chinese students. In M. H. Bond (Ed.), *The handbook of Chinese psychology* (pp. 124–142). New York: Oxford University Press.

Super, C. M. and Harkness, S. (1986). The cultural structuring of child development. In J. W. Berry, P. R. Dasen and T. S. Sarawathi (Eds.), *Handbook of cross-cultural psychology* (pp. 3–39). Needham Heights, MA: Allyn & Bacon.

Wanless, S. B., McClelland, M. M., Acock, A. C., Chen, F.- M. and Chen, J.-L. (2011). Behavioral regulation and early academic achievement in Taiwan. *Early Education & Development, 22*(1), 1–28.

Yang, S.-C. S. and Tsai, C.-Y. (2010). The impact of social ecology on children's play of Taiwan after World War II. *Journal of Early Children & Care, 5*, 133–153 (in Chinese).

11 Japanese preschoolers rule the classroom through play

Satomi Izumi-Taylor and Yoko Ito

A Japanese teacher read a book entitled *Curious George Goes to the Hospital*, to 3-year-old children. One boy remarked, "We need to cure George; he's still sick!" "What do you think we should do?" asked the teacher." A girl replied, "We can put him to bed and care for him." Many suggestions were made: "We have to make his bed, blankets, pillows, and house." "We can make him happy with get-well cards." These children spent a week restoring George's health and curiosity. Later, the same boy who insisted George was still sick implored, "We should send George to America to make him better!" "What does everyone think?" asked the teacher. One girl shouted, "Let's ask the director. My mom says he has friends in America!"

This exchange inspired the teacher to devise a scheme to elicit the director's and his American accomplices' participation in creating a fictitious hospital scene. The director contacted his American co-conspirators, proposing that they be doctors at an imaginary hospital. Such effort demonstrates the degree to which people at this school will facilitate children's imaginative play.

The chief goal was to encourage imaginative play and a caring nature, based on the concept that through play children construct their own knowledge by interacting with their environments in caring, group-oriented communities. To support children's play, teachers cultivate their inquiry, interests, environmental relationships, and capacities for innovation and problem solving.

Introduction

There are two main Japanese definitions of play (Kayo 1993; Yamada 1994). Kayo (1993) describes play as enjoyable and free from external forces. Yamada (1994) defines play from the players' psychological situations, and as having four mental properties: (1) external force vs. independence; (2) seriousness vs. levity; (3) result orientation vs. process orientation; and (4) external vs. internal purpose persuasion. Yamada notes that play oscillates between such opposing aspects, thus play should be examined in the context of the players' psychological situations. Teachers generally support children's involvement in play based on the Japanese cultural belief that play is valued for its own merit rather than its relation to education (Izumi-Taylor 2006; Ogawa and Izumi-Taylor 2010).

This chapter focuses on two professionals' perceptions of and experiences in Japanese early childhood education: The first author is a Japanese native enculturated in American education for 26 years but who works in both systems, possessing both an insider's (emic) and outsider's (etic) knowledge of the Japanese early childhood education system. The second author has studied Japanese early childhood education and home economics for many years with an insider's view of Japan. Together we provide an overall picture of the role of play in current Japanese early education. Some have argued that 'When educators with such varying perspectives offer their views of one phenomenon, people's understanding is richer and authentic' (Ogawa and Izumi-Taylor 2010: 50). We believe that reality is constructed by the observers' perspectives (Lichtman and Taylor 1993; Lichtman 2010). In this chapter, we present a brief history of Japanese early childhood education, theories and conceptual frameworks about play, the traditional Japanese view of the child and early childhood education, an understanding of the relationship between play and early childhood education, and beliefs about play.

Japanese early childhood education history

Play in early childhood education in Japan is based on Japanese traditions, cultural values, and beliefs. Historically, the Japanese believed children grow and change positively if taught appropriately (Nagano 1984). The word "hoiku" captures the Japanese spirit of childrearing—nurturing children's emotional and physical development. This holistic concept (care and education) has been in place for over 130 years. It is evident in kindergartens and childcare centers (Shishido et al. 2006) and acknowledges that the child development process is based on the child's initiative; the adult's role is to facilitate that initiative (Abumiya 2011). Making children do what adults want contradicts the cultural belief of avoiding direct guidance.

Along with Western educational influences, classic Japanese educational philosophies have had a strong impact on children's education (Izumi-Taylor 2006; Ogawa and Izumi-Taylor 2010). Both Kurahashi (1953/1966/1976) and Wada (1932) advocated play-oriented curricula, and their educational philosophies have been transmitted to current classroom practices. Kurahashi valued the relationships between children's everyday lives and play, while Wada was adamant about children's self-initiated play and their need to develop healthy bodies and minds. Kurahashi suggested that kindergarteners' lives should revolve around free play, and if that leads to work naturally, it would be educational. Children can enjoy working if so desired, and it would be the natural course of development. Embodied in the term "yudo hoiku," Kurahashi's child-centered theory was based on the idea that adults and teachers should accept children as they are. For him, the educational process involved the following: children's freedom in appropriate environments; their self-fulfillment; and the teacher's appropriate guidance, facilitation, care, and education (Kurahashi 1953/1966/1976).

Wada (1932) considered play as having three stages: (1) experienced play; (2) pretend play; and (3) expressive play. In experienced play, children naturally play and mimic what they hear and observe. In dramatic play, children pretend participating in events such as riding trains, playing house, shopping, etc. In expressive play, children engage in skill-oriented play such as gardening, manual arts, music, and mental and physical games. Both Kurahashi and Wada recommended that children play freely and spontaneously. However, Nagano (1984) warned that just because children need freedom to play, it does not mean that teachers should allow complete freedom for such activities. He argued that teachers should support children's play unobtrusively and facilitate it. In other words, teachers should consider how children develop and what they can accomplish through play.

These educational philosophies are reflected in the guidelines of the Ministry of Education, Culture, Sports, Science, and Technology in Japan (2008: 1) that recognize play as a child's voluntary activity and as

> an important aspect of learning which cultivates a foundation for the balanced development of physical and mental abilities. Early childhood is a time when children develop their life's foundation upon which everything is built, and with parental involvement, early childhood education provides children with 'a zest for living' ('emotions, will, attitude, etc.').
>
> (Ministry of Education, Culture,
> Sports, Science, and Technology, 2008: 4)

The main focus of Japanese early childhood education is to help children develop basic human attributes rather than just teach academics. The guidelines also describe five aspects of development: (1) physical and mental health; (2) human relationships with others; (3) child-related environments; (4) language acquisition; and (5) expression of feelings and thoughts.

Theories and conceptual frameworks of early childhood education

Japanese educators (Hamaguchi 2001; Ogawa 2010) noted that *jiyu hoiku* (childcare focusing on children's freedom) is based on children's free will, but that does not mean their complete freedom. It also considers teachers' free will, so that they can reflect on their teaching and be flexible in their interactions with children. Ogawa (2010) warned that children's motivation to enjoy everyday activities is manifested through play and diminishes as they develop. Thus, teachers must provide opportunities to revive children's motivation. Peers of different ages are also central in this effort because older children can model play for younger children.

Tsumori was another leading educator who embraced Kurahashi's philosophy about the importance of play in children's lives (Honda 2001). Tsumori (1980) observed that play promotes various skills and offers basic life experiences, but it should also be enjoyable. He, like Nagano (1984), suggested that teachers should facilitate and nurture self-initiative by valuing their first meetings with their charges and touching their

Figure 11.1 Children playing together with sand and water.

hearts. For children to develop, they should experience existence in groups, participation in activities, relationships with others, and self-development (Tsumori 2002).

More recently, Muto (2009) advocated cooperative play in developmentally appropriate environments in which children's cognitive and emotional development can be nurtured (Figure 11.1). Another play advocate, Okano (2011), appreciated children's initiative and freedom. Because children should play at their own pace, adults need not sanction the duration of play time.

The traditional Japanese view of the child

Although there are minority groups in Japan (e.g. Ainu, the Ryuku people) and they have been integrated into Japanese society for over 300 years, the Japanese view of children is dominated by the majority group. Because Japan was an agricultural society, mixed-aged children played together while adults worked the fields. The concept of community was highly regarded among agrarian people who had to work together, and these values were reflected in children's play that focused on cooperative engagement. This tradition of working and playing cooperatively has been transmitted to educational environments in many group-oriented early childhood programs, focusing on promoting harmonious relationships (Kojima 1986; Holloway 2000; Muto 2004; Ogawa and Izumi-Taylor 2010).

Japanese views of children were also influenced by religious beliefs based on the concept of pantheism (Befu 1971; Takeuchi 1994), which leads to the perception of children as having a divine nature who could participate in local religious festivals (Yamamura 1986). As Yamamura suggested, because "children are inherently good at birth, there is no need for strict discipline; left to their own devices, they will naturally come to understanding the surrounding world" (1986: 35). Adults need not control children's inherent nature to play. This Japanese religious background influenced Kurahashi's philosophy of education (1953/1966/1976). Although influenced by Frobel's philosophy (Sakamoto 1976), Kurahashi did not understand the idea of children belonging to God because he perceived children as divine, needing to freely play and grow (Ogawa and Izumi-Taylor 2010).

Japanese views of children are also closely related to morality. White and Levine (1986) suggested that adults raise children to maintain harmonious human relationships. It is important for "cementing one's place in the social environment because it provides evidence of moral character and appropriateness to the milieu" (White and LeVine 1986: 56). Likewise, Shigaki (1983) and Lewis (1984) believed that traits valued in children are associated with their abilities to positively connect with others. Such traits included children's abilities to cooperate (*sunao*), to be gentle, and spirited with bright eyes. Among these traits, *sunao* (cooperation) is very important. In short, *sunao* fosters children's skills in interpersonal harmony and prevents them from causing trouble for others. The Japanese have great regard for this trait in children (Izumi-Taylor 2008). The concept of *sunao* is similar to what Greenberg (1998) described in American children as learning to work cooperatively and making decisions to reach a consensus of the majority.

Another important trait is children's performance or behavior, including persistence, endurance, and reflection (White and LeVine 1986). Persistence (*ganbaru*) is highly valued, and people use the word, *ganbaru*, to encourage children in their tasks (Taylor et al. 1997). *Ganbaru* is similar to the western concept of volition which is defined as "strength of will" (Corno 1993: 14). Taylor et al. (1997) found that children and their families use the word *ganbaru* spontaneously to encourage persistence in tasks, playing games, eating, cleaning rooms, and playing sports. However, adults caution that it should not be used overbearingly.

Enduring hardship (*gamansuru*) is also appreciated by the Japanese people and parents try to instill it in children (White and LeVine, 1986; Izumi-Taylor et al. 2012). The Japanese dictionary, *Kojien* (2008), defines *gamansuru* as enduring hardship, and it is closely related to the Western notion of self-control (Naito 1990), which refers to "voluntary, internal regulation of behavior" (Marion 2007: 51). The Japanese consider it an important skill to learn early in life and practiced when facing difficulties. The common belief is that if one tries hard, one can achieve anything. *Gamansuru* is "used to exhort people to try against all odds because spiritual substance will make it possible to overcome material hurdles—but only by trying very hard" (Befu 1986: 24).

Another salient trait in children is reflection (White and LeVine 1986; Izumi-Taylor et al. 2005; Izumi-Taylor 2009). Japanese people use the word "*hansei*" (to reflect) to promote reflective skills. All, except for the very young, are encouraged to reflect (Izumi-Taylor et al. 2005; Izumi-Taylor 2008; Izumi-Taylor et al. 2010a). Many educators consider *hansei* a cultural learning theory (White 1987; Lewis 1995; Izumi-Taylor et al. 2005; Izumi-Taylor 2009; Izumi-Taylor et al. 2010a). *Hansei* is associated with self-evaluation, improvement, and moral development (Izumi-Taylor et al. 2005). When interacting with children, Japanese adults ask questions to foster *hansei* in children rather than insisting they reflect (Izumi-Taylor et al. 2005; Izumi-Taylor 2009). These observations are supported by some Western educators who consider reflection to be important; teachers are encouraged to ask questions to improve children's thinking skills (Copple and Bredekamp 2009). As the Japanese think that contemplating one's actions can lead to improvement (Sato 1994), they avoid criticizing children; thus, by questioning their behavior, they encourage children to rethink what is needed for improvement (Izumi-Taylor et al. 2005; Izumi-Taylor 2009).

Current Japanese early childhood education in relation to play

Japanese preschools are called kindergartens and enroll children aged 3–5 years (Taylor 2004). The first two years of Japanese kindergarten are equivalent to American preschools, and the third year compares favorably with the American kindergarten. Traditional Japanese preschools (*yochien*) offer relaxed, play-oriented, and child-centered programs in group-oriented environments to promote social skills (Izumi-Taylor 2006). This educational environment is based on play activities that are aimed at unifying and integrating all elements of children's development and learning. This is supported by the National Curriculum Standards for Kindergartens (Ministry of Education, Culture, Sports, Science, and Technology 2008), underlining that children learn best through their everyday play.

Another early childhood educational institution is *hoikuen* (the childcare center). Historically, working parents of children from birth to age 5 enrolled their children in *hoikuen*. However, because of societal changes and with many mothers entering the workforce, children are enrolled in either *yochien* or *hoikuen* (Holloway 2000; Tobin et al. 2009). The main goal of both institutions is to socialize children through play (Takeuchi 1994).

Hoikuen is regulated by the Ministry of Health, Labor, and Welfare. Its guidelines are published by the government (2008) and state that the goal of *hoikuen* is to nurture young children's holistic development, including health, safety, positive attitudes, warm relationships, self-reliance, morality, interest in nature, language development, and creativity. Teachers need to understand children's needs in group-oriented environments during play (Takeuchi 1994) where children learn to work with others and develop their own personalities (Ministry of Health, Labor, and Welfare 2008). Developing children's healthy minds and bodies in caring, group-oriented environments is at the heart of childcare centers. The importance of play is emphasized in the guidelines as a way of supporting children's development and learning.

Japanese beliefs about play

The current philosophy of Japanese early childhood education aligns with constructivism in which one constructs knowledge by interacting with varying environments

(Taylor 2004; Izumi-Taylor 2008, 2009). Constructivist approaches to education are play-based, and are the best modes for children to learn and develop. Japanese early childhood curricula follow detailed guidelines mandating play-oriented programs (Ishigaki 1991), and such programs offer children less structured play activities than do American programs (Bacon and Ichikawa 1988; Taylor et al. 2004). In valuing play, traditional group-oriented early childhood settings provide relaxed, nonacademic classrooms (Izumi-Taylor 2006).

Although Japanese early childhood teachers' perceptions of play vary widely (Taylor et al. 2004; Tobin et al. 2009; Izumi-Taylor et al. 2010b; Izumi-Taylor et al. in press), many studies have found that Japanese teachers intentionally promote children's social skills through play (Takazakura 2007; Sunagami 2008; Liu 2011). These findings align with the guidelines described by governmental bodies where one goal of early education is for children to develop social skills through playing with others (Ministry of Education, Culture, Sports, Science, and Technology, 2008). In this regard, Masami Sasaki, a Japanese pediatrician, recommended that parents and teachers support children's play during early childhood, noting they must experience the joy of playing with friends so they will develop empathy (Sasaki 1989). Moreover, when children's lives revolve around play, they are able to develop their physicality, cognition, language, relationships, and emotions (Okamura and Kaneda 2002) and creativity and artistry (Tatsumi 1990).

Contemporary studies on Japanese children's modes of play

Among contemporary Japanese play researchers, both Kayo (2010) and Muto (2009) believed that children learn best through play and that it promotes the development of the whole child. Muto postulated that when children play cooperatively, they internalize the world around them and develop their cognitive skills (Muto 2009). Kayo (2010) perceived play as the best way for children to experience life because it supports their social and emotional development. It is not appropriate for teachers and adults to let children play freely by just giving them enough time. Instead, it is the time for teachers and adults to facilitate development of the whole child. For Kayo (2010), teachers and adults need to nurture children's social and emotional development by providing developmentally appropriate environments.

Other Japanese play researchers (Ogawa 2010; Akita 2011; Kawabe 2012) have written books on play in relation to early childhood education. For Akita (2011), today's teachers need to develop their observational skills in order to support children's play. To develop such skills, teachers should work together by keeping records of observations, taking photos, and videotaping children's play (Akita 2011). Along similar lines, Kawabe (2012) articulated the importance of teachers keeping effective records of children's play activities in order to assist children. Another play researcher, Ogawa (2010) remarked that teachers should not teach children how to play, but should rather model play behavior to facilitate their play.

At the present time, many children are engaging in pretend play related to the 2011 earthquake (Matsudaira 2013; Sunagami 2013). These children appear to be reliving their experiences and overcoming their fears by resolving emotional conflicts while playing. Such pretend play could be considered therapeutic for children's emotional development. The importance of play in contributing to hospitalized children's recovery is recognized by many pediatricians. Clowns and other play volunteers in Japanese hospitals have been helping ill and traumatized children (Sunagami 2013).

Future directions

What we have described here may be cultural, but "knowing different cultural practices broadens teachers' perspectives" (Izumi-Taylor 2013: 75). When teachers understand others' viewpoints, they rethink and make accommodative shifts in their own teaching (Gonzalez-Mena 2008). Japanese teachers' practices stem from their beliefs that children are active learners who should benefit from the play activities that they facilitate. Teachers' perceptions and social/political systems mediate children's play experiences, and play perception is often rooted in individual and cultural principles.

Culture is one factor that regulates teachers' play perceptions, and we should scrutinize play as a cultural occurrence by constructing more knowledge about the cultural features of play. Teachers' beliefs about play are conceptualized as multidimensional, and when asked about their own practices, teachers are able to describe and reflect on their own values (Izumi-Taylor et al. 2010a; Izumi-Taylor et al. in press). One source of understanding teachers' perceptions of the appropriate implementation of play is to review their teaching practices in different nations. In spite of various differences in political, educational, and religious systems among different countries, many early childhood educators generally value play (Izumi-Taylor et al. 2010b). Because teachers' perceptions of play mediate children's play experiences in the classroom, examining such perceptions among different cultures can further enhance the development of theories and research in early childhood education. Viewing children's activities from different perspectives might help educators "make sound decisions about classroom play" (Frost et al. 2005, p. 58) and better support children's development and learning. The benefits of cross-cultural studies include examining what is typical and atypical in different cultures in order to achieve an integrated universal understanding of human development concepts (Kagitcibasi 1996). Sharing educators' knowledge on how to provide children with authentic play activities may be an important step in developing a complementary, universal understanding of early childhood education (Roopnarine and Metindogan 2006). The manner in which we care for and educate Japanese children can inform such attempts at determining the value of play in a global context.

References

Abumiya, M. (2011). Preschool education and care in Japan. Available at: www.nier.jp/educationinjapan/japan/201109ECEC (accessed 3 Oct. 2012).

Akita, K. (2011). En no asobi gamotarasu manabi no mebae [How play in childcare centers promote children's development]. *Korekarano yojikyoiku o kangaeru*, Spring, 5–7.

Bacon, W. and Ichikawa, V. (1988). Maternal expectations, classroom experiences, and achievement among in the United States and Japan. *Human Development, 31*, 378–383.

Befu, H. (1971). *Japan: An anthropological introduction*. San Francisco, CA: Chandler Publishing Company.

Befu, H. (1986). The social and cultural background of child development in Japan and the United States. In H. Stevenson, H. Azuma and K. Hakuta (Eds.), *Child development and education in Japan*. New York, NY: W. H. Freeman and Company.

Copple, C. and Bredekamp, S. (Eds.) (2009). *Developmentally appropriate practice in early childhood programs serving children from birth to age 8* (3rd. ed). Washington, DC: National Association for the Education of Young Children.

Corno, L. (1993). The best-laid plans: Modern conception of volition and educational research. *Educational Research, 22*, 2, 14–22.

Frost, J., Wortham, S. and Reifel, S. (2005). *Play and child development* (2nd ed.). Upper Saddle River, NJ: Pearson Merrill Prentice Hall.

Gonzalez-Mena, J. (2008). *Diversity in early care and education: Honoring differences* (5th ed.). New York: McGraw-Hill.

Greenberg, P. (1998). Ideas that work with young children. How to institute some democratic practices to pertaining respect, rights, and responsibilities in any classroom. *Young Children, 47*(5), 10–17.

Hamaguchi, J. (2001). Jiyunahoiku to fujiyunahoiku [Free childcare and no free childcare]. In T. Tachikawa, N. Kamigaichi, and J. Hamaguchi (Eds.), *Jiyuhoiku toha nanika* [What is free childcare?] Tokyo, Japan: Fureberukan.

Holloway, S. (2000). *Contested childhood*. New York: Routledge.

Honda, M. (2001). Hitori no kyoshi tositeno Tsumori Makoto [Tsumori Makoto as a teacher]. *Development, 22*, 7–12.

Ishigaki, E. (1991). The historical stream of early childhood pedagogic concepts in Japan. *Early Childhood Development and Care, 75*, 121–159.

Izumi-Taylor, S. (2006). Play of Japanese preschoolers in constructivist environments. *PlayRights, 27*(10), 24–29.

Izumi-Taylor, S. (2008). Sunao (cooperative) children: How Japanese teachers nurture autonomy. *Young Children, 63*(3), 76–79.

Izumi-Taylor, S. (2009). Hansei: Japanese preschoolers learn introspection with teachers' help. *Young Children, 64*(4), 86–90.

Izumi-Taylor, S. (2013). Scaffolding in group-oriented Japanese preschools. *Young Children, 68*(1), 70–75.

Izumi-Taylor, S., Ito, Y., Lin, C. and Lee, Y. (in press). Pre-service teachers' views of play in Japan, Taiwan, and the US. *Research in Comparative and International Education*.

Izumi-Taylor, S., Lee, Y., Moberly, D. and Wang, L. (2010a). Reflective skills of pre-service teachers: A cross-cultural study of American and Japanese college students. *Research in Comparative & International Education, 5*(2), 131–143.

Izumi-Taylor, S., Obana, M. and Kaneda, T. (2012). Terms of endurance: Japanese college students' concepts of enduring hardship and how it relates to early childhood education. Unpublished manuscript.

Izumi-Taylor, S. Samuelsson, I. and Rogers, C. (2010b). Perspectives of play in three nations: a comparative study in Japan, the United States, and Sweden. *Early Childhood Research and Practices, 12*(1), 1–12.

Izumi-Taylor, S., Wang, L. and Ogawa, T. (2005). I think, therefore, I improve: A qualitative study of concepts of hansei (introspection) among Japanese adults. *Journal of Early Childhood Teacher Education, 26*, 79–89.

Kagitcibasi, C. (1996). *Family and human development across cultures*. Mahwah, NJ: Lawrence Erlbaum Associates.

Kawabe, T. (2012). *Asobi o chushintoshita hoiku* [Childcare focusing on play]. Tokyo, Japan: Horinshorin.

Kayo, F. (1993). *Asobi kenkyu no hohoron toshiteno sinrijotaisyugi* [A study of play and its psychology]. Hattatsu, Tokyo, Japan: Minerubashobo.

Kayo, F. (2010). *Asobiniokeru kanjonotagayashi tatatsu* [How play cultivates emotions and development]. Hattatsu, Tokyo, Japan: Minerubashobo.

Kojien (2008). (6th ed.) Tokyo, Japan: Iwanami.

Kojima, H. (1986). Child rearing concepts as a belief-value system of the society and the individual. In H. Stevenson, H. Azuma and K. Hakuta (Eds.), *Child development and education in Japan*. New York: W. H. Freeman and Company.

Kurahashi, S. (1953/1966/1976). *Yochien shintai* [Essays on kindergarten]. Tokyo, Japan: Fureberukan.

Lewis, C. (1984). Cooperation and control in Japanese nursery schools. *Comparative Education Review, 28*, 69–84.

Lewis, C. (1995). *Educating hearts and bodies*. New York: Cambridge University Press.

Lichtman, M. (2010). *Qualitative research in education: A user's guide* (2nd ed.). Thousand Oaks, CA: Sage Publications.

Lichtman, M. and Taylor, S. I. (1993). *Conducting and reporting case studies* (Report No. TM 019 956). East Lansing, ML: National Center for Research on Teacher Learning. ERIC Document Reproduction Service No. ED 358 157.

Liu, H. (2011). Kodomono shakaiseino ikuseio meguru hoikukan no nichichuuhikaku [A comparison of Chinese and Japanese teachers' views of early childhood education regarding children's social development]. Unpublished dissertation: Tokyo Gaugei University, Tokyo, Japan.

Marion, M. (2007). *Guidance of young children* (7th ed.). Upper Saddle River, NJ: Merrill Prentice Hall.

Matsudaira, C. (2013). How play can support children with chronic illness. Workshop presented at the annual international conference of the Association for the Study of Play and the American Association for the Child's Right to Play, The University of Delaware, Newark, Delaware.

Ministry of Education, Culture, Sports, Science, and Technology (2008). Course of study for kindergarten. Available at: http://www.mext.go.jp/english/elsec/1303755.htm (accessed 2 Feb. 2013).

Ministry of Health, Labor, and Welfare. (2008). *Hoikusho hoikushishin* [Childcare guidelines]. Available at: http://www.mhlw.go.jp/bunya/kodomo/hoiku04/pdf/hoiku04a.pdf (accessed 8 Apr. 2013).

Muto, T. (Ed.) (2004). *Early childhood education handbook*. Tokyo, Japan: Yoshimi Kohsan Co., Ltd.

Muto, T. (2009). *Yoji kyoiku no genri* [Principles of early childhood education]. Tokyo, Japan: Minerubashobo.

Nagano, S. (1984). *Hoikugakunyumon* [Introduction to childcare]. Tokyo, Japan: Chairudo Kyoikusensho.

Naito, J. (1990). *Nisai ji shikaranaidemo shitsuke ga dekiru* [2 year olds, you can teach them without scolding them]. Tokyo, Japan: Dobunshoin.

Ogawa, H. (2010). *Asobi hoikuron* [Play and theory of childcare]. Tokyo, Japan: Horinshorin.

Ogawa, T. and Izumi-Taylor, S. (2010). Tech-Knowledge in Japanese early childhood education. In S. Blake and S. Izumi-Taylor (Eds.), *Technology for early childhood education: Developmental applications and methodologies*. Hershey, PA: Information Science Reference.

Okamura, Y. and Kaneda, T. (2002). *Yonsaiji no jigakeisei to hoiku* [Four year-old-children's self-development and childcare]. Tokyo, Japan: Hitonarushobo.

Okano, M. (2011). *Gendai no jikanteki kankyo ni okeru hoiku nikansuru kenkyu* [Current research on childcare and time and environments]. Tokyo, Japan: Kazamashobo.

Roopnarine, J. and Metindogan, A. (2006). Early childhood education research in cross-national perspective. In B. Spodek and O. Saracho (Eds.), *Handbook of research on the education of young children* (2nd ed.) Mahwah, NJ: Lawrence Erlbaum Associates.

Sakamoto, H. (1976). *Kurahashi Sozo sonohitoto shiso* [Kurahashi Sozo, the man and his thoughts]. Tokyo, Japan: Fureberukan.

Sasaki, M. (1989). *Kodomo no kokoro o sodateru hon* [Book that supports children's development of hearts]. Kanagawa, Japan: Maindo Books.

Sato, K. (1994). Doutoku kyoiku to ningen sonzai [Moral education and the existence of human beings]. In Y. Oshitani and T. Naito (Eds.), *Dotokukyoiku* [Moral education]. Kyoto, Japan: Mineruba Shobou.

Shigaki, I. (1983). Child care practices in Japan and the United States: How do they reflect cultural values in young children? *Young Children, 38*(4), 13–24.

Shishido, T., Kaneda, T. and Mogi, T. (Eds.) (2006). Hoiku shojiten [Small dictionary of childcare]. Tokyo, Japan: Otsukishoten.

Sunagami, F. (2008). Children's experiences and their development in pre-schools. In T. Muto and S. Ando (Eds.), *Psychology of child-rearing support: Practice and research in families, pre-schools and communities*. Tokyo, Japan: Yuhikaku.

Sunagami, F. (2013). Play. In The Japan Society for Child Study (Ed.), *Encyclopedia of child study*. Tokyo, Japan: Harvest-sha.

Takazakura, A. (2007). Case study of the formation of intimacy in 3-year-olds. *Research on Early Childhood Care and Education in Japan, 45*(1), 23–33.

Takeuchi, M. (1994). Children's play in Japan. In J. Roopnarine, J. Johnson and F. Hooper. (Eds.), *Children's play in diverse cultures*. Albany, NY: State University of New York Press.

Tatsumi, T. (1990). *Sozosei ni michita geijutsu no umidasu yoji* [Children who produce creative arts]. *Doyo, 22*, 6–8.

Taylor, S. I. (2004). Let it be! Japanese preschoolers rule the classroom. *Young Children, 59*(5), 20–25.

Taylor, S. I., Morris, V., Wasson, R., Lichtman, M., Van Brackle, A. and Ogawa, T. (1997). If at first you don't succeed, ganbare, ganbare, ganbare! *International Journal of Early Childhood, 29*(16), 4–71.

Taylor, S. I., Rogers, C., Dodd, A., Kaneda, T., Nagasaki, I., Watanabe, Y. and Goshiki, T. (2004). The meaning of play: A cross-cultural study of American and Japanese teachers' perspective of play. *Journal of Early Childhood Teacher Education, 24*, 311–321.

Tobin, J. Hsueh, Y. and Karasawa, K. (2009). *Preschool in three cultures revised: China, Japan and the United States.* Chicago: University of Chicago Press.

Tsumori, M. (1980). *Hoiku no taiken to shisaku: Kodomo no sekai no tankyu* [Childcare experiences and contemplation: Quest for children's world]. Tokyo: Dainihontosyo.

Tsumori, M. (2002). Hoiku no chie o motomete [Searching for the wisdom of childcare]. *Kyoikugakukenkyu, 69*(3), 37–46.

Wada, M. (1932). *Jikken hoikugaku* [Empirical childcare]. Tokyo, Japan: Fureberukan.

White, M. (1987). *The Japanese educational challenge: A commitment to children.* New York: Free Press.

White, M. and LeVine, R. (1986). What is an iiko (good child)? In H. Stevenson, H. Azuma and K. Hakuta (Eds.), *Child development and education in Japan.* New York: W. H. Freeman and Company.

Yamada, S. (1994). *Asobironkenkyu: Asobi o kibantosuru yojikyoiku hohorironkeisei notameno kisokenkyu* [A study of play: A basic study of play-based childcare]. Tokyo, Japan: Kazamashobo.

Yamamura, Y. (1986). The child in Japanese society. In H. Stevenson, H. Azuma and K. Hakuta (Eds.), *Child development and education in Japan.* New York: W. H. Freeman and Company.

12 "Children's work is to play": beliefs and practices related to childhood play among Indians

Nandita Chaudhary and Shashi Shukla

The two girls had kitchen-set toys spread out before them: a cooking range, some utensils, cutlery and cups made of brightly colored plastic. Taking a fork and spoon, Anita deftly lifted some make-believe food and tossed it around in a pan placed carefully on the cooking range as if to mix the ingredients. The younger Dina watched with fascination and then picked up a green plastic fork, following the same action with another pan. Persisting with "serious" cooking, Anita picked up a salt container from the variety of things around them. She twisted it open and lifted out a crumpled ball of paper containing some white powder. Pinching a few white grains (salt) between her finger and thumb, she sprinkled them over the dish that was "cooking" with a flourish. Continuing in her careful observation of the older sister, Dina promptly reached out to the paper in Anita's palm, picked out some salt, and sprinkled her dish as well, licking her finger and thumb for a taste as she went about her cooking. The salt was real!

Introduction

When children play in informal circumstances, undirected by adult supervision as in the above vignette, we encounter a seamless movement between fantasy and reality. At a distance from the watchful supervision of concerned adults, children are likely to express a constant and dynamic arrangement between real and playful activity.

It is not only under circumstances of relative affluence and adult arrangement that children play meaningfully, as has sometimes been suggested within structured global standards of early childhood education and care. Children are acutely aware of events and objects in their environment as their minds soak up the various experiences with wonder. As Kumar remarks, "Children have the sensitivity to notice; certain kinds of detail about life that adults are unlikely to treat as important" (1998: 46), despite the fact that the spaces are shared. Perhaps because of the fact that their minds are not yet fully patterned by culture, they approach their environment with spontaneity and primal interest. The active intervention of play activities by adults is relatively recent in the history of the family. Even now, in many parts of the world, children spend more time with other children in groups under the marginal supervision of known adults (Rogoff 2003; Lancy 2008; Gottlieb 2009; Nsamenang and Joseph 2012; Chaudhary 2013) than we care to discuss in developmental psychology (Burman 2008).

Play has always been an important process in children's learning about culture, even in ancient times. The National Museum in New Delhi has exhibits from the Indus Valley civilization (3300–1300 BC) that display terracotta, wooden and metallic articles that were meant for play among children—objects that adults made for their children to play with and objects that children created in the company of adults as they went about their daily lives. However, the ways in which the activity is constructed and the organization of play and materials have always responded to economic and social movements within cultural settings.

Play as cultural learning

Play in the lives of young children is an important means of promoting cultural aware-ness. Traditional games, especially games with rules, generally form an integral part of a culture since they provide a means of communication for social norms, assist in the assimilation of group members, and allow for differentiation within any grouping. The games children play and the playthings they use are intricately adapted to the culture in which they live and provide a way for children to practice skills needed as adults (Scribner 1976). Play thus serves as an important medium for enculturation.

Vygotsky (1978) believed that through play, children develop social competence and that play is a way for young children to learn about the cultural norms and values of a society. Play activities are, by their very nature, adaptive to the social setting in which a child lives. Vygotsky's proposal that children are a head taller when they play suggests that they are able to express themselves in mature ways when they are engaged in non-directed activities, contributing complementarity to the notion of the zone of proximal development. When children are playing, they express themselves freely, thereby demonstrating abilities that may otherwise go unnoticed. Play teaches children about themselves, others, rules, consequences, and how things go together or come apart (Klein et al. 2004).

Childhood in India

The immense diversity among Indians, both within the country itself and among the large populations of people of Indian descent living in other parts of the world, is sometimes impossible to grasp. Characterized by variety in every aspect of life includ-ing religion, language, ecology, clothing, food and family, Indian culture is unified by this diversity (Saraswathi and Dutta 2010) with several underlying and common ideol-ogies, particularly among Hindu communities (Malhotra 2013). Similarly, the experi-ence of childhood is also varied, depending heavily on the context within which children are reared. However, the fact of variation does not preclude several underly-ing ideas about children and their care which cut across communities and are even found to prevail among people of different ethnic groups and religions living in close proximity. The "constant barrage of humanity" that Wadley noted in her early visits to Karimpur still frames the lives of Indians—something that she, as an American, found as alien as the festivities and friendships (Wadley and Derr 1994: xxii). This first-hand experience of everyday liveliness alongside the despair of the human experience persists in present-day India, where life is transacted between the home and street with earthy openness, often daunting for the foreign traveler. On account of the continuity principle, children are very much a part of this reality both as participants and observers of these circumstances, favorable and otherwise. Children's engagement with playful activity is transacted within this cultural truth.

It is a shared belief in Indian society that childhood is a continuous stage in development from birth to adulthood (Saraswathi 1999a), and as a consequence, children are part and parcel of everyday activity; they share spaces and events with adults in most social settings. In family life, living spaces, sleeping arrangements (Shweder et al. 1995), schedules (Seymour 1999), and social events (Trawick 1990) display the ideology of inclusion of all members; thus, children are always in the company of others of all ages. There is a constant, loose supervision of children within the rural model of family life that is trans-national. This is the most frequent social context within which play occurs in the Indian family. Urban Indian nuclear and extended families are different in their focus and strategy, not in their ideology.

An important articulated goal of children's development is the consideration for family relationships; responsibility rather than reason is a dominant objective of socialization, quite similar to the findings in some other non-Western communities (Nsamenang and Joseph 2012). Indians are deeply conscious of social status, socialized within the family to engage differently with people who are "seen" as different based on age, status, or gender. Social discourse and even the style of language used (forms of address, other markers) are sensitive to social status. Children are expected to learn this rule quickly—that they have to behave differently with different people (Chaudhary 2004). Older children are expected, encouraged, and supported to take care of younger children every day, not always as substitute caregivers, but as mentors during play (Figure 12.1). Birth order and age are important details that children note in each other, and younger children listen to and follow older ones. Younger children enjoy the benefits of older children's more advanced knowledge. For their contributions, older children receive respect, followership, and the constant companionship of their younger siblings. They, in turn, protect them in the company of other children, even adults, but sometimes relinquish their protection if some relationship is to be preserved with another child. Care of children by children, the learning from other children, and the social dynamics among children were found to have an important contribution in the experience of childhood (Chaudhary 2004, 2013).

Adult ethnotheories about play among children

Parents believe that "children's work is to play," and since children play anyway, the modern trend to learn through playful activity in preschools is sometimes undermined.

Figure 12.1   Children in the care of older children.

Commonly heard complaints from many parents include that if children go to school, they should learn how to "sit properly and read and write." This is particularly so for low-income families (Chaudhary 2013). Most middle-class parents believe play to be universal and that children spontaneously learn games, rules and boundaries. The awareness about non-formal education is on the increase in India, but parents are anxious about admission into "good" schools and hope to have an additional head-start through preschool. Play, therefore, often has to take a back seat in family life because children are believed to play anyway. The desire for children to emerge as "better than us" is omnipresent, and education is seen as its route. Play is an indulgence as the child grows older, though what is considered good education seems to vary (Chaudhary 2013).

Adults believe that there are clear differences in the play preferences of boys and girls, both in activities as well as in the materials they choose (Gupta 2005). These beliefs seemed more exaggerated than findings related to play preferences in ethnographic accounts of children's play would indicate (Bhargava 2010; Chaudhary 2013). However, some studies do report a greater engagement of girls in fantasy play related to food, and boys in activities with automobiles and aeroplanes (Subhash 2010).

Children's play activities: research on play in India

Play during childhood is found to be primarily unstructured and informal, taking place within the spaces children share with others, both adults and children. After consolidating research on play among children, we concluded that children play more frequently with other children using materials that are around them and are easily available. The purchase of a variety and an abundance of play materials with due consideration to developmental needs is experienced mostly among urban, educated and wealthier families where adults "playing" with children is also more commonly observed. Among urban families in Delhi, children were found to enjoy playing with people and objects together rather than only with objects (Mehra 1995); and when they were given dolls to play with, they showed a wide variety of activities like attempting to feed the doll, making dolls fight with each other, dressing them up, and simply manipulating them (Bhargava 2010).

In a recent study of 58 rural, small town, and city families with young children in and around Delhi, it was found that children had no hesitation in accepting and playing with the material provided by the researcher. In one event from a low-income area, a group of children found an unfinished house where some rubble was lying. They spent long hours in a space above this house where construction was in progress, sometimes even crossing somewhat precarious spaces. The children carried building material to one corner and made a sort of shrine and put pictures of gods against the wall (Chaudhary 2013: 98). These 3-year-old children, their siblings and friends were seen to play all the time—while they bathed, ate, got ready, in school, at home, on the street, with friends, with adults, alone, with siblings, using toys, playing games, or using household materials. Further, children's play, work, and learning were seen to be wonderfully mixed at this young age, although adults often had separate categories for this as was demonstrated by reactions to children's "play."

In rural India and among the urban poor families, availability of toys or equipment for children to play with is a rare sight; children mostly play with natural materials like tree branches, leaves, animals, wood, sand, etc. (Figure 12.2).

In urban homes, children have toys of different types and sizes depending on the gender of the child; girls will have dolls, doll houses, and soft toys, and boys will be seen playing with cars, guns, blocks or more mechanical things (Bhargava 2010). Pretend play is also commonly observed among young children in both rural and urban India. Children take on adult roles and play with other children. In instances during make-believe play with objects, children display very detailed observations of adults in action. Although gender differences in domestic work among adults persist, children do not always display similar preferences during play. In one study, boys were more frequently playing with cars, yet they also actively engaged in playful cooking, making tea, and serving others. Many of these cooking sessions were dramatic and detailed, where careful placement of pots and pans and elaborate rituals of tea-drinking were followed (Chaudhary 2013). Subhash (2010) also found a similar trend in his study of children in Kerala.

Although not as common, solitary play was also evident (Trawick 1990; Chaudhary 2013). When children played in groups, the older ones guided play activities. And when children played in the absence of adults, it was possible to see unmediated dominance and leadership as well as subordination among them. Very few encounters of pushing and shoving were seen during spontaneous play sessions; dominance and leadership were mostly acceptable. Other findings related to dynamics among children were that

Figure 12.2 Toys are made from materials in the immediate environment.

among children close in age, there was a lot of imitation. If one child did something, so did the other children. If one child picked up a particular thing, it was seen to become the coveted object, even if it was a discarded stick (Chaudhary 2013).

Children's play and the family

An overview of research with children and families found that adults in Indian families tend to let children play. When they entered the scene, it was mostly with an additional objective beyond the simple engagement with children. In some instances the objectives were to feed the child distracted by play (very common among urban educated families), to teach the child numbers or the alphabet, to encourage the child to engage with others, or simply to guide the child in specific directions, for instance, to draw pictures of family members (Chaudhary 2013).

Regarding interactions between mothers and infants, Keller (2007) identified different parenting systems of care: namely primary care, body contact, body stimulation, object stimulation, face-to-face, and narrative envelope. Although all cultures manifest all parenting systems at some given time or another, there are differences in the dominant modes that are essentially adaptive, moving from physical proximity and body contact among agricultural and pastoral communities to face-to-face and object stimulation as dominant modes in technologically advanced cultures. This creates what Keller (2007, p. 22) identified as cultural styles of parenting. Over and above cross-cultural differences, Indian rural and urban families have different orientations, according to Keller. Whereas the rural (Gujarati) families displayed a higher frequency of body contact and body stimulation, a model of caregiving that facilitated inter-dependence, urban educated families expressed what was identified as an autonomous-relational model of parenting (Keller 2007).

With higher mobility, migration, and departure from native places, there is inevitably an increase in the prevalence of the nuclear family despite persistent long-distance connections with the larger family network. However, there is evidence to suggest that this change is important for the role of the father since the involvement of fathers and the closeness to his own children have been found to be significantly higher in nuclear families (Roland 1988). Roopnarine et al. (1992) found that physical play was not common for both mothers and fathers. However, a more recent study reported that the North American proposition of the dominance of rough play by fathers for the development of attachment (between the baby and the father) may not apply to the Indian family or to several other cultures as well (Roopnarine et al. 2013). Over the years close observations of Indian families (Chaudhary 2012, 2013), found that fathers' engagements with children were prone to reduced attention on account of some important features of the research experience in India, over and above the existing patterns. Predominantly, researchers working on issues related to family life in general and children in particular have tended to be young women. This created a definite distance in the spontaneous involvement of the father, as well as of selected others, and tends to highlight and zone in on mothers. On account of habitual research practices as well as the dominance of women in fieldwork of this nature, these findings persist. There is no doubt that conventionally, men are shy about interacting with their own children in the presence of others, as Kakar has noted in his writings (Kakar and Kakar 2007), but that such patterns also persist away from the researchers' glance is an assumption often made without sufficient reason.

Play with other members of the family, particularly grandparents, also needs attention. Several studies have found a great sense of engagement in play between children and grandparents (Seymour 1999; Sharma 2000; Gupta 2005; Singh and Srivastava 2008; Tuli and Chaudhary 2010). Apart from the fact that grandparents spent significant amounts of time with children, parents mention that they really value these interactions, both for the older generation as well as for the continuity in culture that they assume is facilitated for the next generation (Saraswathi 1999b; Chaudhary 2004; Gupta 2005).

Implications for policy on early childhood education and care

Early childhood education and care (ECCE) programs are now a global phenomenon. Tasks that were earlier fulfilled by the family prior to schooling have now been taken over by institutions, and the pressure is mounting to universalize preschool education since it is believed to be the magical solution for retention and participation in school, particularly for the poor (Ball 2011). As a country with a large population of young children, many of whom live in difficult circumstances, some of the important issues related to planning for early childhood education and play are discussed in the following sections.

Government policy and ECCE programs

The Indian government has repeatedly demonstrated its commitment to early childhood care and education within which the provision for play for children through non-formal activity is a large and significant component. The policy promotes the provision for care, nourishment, health and play for children between birth and 6 years, especially in disadvantaged settings.

The Integrated Child Development Services Scheme (ICDS), a holistic welfare programme for young children and families that was initiated in 1975, primarily targets the preschool years and now covers a significant population through its centers nation-wide, covering around 72 million children (aged 6 months to 6 years of age) for supplementary nutrition and around 34 million for preschool education as per one estimate (Planning Commission 2012). However, repeated evaluations of the ICDS program nationwide have revealed several important problems which dilute the outreach of the services. The non-formal play services are believed to be the weakest link, with health and nutrition receiving greater attention than coverage in planning and delivery. In spite of these challenges, the ICDS programme is the largest of its kind in the world, and several important experiments in conjunction with local non-governmental organizations (NGOs) and international agencies have resulted in effective delivery and provision for play for children in many of the centers. Local collaborations have proved to be very productive for facilitating conditions where children can learn through play among families who do not have access to resources, but much more work needs to be done in this area (CECED 2013b).

Multilingualism and the young child

Language is a critical issue for India. In the latest survey (Devy 2013), in India, a total of 850 languages were counted, with 22 of them being registered as "official." Regarding young children and play, this becomes an issue of concern for early childhood education programs. At home and on the street, children have the benefit of hearing and learning languages within the family and community. However, once they leave for preschool, the language of the teacher and other children comes into play. It has been found that when the teacher and/or the other children are from different linguistic backgrounds, learning can be seriously compromised for the young child from a minority language if her mother tongue is silenced in the classroom (Mohanty 2008). Contemporary scholars are working hard towards developing culturally and developmentally appropriate curricula for multi-lingual education (MLE) (Mohanty 2008). It is recommended that the movement of a child from home into the larger world must be based from the familiar outwards, rather than on replacement, whether this is for language or other cultural practices. The international focus is on mother-tongue education, after considering the fate of children from minority groups (Ball 2011). However, since India has a much more complex and textured linguistic map, simply referring to the mother tongue as the child's language can be misleading since there may be several languages being spoken in the home and the neighborhood. The focus is thus on multi-lingual education as social justice rather than bilingual education.

Art and children

Another important initative is the integration of art in education. Gandhian scholar, artist and educator, Devi Prasad (1997), advocates that, rather than teaching art, the incorporation of different forms of art in education provides a fundamental grounding of children's learning in their daily aesthetic engagement with the world, something that seems to be lost in our modern interpretation of education in general, and art education in particular. A child's creative expression needs to be nurtured in a classroom. When the reverse is promoted, where a child's product is evaluated and worse still, berated, the impact is far from favorable, Prasad argues, articulating the developmental and cultural significance of art activities for children (Prasad 1997).

The infrastructure

Several important concerns emerge from a careful study of research findings regarding planning for children's play, among them is the availability of open and safe spaces for children to play; this is becoming a serious issue in urban settings, especially in lower-income areas. People are moving rapidly to cities and there needs to be concerted effort towards play space provisions for children of all ages. Second, the inclusion of children with special needs is an urgent need. We need greater access, visibility and resources allocated to this concern. In traditional society, people with special needs were not excluded, albeit without any specific resources allocated to their care and mainstreaming; but they were always around. Urban environments are increasingly competitive, and therefore exclusion becomes a serious issue leading to the distancing of people with special needs.

Training the teacher

The quality of an early childhood program depends on the adults who lead the group. Research has shown repeatedly that investment in teacher training carries long-term impact in the improvement of child-centered and developmentally appropriate learning environments (CECED 2013a). Good programs require a constant revision of strategies on account of the special features of young children. However, a program for children also functions in a cultural context, and being prepared for specific characteristics and challenges in a given situation is essential for a program's success. Language use, attitudes towards the local community, knowledge of local practice, ease and comfort with playful activity and innovativeness, and a general sense of joy in being with children are some of the important ingredients of a teacher's disposition. Investing in teacher training has repeatedly proven to be extremely valuable for enhancing the quality of services available to children.

Conclusion

Play during childhood in India is primarily unstructured and informal for the vast majority of children, taking place in the spaces children share with several others. Children play more frequently with other children using materials that are around them and easily available. The purchase of a variety and abundance of play materials with due consideration to developmental needs is seen primarily among urban, educated and wealthier families where adults "playing" with children is also more commonplace. Adult intervention in children's spontaneous or structured play always seems to carry an additional objective, e.g., to feed, teach or guide the child in specific ways. Participation in family relationships and social exchanges are important themes during play among children. By and large, play between and among children of all ages, informal and unstructured, under the marginal supervision of adults prevails. The child-to-child model for play was found to be the most prevalent in Indian communities, where adults participate mostly when other children are not available for companionship (Chaudhary 2013). This supports observations of children's play in the majority world by Lancy (2008) and Rogoff (2003), who conclude that the Euro-American structuring of dyadic and didactic play activities between adults and children is quite specific to societies where Western schooling prevails, both historically and culturally.

References

Ball, J. (2011). *Enhancing learning of children from diverse language backgrounds: Mother-tongue-based bilingual or multi-lingual education.* Paris: UNESCO.

Bhargava, P. (2010). Children's understanding of self and others. Unpublished doctoral dissertation, University of Delhi, India.

Burman, E. (2008). *Developments: Child, image, nation.* London: Routledge.

CECED. (2013a). Conference on Early Learning: Status and the way forward. New Delhi: Ambedkar University, 25–27 October 2013.

CECED. (2013b). *Annual report of the Centre for Early Childhood Development and Education.* New Delhi: Ambedkar University.

Chaudhary, N. (2004). *Listening to culture: Constructing reality in everyday life.* New Delhi: Sage.

Chaudhary, N. (2007). The family: Negotiating cultural values. In J. Valsiner and A. Rosa (Eds.), *Cambridge handbook of social psychology* (pp. 524–539). Cambridge: Cambridge University Press.

Chaudhary, N. (2012). Father's role in the Indian family: A story that must be told. In D. Shwalb, B. Shwalb and M. Lamb (Eds.), *The father's role: Cultural perspectives* (pp. 68–94). New York: Routledge.

Chaudhary, N. (2013). Parent beliefs, socialisation practices and children's development in Indian families. Unpublished report of a major research project funded by the University Grants Commission, New Delhi.

Devy, G. (2013). People's linguistic survey of India. Available at: http://peopleslinguisticsurvey.org/sitemap.html (accessed 23 August, 2013).

Gottlieb, A. (2009). Who minds the baby? Beng perspectives on mothers, neighbors, and strangers as caretakers. In G. Bentley and R. Mace (Eds.), *Substitute parents: Alloparenting in human societies* (pp. 115–138). Oxford: Bergahn.

Gupta, D. (2005). Why do young children play? Exploring parental beliefs. Unpublished master's thesis, University of Delhi, India.

Kakar, S. (1981). *The inner world: The psychoanalytic study of childhood and society in India.* New Delhi: Oxford.

Kakar, S. and Kakar, K. (2007). *The Indians: Portrait of a people.* New Delhi: Penguin.

Keller, H. (2007). *Cultures of infancy.* Mahwah: NJ: Lawrence Erlbaum.

Klein, T., Wirth, D. and Linas, K. (2004). Play: Children's context for development. In D. Koralek (Ed.), *Spotlight on young children and play* (pp. 21–47). Washington, DC: National Association for the Education for Young Children (NAEYC).

Kumar, K. (1998). Study of childhood and family. In T. S. Saraswati, and B. Kaur (Eds.), *Human development and family studies in India* (pp. 45–61). New Delhi: Sage.

Lancy, D. F. (2008). *The anthropology of childhood: Cherubs, chattels, changelings.* Cambridge: Cambridge University Press.

Malhotra, R. (2013). *Being different: An Indian challenge to Western universalism.* New Delhi: HarperCollins.

Mehra, V. (1995). Parental perceptions and patterns of young children's play. Unpublished Master's dissertation, University of Delhi, India.

Mohanty, A. (2008). Perpetuating inequality: Language disadvantage and capability and deprivation of tribal mother-tongue speakers of India. In W. Harbert, S., McConnell-Ginet, A. Miller and J. Whitman (Eds.), *Language and poverty* (pp. 102–124). Clevedon: Multilingual Matters.

Nsamenang, B. A. and Joseph L. L. (2012). Afrique noire. In M. H. Bornstein (Ed.), *Handbook of cultural developmental science* (pp. 383–407). New York: Taylor & Francis.

Planning Commission (2012). *Evaluation report of the Integrated Child Development Services: Programme Evaluation Organisation.* New Delhi: Planning Commission. Available at: http://planningcommission.nic.in/reports/peoreport/peo/peo_icds_vol1.pdf (accessed 8 October, 2013).

Prasad, D. (1997). *Art as the basis of education.* New Delhi: National Book Trust.

Rogoff, B. (2003). *The cultural nature of human development*. New York: Oxford University Press.

Roland, A. (1988). *In search of self in India and Japan: Towards a cross-cultural psychology*. Princeton, NJ: Princeton University Press.

Roopnarine, J. L., Krishnakumar, A. and Vadgama, D. (2013). Indian fathers: Family dynamics and investment patterns. *Psychology and Developing Societies, 25*(2), 223–247.

Roopnarine, J. L., Talukder, E., Jain, D., Joshi, P. and Srivastav, P. (1992). Characteristics of holding, patterns of play, and social behaviours between parents and infants in New Delhi, India. *Developmental Psychology, 26*(2), 867–873.

Saraswathi, T. S. (1999a). Introduction. In T. S. Saraswathi (Ed.), *Culture, socialization and human development: Theory, research and applications in India* (pp. 13–42). New Delhi: Sage.

Saraswathi, T. S. (1999b). Adult-child continuity in India: Is adolescence a myth or an emerging reality? In T. S. Saraswathi (Ed.), *Culture, socialization and human development: Theory, research and applications in India* (pp. 213–232). New Delhi: Sage.

Saraswathi, T. S. and Dutta, R. (2010). India. In M. Bornstein (Ed.), *Handbook of cultural developmental science* (pp. 223–238). New York: Psychology Press.

Scribner, S. (1976). Situating the experiment in cross-cultural research. In K. E. Reigel and G. A. Meacham (Eds.), *The developing individual in a changing world* (pp. 310–321). The Hague: Merton.

Seymour, S. (1999). *Women, family and child care in India: A world in transition*. Cambridge: Cambridge University Press.

Sharma, D. (2000). Infancy and childhood in India: A critical review. *International Journal of Group Tensions, 24*(3–4), 219–251.

Sharma, D. (2003). Infancy and childhood in India. In D. Sharma (Ed.), *Childhood, family and sociocultural change in India* (pp. 13–47). New Delhi: Oxford University Press.

Sharma, N. (1996). *Identity of the Indian adolescent girl*. New Delhi: Discovery.

Sharma, N. and Chaudhary, N. (2004). From home to school. *Seminar, 546*. Available at: http://www.google.co.in/search?q=neerja+sharma+nandita+chaudhary+seminar&ie=utf-8&oe=utf-8&aq=t&client=firefox-a&rlz=1R1GGGL_en-GBIN334IN334 (accessed 23 January, 2011).

Shweder, R. A., Jensen, L. A. and Goldstein, W. M. (1995). Who sleeps by whom revisited: A method for extracting moral goods implicit in practice. In J. J. Goodnow, P. J. Miller, and F. Kessel (Eds.), *Cultural practices as contexts for development* (pp. 21–40). San Francisco, CA: Jossey-Bass.

Singh, A. and Srivastava, P. (2008). Exploring children's understanding of play and games. Unpublished master's thesis, University of Delhi, India.

Subhash, P. D. (2010). Gender differences in free play of preschool children in select cultural settings of Kerala. Kottayam, Kerala: Mahatma Gandhi University. Available at: http://shodhganga.inflibnet.ac.in/handle/10603/499 (accessed 7 October, 2013).

Trawick, M. (1990). *Notes on love in a Tamil family*. Berkeley, CA: University of California Press.

Tuli, M. and Chaudhary, N. (2010). Elective interdependence: Understanding individual agency and interpersonal relationships in Indian families. *Culture and Psychology*, *16*(4): 477–496.

Vygotsky, L. (1978). The role of play in development. In L. Vygotsky, *Mind in society: The development of higher mental processes* (trans. M. Cole) (pp. 92–104). Cambridge, MA: Harvard University Press.

Wadley, S. and Derr, B. W. (1994). *Struggling with destiny in Karimpur, 1925–1984*. Berkeley, CA: University of California Press.

13 Woolloomooloo and cross the Domain . . . Australian children's play

Gwenda Beed Davey

> Johnny and Jane and Jack and Lou
> Butler's Stairs through Woolloomooloo;
> Woolloomooloo and cross the Domain;
> Round the Block, and home again!
> Heigh Ho! Tipsy toe,
> Give us a kiss and away we go.

Introduction

Play is integral to childhood, and every one of the many diverse cultural and linguistic groups in Australia has a play culture, which includes running, skipping, counting out, handclapping, role-playing and imaginative games and rhymes. More than 12,000 items are documented at Museum Victoria in Melbourne, in the Australian Children's Folklore Collection, one of the world's largest collections of children's traditional playlore.

According to the Australian Government report, *Our Country Our People 2013*, 20 percent of the Australian population speaks a language other than English at home, but the national and majority language in Australia is English, and most playground lore follows the British canon, as documented by Iona and Peter Opie in their classic studies such as *The Lore and Language of Schoolchildren* (1959) and *Children's Games in Street and Playground* (1969). One of the earliest publications of a rare Australian children's rhyme, noted above, is *Woolloomooloo and cross the Domain*. The rhyme refers to a number of Sydney landmarks, and was published in *The Bulletin* magazine in March 1898. It was sent in by a correspondent as a contradiction to a *Bulletin* article by the poet Victor Daley, who thought it would take "five hundred years" to have an Australian child-literature that will supersede the old nursery favorites.

Of particular interest in Australia is Aboriginal children's play, which comes from the world's oldest continuous culture, albeit one which consists of many disparate groups and languages (*Science*, 7 October 2011. pp. 94–98). Australia's Indigenous population was, by 2013, about 460,000, 2.4 percent of the almost 23 million who make up modern Australia's diverse, multiethnic population (Australian Bureau of Statistics 2010).

What do we know of early Australian Aboriginal children's play? There are substantial archival holdings in the Australian Institute for Aboriginal and Torres Strait Islander Studies (AIATSIS) in Canberra, and a detailed account is contained in June Factor's scholarly work from 1988, *Captain Cook Chased a Chook: Children's Folklore in Australia* (Factor 1988). Somewhat earlier, Lyn Love, the President of the Anthropological Society of Queensland, presented *A Selection of Aboriginal Children's Games* to the Society in July 1983. She described imitative games, play with fire, listening to stories, songs, string figures, hiding, skipping, swinging and toys such as a hobby horse made from tree branches to represent an emu. She considered that children's favorite games were those which involved singing and dancing. Her sources were both old and recent, and included well-known anthropologists such as Malinowski, Berndt, Petrie, Mountford and Kartomi (Love 1983).

How might Aboriginal play be considered similar to or different from non-indigenous play in Australia? Judy McKinty's chapter in *Antipodean Traditions* (2011) describes some of the earliest reports of string games played by Aboriginal people in the nineteenth and twentieth centuries. She also wrote an account of her work on the Aboriginal Children's Play Project in Victoria (The Stegley Project) between 1991 and 1997. She found that many of the games described by Aboriginal children and adults were

> [games] common to Australian childhood and usually found in schoolyards – marbles, skippy, chasey, ball games, racing games, and various sports. The games at home were also similar – riding bikes, playing with pets, collecting things, making things, and just "mucking around". Generally speaking, the strong Aboriginal traditions in childhood were found where there was an ongoing connection or re-connection to the land and someone to pass the traditions on to the children.
>
> (McKinty 1998, pp. 4–6)

Uncle John "Sandy" Atkinson AM (Member in the Order of Australia) is a Bangerang Elder and leader in Aboriginal affairs in Victoria. In 1988, he spoke about his childhood on Cummeragunja, an Aboriginal mission on the Murray River on the Victorian/New South Wales border. The river was a major feature of children's play. The types of play taking place at the river included swimming across its width, diving for bricks in the water, and making canoes from sheets of iron found at the local tip in order to make trips to find ducks' and swans' eggs. A popular game was Mud Switches, made from red gum suckers and clay pellets, mainly used for target practice rather than for "warfare." Children were often taught by adults to avoid snakes, to beware of the giant Murray Cod (fish) and especially to keep away from the deep water holes, homes of the fearsome (and mythical) Bunyip. Empty Golden Syrup (treacle) tins were made into pull-along trains and paddle steamers. Sandy Atkinson also spoke about adults frequently joining children in their play (Atkinson 2011, pp. 14–16).

Somewhat earlier (1905), Kate Langloh Parker, writing about the Euahlayi people, had indicated that there was less division between Aboriginal adults and children in their play. She wrote:

> A very favourite game of the old men was skipping – Brambahl, they called it. They had a long rope, a man at each end to swing it. When it is in full swing in goes the skipper. After skipping in an ordinary way for a few rounds, he begins the variations, which consist, among other things, of his taking thorns out of his feet, digging for larvae of ants, digging grass seed, jumping like a frog . . . The one who can most successfully vary the performance is victor. Old men over seventy seemed the best at skipping.
>
> (Langloh Parker 1905: 127)

Today, skipping in Australia is usually thought of as a girls' activity, but it was not so in earlier times, even in non-Aboriginal circles. One of my favorite sound recordings from the National Library of Australia's Oral History and Folklore Section is about skipping in the street, around the time of the First World War (1914–1918). Mr Bernie Johnston was born in 1906, and was interviewed by the Library in 1987 for the New South Wales Bicentennial Oral History Collection. Mr Johnston spoke of doing 'a lot of skipping' during his childhood in the inner Sydney suburb of Surry Hills: "We'd cross a long rope across the street and I used to have a dozen kids skipping down there. Even Mrs. Munro came out – seventeen stone, and she had no shoes on. She'd come out and skip" (Johnston 1987).

How is play viewed in Australia?

Adult attitudes towards children's play in Australia vary from benign to malign; in between is indifference. The popular media is mainly indifferent, though thoughtful journalists may occasionally place an article in a daily newspaper, such as Geoff Maslen's "The kids are All Right, Vegemite," which featured an extensive interview with June Factor about the persistence and value of children's traditional playlore (Maslen 2013). Academia is also largely indifferent, apart from early childhood studies. Although the primary school years and primary school playgrounds are the main times and places where traditional play is found, play appears to have little part in the curricula of many primary education teacher training courses in Australia, a fact which might be considered as astonishing as a medical course without studies of anatomy. As part of the Childhood, Tradition and Change project which is discussed below, an examination was carried out of the 32 Bachelor of Education (Primary) courses in universities listed by the Australian Government's Department of Education, Science and Training as offering primary teacher training.

Play as a topic for study was conspicuously absent in most course outlines, and curricula in general seemed to take a heavily instrumental approach to instruction. Most of the B.Ed. (Primary) courses have about 30 separate units, so that for the 30 or so different courses studied, there are about 900 units. Out of these 900 units, only 19 dealt specifically with either play or child development, and only one university included a core subject focusing on play, namely AEB1181 *Play, Development and Learning*, from Victoria University of Technology in Melbourne (Davey 2008). In terms of teacher training in Australia, play seems to be seen as belonging exclusively to early childhood education, where it has a proud history. The Sydney Kindergarten Teachers' College was founded in 1897, emphasizing Froebel's theories on the importance of self-directed play. Other preschool training colleges were established soon after, such as Melbourne Kindergarten Teachers' College, now part of the University of Melbourne, which was founded by the Free Kindergarten Union (FKU) in 1916. The FKU also established the Multicultural Resource Centre in Melbourne in 1978, which pioneered many imaginative responses to Australia's immigration programs.

Hostility to children's play mainly derives from some fearful teachers and parents who have succumbed to the climate of fear which surrounds children in many Western countries in the twenty-first century (Furedi 2002). The role of adults as either friends or enemies of children's play is an important one, even though the culture of childhood is normally passed on from one generation of primary school-aged children to the next. In many ways the late twentieth and early twenty-first centuries have become the age of adult fears with regards to children; fears of accidents, fears of "stranger danger," and fears of parental litigation against school authorities (Furedi 2011). Although many of these fears have been shown to be unrealistic (Davey 2011), some schools are increasingly forbidding various activities. This is reflected in the following statement from the Childhood, Tradition and Change project:

> As for my 'forbiddings', they're plentiful, alas, and include no marbles (cause arguments), no playing in garden areas (garden is for show), no throwing balls (may hit someone), no climbing (may fall), no water play (too messy) . . .
> Then there was the Catholic primary school in Melbourne which commanded that its children not play at all before school started, so that they would be calm when they entered the school. The combination of parental fury, public ridicule (it was reported in the media), and the swift action of Susan Pascoe, then head of the Catholic Education Office, put a stop to that rule.
>
> (Factor 1988)

Some of the forbiddings I collected during the CTC project included: No play with sticks. No digging in the dirt. No holding stones in your hand (even to admire them). And in some extraordinary cases "no running." As one child said, "They might as well try to stop us breathing."

A rueful side effect of the contemporary climate of fear is the increasing difficulty researchers are finding in making visual records of children's play. In Australia, the twenty-first century is not only the century of fear, but is fast becoming the century of faceless children. In both television and print media, children's faces are now distorted to prevent recognition by undesirable adults; even the public database for the Childhood, Tradition and Change project has all images of children shown with colors inverted, for the same reason. How might these practices affect national collections such as the National Film and Sound Archive, whose mission statement holds that the NFSA collects, preserves and aims to ensure the permanent availability of the nation's audiovisual heritage? Is the NFSA to go for a century, or even longer, without any naturalistic representations of children in its collections?

Research on play in Australia

Children's play in Australia has been documented in a number of studies in the twentieth and twenty-first centuries, and there are also a few significant accounts from colonial days, in the nineteenth century. Sir Joseph Verco, born in 1851 and a distinguished physician in Adelaide, left to the State Library of South Australia a number of papers including a hand-written document entitled, "Early Memories 1860–1870." In this manuscript, Verco describes in great detail a number of different games of marbles played by boys: nux or nucks, in the ring, in the hole, and on the line. He also writes about fishing and swimming in the River Torrens, playing cricket in the neighborhood, a number of games played with tops (less common in the twenty-first century) and the keeping of animals such as rabbits, possums, and silkworms (Verco 1860–1870, passim).

In the twentieth century, a major research project was carried out in Australia by the American Fulbright scholar, Dr. Dorothy Howard, during 1954 and 1955. She visited every Australian State and Territory except the Northern Territory, meticulously documenting her observations, and publishing ten scholarly articles on topics such as hopscotch, knucklebones, string games and counting-out rhymes. Before her death in 1996, she donated all her Australian research materials to the Australian Children's Folklore Collection at Museum Victoria. The ACFC was placed in 2004 on the UNESCO Australia Memory of the World Register, as an important part of Australia's significant documentary heritage. Howard's ten articles, together with other scholarly commentary, were republished by Museum Victoria as *Child's Play: Dorothy Howard and the Folklore of Australian Children* (Darian-Smith and Factor 2005).

Only one of Dorothy Howard's ten papers was published in Australia, in 1955, but her work encouraged the publication in 1969 of a best-selling book, *Cinderella Dressed in Yella: Australian Children's Play-Rhymes*, collected by Ian Turner, an Associate Professor of History at Monash University in Melbourne. This scholarly production of Rhymes for Games, Rhymes for the Playground, and Rhymes for an Autograph Album, nevertheless became notorious when it ran into trouble with postal regulations on the grounds of obscenity. Turner had not backed away from including some of Australian children's vulgar and scatological interests, as well as their satirical comments on adult hypocrisies and taboos, such as

> Jack and Jill
> Went up the hill
> To fetch a pail of water;
> I don't know
> What they did up there
> But now they've got a daughter.

A collection of such subversive material was published in 1974 by historian Wendy Lowenstein as *Shocking, Shocking, Shocking: The Improper Play Rhymes of Australian Children*:

> Shocking, shocking, shocking,
> A mouse ran up my stocking;
> He got to my knee
> And what did he see?
> Shocking, shocking, shocking.

In the 1970s, two Queensland physical education lecturers, Peter Lindsay and Denise Palmer, carried out a study published in 1981 as the *Playground Game Characteristics of Brisbane Primary School Children*. They observed nearly five thousand children at play from 21 Brisbane schools and analysed their observations for basic play characteristics, play elements, area of play, touch characteristics, and group characteristics. Of particular interest are their comparisons between spontaneous playground games and teacher-directed syllabus games, where spontaneous games were found to show superiority in strategy, cardiovascular endurance, rhythm and touching.

In the twenty-first century, a widespread research project on Australian children's play was Childhood, Tradition and Change: A National Study of the Historical and Contemporary Practices and Significance of Australian Children's Playlore (2006–2010). For this project, fieldworkers visited primary schools in every Australian State and Territory, documenting children's playground activities using sound and video recordings, photographs and written notations (Figures 13.1 and 13.2). The Final Report was published in June 2011, and a public database was also posted online.

One of the most commonly asked questions addressed to members of the CTC research team was "Do children play the way they used to?" And the most common answer was: "Yes, and no." Many traditional games are still played, but some changes have occurred. The Final Report of the CTC project listed a number of issues in its Table of Contents, such as "The need to run and play chasey crosses all school contexts," "Fieldworkers described seventy-five forms of imaginary play," "Forbidden games," "Technology and computers," "School size and playground space" and "Weather and seasonal differences."

Children's play not only varies with seasonal playground differences (such as "the marbles season") but games can also appear and disappear for no apparent reason. Games popular in the nineteenth and early twentieth century such as spinning tops and circle singing games have largely disappeared from contemporary playgrounds in Australia, and in April 2013, the international online *Childlore List* posted a number of comments about whether the game of Elastics was still played. The consensus seemed to be that it had fallen from favor in a number of places, although the CTC Public Data Base lists a number of schools in Australia where Elastics was still being played.

The Final Report of the Childhood, Tradition and Change also included in its contents a section on cultural diversity and play, and quoted the Australian Bureau of Statistics to identify Australia today as a culturally diverse nation with a population

Figure 13.1   Hand stands.

that speaks almost 400 languages and identifies more than 270 ancestries. The Report states:

> Since World War II Australia has been profoundly shaped by successive waves of migration: from the post-war migration of Europeans, to the arrival of South-East Asian refugees from the late 1970s, to the more recent influx of migrants from parts of Africa and Afghanistan.

By 2006, almost a quarter of all Australians were born overseas, and just over a quarter of Australian-born people had at least one parent born overseas (Australian Bureau of Statistics, Yearbook Australia 2009–2010). A more recent national census was carried out in 2011, but data analysis is not yet complete.

There have been some useful studies of immigration and children's play, although they do not point to substantial or widespread alterations in the traditional games played across Australia as a whole. Kathryn Marsh's prize-winning study *The Musical Playground* (2008) studied children in schools in Sydney, central Australia, Norway, the United Kingdom, the United States, and Korea. In Chapter 7 of her book, she examined "the ways in which the singing game tradition in a range of playground localities is changed through the influences of inter-ethnic transmission, audiovisual and written

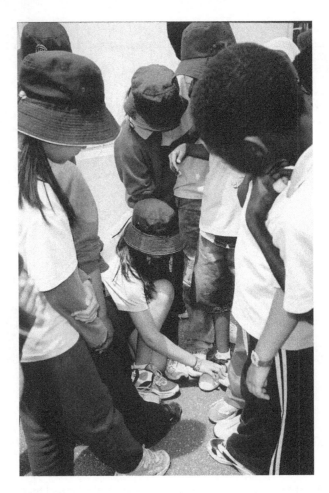

Figure 13.2 Coconut crack.

media, classroom transmission, and material from other sources external to the school" (Marsh 2008: 156). Inter-ethnic transmission is only one source of alteration, and the changes are usually confined to one particular school. Of interest is Kathryn Marsh's description of the reluctance of some non-Anglo children to use their own language in playground games, as they see this as challenging the culture of the playground (Marsh 2008, pp. 157–159).

Heather Russell's detailed study of one inner-suburban school in Melbourne in the 1970s was entitled *Play and Friendships in a Multi-Cultural Playground* (Russell 1986) and documented playground activities and friendship patterns, including "prejudice in the playground." Most of the children in "Hightown" Primary School lived in multi-story public housing, often in transition to other locations, so that the school population could be described as *high rise, high migrant, high turnover*. Children tended to play with their own ethnic group, though some special skills such as Vietnamese girls' mastery of the game of Elastics (particularly high jumps) and Vietnamese boys' skillful 'Chinese flick' in marbles did occasion admiration and imitation. Some immigrant pupils did not carry play traditions from their home countries to the school setting because of disruptions in schooling. Some ethnic groups were excluded from joining others. Following Heather Russell's study, the school introduced a successful cooperative play program to assist socialization, which continues today.

Sociocultural models/theories on play in Australia

For many years, play theory in Australia (e.g., Peterson 1984) was dominated by the cognitive developmental approach of the noted Swiss psychologist, Jean Piaget, who posed a combination of biology and experience to lead to a series of stages in children's development, including their play (Piaget 1962). In more recent years, play has been increasingly linked to pedagogy (e.g., Dockett and Fleer 1999), and even more recently, to cultural contexts (e.g., Ebbeck and Waniganayake 2010).

It is, however, not only early childhood educators who are interested in sociocultural models in play in Australia. Historians, architects, and landscape architects are increasingly involving themselves in this field. An important historiography is Simon Speight's *Young People and the Shaping of Public Space in Melbourne, 1870–1914* (Speight 2013). The year 1871 was part of an extraordinary period when Melbourne was bursting with juveniles; 42.2 percent of the population of the city were aged 14 or under, the result of a baby boom "in the wake of the gold rushes during the 1850s" (Speight 2013: 3).

As well as recounting social anxiety about the anti-social behavior of the larrikin gangs, Speight vividly describes the many uses to which city children appropriated many public spaces in Melbourne for their "larrikin repertoire" of activities. His book is prescient in terms of contemporary anxiety about children's shrinking opportunities for informal, outdoor play.

Concern for children's freedom to play naturally is widespread in Australia today, and the historian Carla Pascoe's book *Spaces Imagined, Places Remembered: Childhood in 1950s Australia* (Pascoe 2011) is an important contribution to this discourse. In the Preface to her book, Pascoe recalls her preference as a child for a "strange, unkempt, ugly-yet-beautiful place in the shadow of a freeway" instead of "a large recreation reserve complete with play equipment, sports field and tennis courts" (pp. xii–xiii). Of particular interest are her interviews with a number of adults about their memories and "mental maps" of their neighborhoods in post-war Carlton and North Balwyn, two very different Melbourne suburbs. Carla Pascoe is a historian, but there are members of a variety of disciplines who share her concerns. In September 2007, a symposium was held in Perth, Western Australia, entitled Come and Play Outside. Participants included architects, landscape architects, naturalists, educators, and historians, and overseas visitors came from England, America, and Denmark. Margaret Grose, the symposium convener, is a University of Melbourne lecturer in the School of Architecture, and she "argued that over-design is common in children's playgrounds, when actually such spaces should be wild enough to enable a sense of discovery" (Grose 2007, quoted in Pascoe 2008).

There are a number of Australian organizations dedicated to defense and advocacy as regards to children's play. *Play for Life* is a Melbourne-based not-for-profit organization that is advocating for and acting to enrich children's free play in schoolyards and communities. *Play Australia* is the Australian member of the International Play Association. It has grown from an earlier body, the *Playgrounds and Recreation Association of Victoria* (PRAV, founded in 1913). The *Australian Research Alliance for Children and Youth* (ARACY) is also a national body, although regrettably it does not specifically consider play in its measures of children's health and well-being. *Play and Folklore* is the online publication associated with the Australian Children's Folklore Collection at Museum Victoria, and the three editors of the publication (June Factor, Gwenda Beed Davey, and Judy McKinty) and other Museum staff work as a *de facto* advocacy organization through media and conference presentations, both in Australia and overseas. Of importance is the appointment by the Federal Government in February 2013 of Megan Mitchell as Australia's first National Children's Commissioner, to be a dedicated advocate for children and young people and for the United Nations Convention on the Rights of the Child. She will be based at the Australian Human Rights Commission in Sydney. Many advocates of children's play are hopeful that Megan Mitchell will not only respond to things which happen to children, but will also advocate on behalf of the brilliant culture which is children's independent playlore.

Future directions and policy implications

An ever-present source of concern about Australian children is whether spending too much time on electronic play media can encourage obesity and damage children, both physically and neurologically (Stanley et al. 2005). Most Australian schools do not permit electronic toys at schools, though computer games are sometimes played. It is interesting that some computer terminology such as pause and rewind has found its way into children's games, sometimes as an update on the older concept of barley, to indicate a desire for a break in a game. In Issue No. 59 of *Play and Folklore*, a photograph shows two children with a large cubby house they built in bushland near their home. These two children also regularly play computer games, Nintendo Wii and other video games, and use Nintendo DS consoles, iPods, and iPads. They live in both worlds.

The conclusion to the Final Report of the Childhood, Tradition and Change project included the following observations:

> The preliminary findings of the **Childhood, Tradition and Change** project reveal much about children's schoolyard play in Australia, not least the inventiveness of children and their capacity to engage with each other and

their environment in all forms of play. Further analysis of the data collected by fieldworkers . . . will reveal in further detail how children in Australia play in schools in the early twenty-first century, and the diversity and similarity of their play practices from school to school, and state to state. The research findings will also focus on the ways that children's play has altered and remained constant since the mid twentieth century, drawing upon the earlier studies of scholars, such as Dorothy Howard, and Peter Lindsay, and Denise Palmer, and Heather Russell . . . The project reveals the richness of children's games and language, and the diversity and similarity of play across the nation attests to the vibrancy of children's cultures.

(Darian-Smith and Henningham 2011: 446)

A particular challenge in twentieth-century Australia concerns the need to protect children's traditional playlore, to defend its value, and the time and space children need to practice their own culture. Perhaps primary school playgrounds could be declared Sacred Sites, or at least sites worthy of heritage protection.

References

Atkinson, S. (2011). Childhood on Cummeragunja. *Play and Folklore, 55,* 11–15.

Australian Bureau of Statistics (2010). *Yearbook Australia, 2009–2010.* Available at: Australia gov.au http://australia.gov.au/about-Australia/our-country/our-people (accessed 9 March 2013).

The Bulletin magazine (1898 and 1917). Sydney.

Childhood, Tradition and Change: A National Study of the Historical and Contemporary Practices and Significance of Australian Children's Playlore (2006–2010). This Australian Research Council project was also supported by Melbourne, Deakin and Curtin Universities, the National Library of Australia and Museum Victoria.

Childhood, Tradition and Change Public Data Base. Available at: ctac.esrc.unimelb.edu.au/resources.html (accessed 17 April 2013).

Darian-Smith, K. and Factor, J. (Eds.) (2005). *Child's play: Dorothy Howard and the folklore of Australian children.* Melbourne: Museum Victoria.

Darian-Smith, K. and Henningham, N. (2011). *Childhood, Tradition and Change final report.* Available at: ctac.esrc.unimelb.edu.au/objects/project-pubs/FinalReport.pdf (accessed 17 April 2013).

Davey, G. (2008). The last frontier? Primary school playgrounds and children's play. Address to Australian Teacher Education Association Conference, Mooloolaba, Queensland. Published by ATEA as CD.

Davey, G. (2011). Rights and representations of Australian Childhood. Final Report of Scholars and Artists in Residence Fellowship, National Film and Sound Archive, Canberra, 2011. Available at: www.nfsa.gov.au › Research › Papers and projects.

Dockett, S. and Fleer, M. (1999). *Play and pedagogy in early childhood: Bending the rules.* Marrickville, NSW: Harcourt Brace & Company Australia.

Ebbeck, M. and Waniganayake, M. (2010). *Play in early childhood education: Learning in diverse contexts.* South Melbourne, Victoria: Oxford University Press Australia & New Zealand.

Factor, J. (1988). *Captain Cook chased a chook: Children's folklore in Australia.* Ringwood, Vic. Penguin Books Australia, p. 119.

Furedi, F. ([1997] 2002). *The culture of fear.* London: Continuum.

Furedi, F. (2011). The real danger to our children. *The Australian,* 9 September.

Hall, T. (2010). *The life and death of the Australian backyard.* Collingwood, Vic.: CSIRO Publishing.

Howard, D. (1955). Folklore of Australian children. *Journal of Education, 2*(1), 30–35.

Johnston, B. (1987). New South Wales Bicentennial Oral History Collection, sound recording, TRC 2301/115. National Library of Australia, Canberra.

Langloh Parker, K. (1905). *The Euahlayi tribe: A study of Aboriginal life in Australia.* London: Archibald Constable.

Lindsay, P. L. and Palmer, D. (1981). *Playground game characteristics of Brisbane primary school children,* ERDC Report No. 28. Canberra: Australian Government Publishing Service.

Love, L. (1983) A selection of Aboriginal children's games. *Newsletter of the Anthropological Society of Queensland.*

Lowenstein, W. (1974). *Shocking, shocking, shocking: The improper play rhymes of Australian children.* Prahran, Vic.: Fish and Chip Press.

Marsh, K. (2008). *The musical playground: Global tradition and change in children's songs and games,* Oxford: Oxford University Press.

Maslen, G. (2013). The kids are all right, Vegemite. *The Age,* 12 September 2013.

McKinty, J. (1998). Aboriginal children's play project: a researcher's experience. *Play and Folklore, 34,* 4–6.

McKinty, J. (2011). String games in Australia. In G. Seal and J. Gall (Eds.), *Antipodean traditions: Australian folklore in the 21st century* (pp. 42–58). Perth, WA: Black Swan Press.

Opie, I. and Opie, P. (1959). *The lore and language of schoolchildren.* Oxford: Oxford University Press.

Opie, I. and Opie, P. (1969). *Children's games in street and playground.* Oxford: Oxford University Press.

Pascoe, C. (2008). The joy of playing naturally. *Play and Folklore,* No. 50. Melbourne: Museum Victoria.

Pascoe, C. (2011) *Spaces imagined, places remembered.* Newcastle upon Tyne: Cambridge Scholars Publishing.

Petersen, C. C. (1984). *Looking forward through the life span: Developmental psychology,* Sydney: Prentice-Hall of Australia.

Piaget, J. (1962). *Play, dreams, and imitation in childhood.* New York: Norton.

Russell, H. (1986). *Play and friendships in a multi-cultural playground.* Melbourne: Institute of Early Childhood Development.

Science Magazine (2011). 7 October, pp. 94–98. Published online 22 September 2011. American Association for the Advancement of Science.

Speight, S. (2013). *Young people and the shaping of public space in Melbourne, 1870–1914*. Burlington, VA: Ashgate.

Stanley, F., Richardson, S. and Prior, M. (2005). *Children of the Lucky Country? How Australian society has turned its back on children and why children matter*. Sydney: Pan Macmillan Australia.

Turner, I. (1969). *Cinderella dressed in yella: Australian children's play rhymes*. Melbourne: Heinemann Educational.

Verco, J. (1860–1870). Early Memories 1860–1870. Unpublished manuscript, State Library of South Australia, Passim.

Part IV

Europe and Turkey

14 Play in a Swedish preschool context

Anne Lillvist and Anette Sandberg

> If someone would ask me what I remember from my childhood, my first thought would not be the people. Instead, I would say the nature that embraced my days and filled them so intensely, that as an adult, you can't even believe it. Places with wild strawberries, meadows with hepatica and primrose, blueberries and the forest with pink flowers in the moss. The pasture around Näs, where we knew every trail and rock, the river with water lilies, the ditches, streams and trees, all this I remember more than the people. Stones and trees, they were like living beings, and nature protected and nurtured our play and our dreams.
>
> (Astrid Lindgren et al. 1987: 20)

Introduction

The quote above is from the famous Swedish author Astrid Lindgren, the author of Pippi Longstocking, and several other well-known characters in children's books. Lindgren's child characters always portray the child as competent, creative, free-roaming, independent, and playful, living in close proximity to nature. Although the characters are fictional, some similarities to the views on childhood and play in Swedish society today can be discerned. The aim of this chapter is to illuminate these views by discussing the status of play within a Swedish preschool context, the theoretical frameworks for emphasizing play, research on play and finally, future directions and policy implications.

The status of play within the Swedish preschool context

Sweden, along with the other Nordic countries, shares international recognition for high quality preschools, and for the status of play in society (UNICEF 2008; Izumi-Taylor et al. 2010). In Sweden, early childhood education is unique in the way in which it combines learning and play with care and the fostering of fundamental values. The main aim of this chapter is to describe and discuss the status of play in

Sweden, specifically focusing on the preschool context. When discussing play in Sweden, it is important to focus on it from different conceptual levels: societal, preschool, and children. We describe the status of play given in policy documents such as the curriculum for preschool, and give examples of the status of space or freedom for play provided by preschool teachers. We also focus on how children create their own culture of play in preschool settings.

In the autumn of 2011, approximately 470,000 or 83 percent of all children aged 1–5 years were enrolled in preschools in Sweden (National Agency for Education 2013). The high percentage of children enrolled in preschools is a consequence of both parents being in the workforce in the majority of families (at least part-time) as well as the different educational and social reforms that have reduced the cost of preschool for parents. A national reform enabling 15 hours of free preschool per week for children whose parents are unemployed or on parental leave, as well as 525 hours of preschool free of charge for all children from their fourth birthday on was introduced in 2001–2003 (National Agency for Education 2003). Beginning in 2010, preschool became free of charge for 3-year-olds as well. These reforms are based on the assumption that preschool is beneficial for children and an important preparation for school. What this means is that preschools serve as an important play context for children, teachers facilitating children's play but also setting boundaries for it. Due to economic restraints, the size of children's groups in preschools has increased in recent years. Data from the National Agency for Education (2013) show that the staff to child ratio is 1: 5, with an average of 17 children per preschool unit. Approximately every fifth child comes from a cultural background other than Swedish. The staff in preschools consists of child minders and preschool teachers.

Play is emphasized in the curriculum, and preschool teachers support children in actively engaging in the learning process. Learning and playing are seen as inseparable with children viewed as learning-playing agents within the social context of preschool. The curriculum is based on the sociocultural theory developed by Vygotsky (1976, 2012). The curriculum of the preschool states that:

> Play is important for the child's development and learning. Conscious use of play to promote the development and learning of each individual child should always be present in preschool activities. Play and enjoyment in learning in all its various forms stimulate the imagination, insight, communication and the ability to think symbolically, as well as the ability to co-operate and solve problems. Through creative and gestalt play, the child is given opportunities to express and work through his or her experiences and feelings.
>
> (National Agency for Education 1998/2010: 6)

The curriculum also states that preschools should strive to ensure that children develop their ability to play and learn. Hence, this can be interpreted as the ability to play is not seen as static, one that children are born with and either have or do not have. Rather, play is something changeable that can be promoted and further developed by social interaction with other children and adults. In a study examining preschool teachers' beliefs about play, playfulness was perceived by the teachers as an inherent capacity as well as a learned ability. Approximately 40 percent of the teachers believed that playfulness was either completely or mostly an inherent capacity. A minority of 10 preschool teachers reported playfulness to be completely learned (Sandberg et al. 2012).

The role of play in preschools has come under pressure, however. The curriculum for preschools was revised in 2010 (National Agency for Education 1998/2010) to include new goals in the areas of science, language, and mathematics. According to a clarification to the curriculum offered by the National Agency for Education in 2010 (National Agency for Education 2010), the goals of the curriculum are not standards against which the children should be evaluated or judged, but rather they are goals to strive towards. In addition, the only focus for evaluation should be the activities in the preschool, and not the abilities of individual children. The curricular goals can be interpreted in many ways. For example, there are some indications that the goals of mathematics or science are seen as subjects that should be taught to the children. An extended and deepened focus on subjects such as mathematics, science, and language development threatens the status of play if the ambition is to turn preschool into school for early learners. Tendencies towards this "schoolification" with a clearer focus on learning are evident in both international and national policy documents, for example, the European Commission (2011) states the importance of laying the foundation for lifelong learning in preschool and, with the revision of the Education Act in Sweden, preschool was included as the first level in the educational system and as a form of school on its own.

Pramling-Samuelsson (2011) discussed the relationship between learning and play in terms of quality. What is characteristic for high quality preschools is that play is not separated from learning. Johnson et al. (2005) offered a holistic view on play and learning, describing play in high quality preschools as grounded in the educational content initiated by the teachers, and learning as grounded in the content of play initiated by the children. Simeonsdotter Svensson (2009), who studied circle time of Swedish 6-year-olds in the preschool classroom, presented some results that support these perspectives. Children experienced circle time more positively when it included aspects of play; they also often used play as a coping strategy for creating meaning in difficult-to-comprehend situations. The author points out the importance of including children in the planning of different activities such as circle time as a way of fostering participation and engagement by children. Two other Swedish studies that interviewed children about their abilities to make decisions regarding the everyday activities in preschool showed that children had very little influence on the activities carried out in preschool (Pramling-Samuelsson and Sheridan 2003; Arnér 2009). When children were able to make their own decisions, it was mostly concerning activities or topics that were not seen as very important. Such findings suggest that though statements about the importance of play are included in different policy documents on the curriculum, there are limitations in how these documents are interpreted or implemented in practice in the everyday life of preschools—at least from the children's point of view.

Theoretical framework for understanding play in a Swedish preschool context

The construct of play has been the focus of interest for scholars for hundreds of years, with its roots in the ancient Greek philosophy of Plato and Aristotle. Play is a necessity for our existence as human beings. Berg (1992) argues, for example, that play is a central and essential part of human development of identity, and essential for the formation of close relations as well as the ability to coordinate reality and the parts of reality into a whole. Symbolic play, according to Berg, is a way of handling reality by distancing oneself from it, by having something representing something else, for example, the banana becomes a telephone. The human being is biologically wired for play. We are herd animals, socially responsive and conditioned to respond to other people around us. From a biological perspective, play develops around these responses, and starts even before the child is born. From an evolutionary perspective, we have to be sociable and likable in order to get along with other people, not to be excluded, and as an adult to attract a mate. Viewing play from the point of a life-span perspective, these abilities or competencies are grounded in the play experiences and social interactions of our childhood and are closely connected to learning, development, positive feelings, and participation. Historically, play has been described as preparation for a working life (Dewey 1913), as sensory learning (Montessori 1972), as intellectual development (Piaget 1962), and as social development (Vygotsky 1976).

Thus, it is important for many reasons to discuss the status of play internationally and nationally. Vygotsky conceptualized play as emerging from unmet desires that the child feels a need to realize through play. Play is seen as an important part of socialization and as both an inter-individual and an intra-individual process. Further, play is seen as an internalization of the values and culture of a given society. As noted earlier, sociocultural theories serve as the theoretical framework for the Swedish curriculum for the preschool. The sociocultural approach corresponds well with a view in which children are seen as both beings and becomings, concepts recognizing the value of childhood and seeing children as competent and actively engaging in making meaning of their world while undergoing continuing development. This view balances the acknowledgment of children as independent and fairly competent, but still needing guidance and support from others in their learning and development (Sommer et al. 2010).

The concept of the zone of proximal development is widely recognized and is sometimes given as a reason for the mixed-age group constellations of children in preschools. Children learn from each other, but the extent to which children actually turn to each other for problem solving, help or instructions is very much dependent on the adults' views of children's collaborative learning. Research by Williams et al. (2000) showed that the collaborative learning of children was more frequent and more encouraged by preschool teachers in high quality preschools than in those identified as of low quality.

The framework of sociocultural theory, by emphasizing the cultural and social experiences for learning, provides the foundation for the pedagogical approaches found in the Swedish preschool. Communication is seen as a collective act where all the participants are active in the construction of meaning within social and cultural experiences. Pedagogical approaches are based on interaction and the variety of experiences; ways of making meaning are, at least on a conceptual level, seen as an asset. Thus, children's various experiences and manifestations of play are the focal point for all preschool didactics. Preschool teachers need to be flexible and attentive, capturing the themes or experiences that children demonstrate in play, in order to share the meaning-making of individual children in a specific situation.

Research on play

The research field of play in Sweden encompasses a variety of topics. Extensive research has been carried out regarding topics that are either conceptually related to play, such as interaction, participation, the children's own perspective and meaning-making, or topics that have consequences for play, for instance, professionalism and quality in the preschool. Even though the latter research may not directly focus on play, it is nevertheless relevant to the current status of play in Swedish preschools.

Sandberg and Vuorinen (2005) investigated the play memories of Swedish preschool teachers and students in preschool teacher education programs. One characteristic of many of the memories described was that they resembled flow, a state of total engagement, arousal and inspiration (Csíkszentmihályi 1992). The participants described how they lost track of time and space in play; some even described it as meditative state close to an out-of-body experience. Several researchers have linked this type of very intense experience of play to positive health effects (Csíkszentmihályi and Hunter 2003; Almqvist et al. 2007). To reach this meditative state of play, children must be given time and space to play.

In Swedish preschools usually some time is devoted every day for what is called free play. Free play is characterized by freedom to choose what and where to play, and sometimes also with whom to play. The wording of play in preschools as "free" has been discussed and to some extent challenged since children typically encounter a variety of limitations and constraints, even if the play is supposed to be free (Hangaard Rasmussen 1992). One common limitation is time. The Swedish researcher Margareta Öhman (2011) reported on her interview with a boy about play in preschool. When asked what he usually plays in the preschool, he replied: "I usually don't play at the preschool, because there is never time to finish the play. So I wait and play at home instead, where I can play until I'm done." Although the aim was to keep the free play period as free as possible, children constantly find interruptions and limitations which interfere with their desire to play. Resilient children will probably find a way of playing even in preschools of very low quality, but sensitive children who have difficulties in tuning into the mode of play are the ones who may only reach a very shallow state of play in such preschools.

Another restriction that children typically encounter is that toys or artifacts can only be played with in a specific room. For example, it may be forbidden to make tire tracks of small cars in the play-dough, or to move chairs from one room to the other. Thus, play is often conditioned. Sometimes these limiting conditions are due to safety regulations but sometimes the restrictions that children encounter while playing are merely based on what is the most convenient option for the teachers (Pramling-Samuelsson and Sheridan 2003). The nature of play is creative and rapidly changing, and this calls for a flexible environment, one that facilitates play rather than suppresses it. How well this is done is dependent on the attitude and competencies of the preschool teachers.

Parents and preschool teachers in Sweden seem to have a good deal of respect for children's play and recognize it as something special. However, it also seems that play almost has a mystical aura around it and adults do not know how to approach it. At times, this confusion may be due to a lack of understanding and sometimes due to a fear of intruding on it and thereby destroying the play. High quality preschools require competent preschool teachers who are able to support children in their meaning-making. To illustrate, Sheridan and Pramling-Samuelsson (2001) showed how quality in preschool varied depending on the teachers' attitudes towards play, learning, and participation by children. Lower quality preschools were less flexible regarding the possibilities for children to be creative. Their communication was at a shallow level, with few conversations occurring with the children. The higher quality preschools evidenced more teacher–child dialogues and play interactions; the activities provided were based on the interests of the children and not just the interests of the adults. Preschools of high quality were also characterized by freedom of choice, with fewer restrictions concerning what the children could play with and where.

The outdoor natural environment has a long tradition of being an important play context in Sweden and the other Nordic countries. The tradition is rooted in the movement of European Romanticism, based on the thoughts of Rousseau and, at a later point, Froebel. Central to the theories spun from the Romantic movement is the thought of the child and nature as intertwined. The legacy of these thoughts has had a great impact on the Swedish preschool until today. Preschool children usually have time for outdoor free play at least once a day. Regardless of the weather, children are often outside in the morning and in the afternoon, either in the preschool yard or having an outing to a nearby wooded area, park, or meadow. Some preschools have as many activities as possible outdoors, including meal preparation, play, and even napping (Halldén 2011; Ärlemalm-Hagsér and Sandberg 2013).

In a review of Swedish educational policy documents, Ärlemalm-Hagsér and Sandberg (2013) summarized the content related to nature and outdoor play. The results showed that nature and outdoor play were described as promoting children's development. Being in nature also furthers respect for all living things, and is thought to foster awareness of nature. Furthermore, nature and outdoor play have also been described in terms of freedom and health promotion (Halldén 2011). Other research on children's outdoor play has focused on gender issues. For instance, some research has shown that the outdoor, natural environment might increase gender equality, since nature itself is not gender coded, as many of the materials indoors might be (Änggård 2011). By contrast, in Sandberg and Vuorinen's (2010) study, children's narratives indicate that girls and boys gain qualitatively different experiences from playing in the natural outdoor environment. Even in Niklasson and Sandberg's (2010) study, some differences between gender and ages concerning perceived and used affordance in outdoor environments were obvious. For example, it is more common for girls to stay closer to the preschool teachers than boys do, and if a choice is given between staying inside or going outdoors to play, many girls prefer to stay inside. Ärlemalm-Hagsér and Sandberg (2013) point out the importance of raising critical awareness of gender structures and hierarchies in children's outdoor play.

Others have pointed out the positive effects that outdoor play has on gross motor skills (Fjørtoft 2004) as well as how the outdoor area offers a different vocabulary, and that children and adults use different types of words when they are outdoors (Norling and Sandberg submitted). The tradition of seeing the outdoors as an extended pedagogical play space has affected preschool teacher education programs as well as teacher education programs for school children in several ways, including the training of pre-service students in addressing the outdoor environment as a valuable asset for play and learning. There is a trend for schools to use the outdoors as an extended classroom, and many scholars have pointed out the importance of acknowledging playfulness and play in school in the way it traditionally has been recognized in preschools (Szczepanski et al. 2006). However, moving the classroom outside without changing teaching approaches and curricular activities accomplishes little. The outdoors should be perceived as another context that adds a new and different dimension to the play of children. A mathematics lesson outdoors could include children investigating the concept of the circumference of a tree, or investigating distance, weight and other concepts by using the natural materials that can be found there.

Play is one of the most common activities in preschool, and when children are asked about their engagement and participation in preschool, they often respond that the most important thing is to play and have friends (Vickerius and Sandberg 2006; Öhman 2011). Extensive research has shown that social interaction with peers has a positive impact on children's well-being, social competence, and school achievement (see, for example, Howes et al. 1992; Coolahan et al. 2000; Laine et al. 2010). A comparative study on preschool teachers' views on children's learning in Sweden and Denmark found that most preschool teachers reported that children learned best from playing with other children (Broström et al. 2012). With this in mind, it is alarming that, according to a study conducted by Lillvist and Granlund (2009), the majority of children perceived to be in need of special support were identified as being in need of this support due to difficulties in interactions with other children. How to support and facilitate children's peer interactions thus continues to be an important task for preschool teachers.

Implications for child development and preschool teacher education

There is very little disagreement as to how important play is for the development of young children. The preschool environment and especially the preschool teacher thus play an essential role in how children can achieve this developmental opportunity. The role of preschool teachers has traditionally been to organize and structure children's play (Jones and Reynolds 1992); but even as the importance of the role of adults in play has been elaborated, additional research is warranted concerning preschool teachers' perceptions of the competencies they need in facilitating and promoting children's play.

A study by Wood (2004) showed that preschool teachers express the importance of having support frameworks to develop and assess children's skills in learning and in play, while not being overly monitoring and guarding. Rather than viewing play as a predefined learning objective, teachers argue that it is necessary to understand and follow the children's own meaning of play. Other research has described the multifaceted nature of preschool teachers' play competence (see, for example, Ashiabi 2007; Sandberg et al. 2012). Pramling-Samuelsson and Johanson (2009) found that children want preschool teachers to help and support them in their play and learning. Thus, the complexity of the concept of play competence is a challenge for preschool teacher education. Research also indicates that play competence develops from play experiences. This means that the combination of theory and practice is important to emphasize and possibly develop even further in teacher education.

Swedish society is rapidly changing and so are the conditions for children. This rapid change has been brought about by technical equipment such as computers, tablets, mobile phones, and interactive boards that today constitute a wide base for children's play experiences, both in the home and in preschools and schools. Digital competence is one of the key competencies for lifelong learning, according to the European Commission (OECD 2007). According to a report from the Swedish Medieacouncil (Medierådet 2010) 75 percent of children aged 3–5 years regularly use computers. Some years ago technology tools were used mainly in preschools as a resource for children in need of special support (Brodin and Lindstrand 2003); but the use of computers, tablets, etc. from a pedagogical perspective has grown rapidly recently, affecting all children. Sheridan et al. (2013) point out that digital technology has created new possibilities for children to make their voices heard and to participate in documentation processes; this has also elevated the status of the child as co-constructors in the pedagogy of play. This places high demands on the digital competence of the preschool teacher, and thus preschool teacher education. In several ways there is still a gap between the knowledge of the children, who in many respects are the experts, and the preschool teachers' competencies to use digital tools in order to support and challenge children's play and learning.

Another challenge for preschool teacher education is to prepare teachers-in-training to work in a client-centered way with parents and children from a variety of different cultural backgrounds. Many nationalities are now represented in Swedish preschools and in some areas the vast majority of children do not have Swedish as their mother tongue. Play is a phenomenon that is universal, but it is culturally dependent, and this calls for preschool teachers to be responsive and flexible to be able to support all children in their play. Although the intention of the Swedish government is to provide all children with equal opportunity to obtain a high quality preschool experience, the preschool provision is becoming more and more segregated, leading to differing opportunities of play, learning, and development for children. In segregated areas the quality of preschool might be lower due to economic restraints, high staff turnover, and fewer educated preschool teachers (Nordfeldt and Segnestam Larsson 2011). The lack of qualified teachers possibly has implications for the support and challenges that children are given in their play.

Commentary on future directions and policy implications

As outlined in this chapter, play has traditionally had a strong status in the Swedish preschool context and among parents. However, during the past decade the focus has shifted towards emphasizing play as a tool or as a method for reaching developmental outcomes. One explanation for this shift might be the media concerns that frequently highlight the declining school achievement results of Swedish children. In these discussions of how to improve the achievement results of children, preschool has been identified as central to prepare children for school. The foundations for learning are established in preschool; and the expectations of preschool as the child's first educational experience has grown, along with the focus on learning. In this climate, it is important to see that play and learning are not opposites; rather, it is a question of perspectives and how to integrate these perspectives into a whole. The challenge is how to give the preschool teacher profession a higher status without making preschool into a traditional school. This chapter has suggested two major challenges that future research and policy need to take into consideration. First, play still needs to be defended and not eroded. Although extensive research has demonstrated the importance of play, this knowledge needs to be disseminated more widely in Swedish society, reaching all adults who work with children and those adults whose decisions have an impact on the lives of children in some way. Second, in order for this to happen, the professional training and development of current and future preschool teachers need to be of high quality and prioritized throughout Swedish society.

References

Almqvist, L., Uys, C. J. E., Uys, K. and Sandberg, A. (2007). The concepts of participation, engagement and flow: A matter of creating optimal play experiences. *South African Journal of Occupational Therapy, 11*, 1–6.

Änggård, I. (2011). Children's gendered and non-gendered play in natural spaces. *Children, Youth and Environments, 21*(2), 5–33.

Ärlemalm-Hagsér, E. and Sandberg, A. (2013). Outdoor play in a Swedish preschool context. In S. Knight (Ed.), *International perspectives on Forest School: Natural spaces to play and learn* (pp. 42–52). London: Sage.

Arnér, E. (2009). *Barns inflytande i förskolan: en fråga om demokrati.* [Children's participation in preschool: A question of democracy]. Lund: Studentlitteratur.

Ashiabi, G. S. (2007). Play in the preschool classroom: Its socioemotional significance and the teacher's role in play. *Early Childhood Education Journal, 35*(2), 199–207.

Berg, L. E. (1992). *Den lekande människan: En socialpsykologisk analys av lekandets dynamik.* [The playing human being. A socio-psychological analysis of the dynamics of play]. Lund: Studentlitteratur.

Brodin, J. and Lindstrand, P. (2003). *Perspektiv på IKT och lärande.* [Perspectives on ICT and learning]. Lund: Studentlitteratur.

Broström, S., Johansson, I., Sandberg, A. and Frøkjær, T. (2012). Preschool teachers' views on learning in preschool in Sweden and Denmark. *European Early Childhood Education Research Journal, 68.*

Coolahan, K., Fantuzzo, J., Mendez, J. and McDermott, P. (2000). Preschool peer interactions and readiness to learn: Relationships between classroom peer play and learning behaviors and conduct. *Journal of Educational Psychology, 92*(3), 458–465.

Csíkszentmihályi, M. (Ed.) (1992). *Optimal experience: Psychological studies of flow in consciousness.* New York: Cambridge University Press.

Csíkszentmihályi, M. and Hunter J. (2003). Happiness in everyday life: The uses of experience sampling. *Journal of Happiness Studies, 4,* 185–199.

Dewey, J. (1913). Play. In P. Monroe (Ed.), *An Encyclopedia of Education* (pp. 725–727). New York: Macmillan.

European Commission (2011). *Early childhood and care: Providing all our children with the best start for the world of tomorrow* (Vol. 17.2011). Brussels: EU.

Fjørtoft, I. (2004). Landscape as playscape: The effects of natural environments on children's play and motor development. *Children, Youth and Environments, 14*(2), 21–44.

Halldén, G. (Ed.) (2011). *Barndomens skogar: Om barn och natur och barns natur* [Forests of childhood: Children and nature and children's nature]. Stockholm: Carlsson.

Hangaard Rasmussen, T. (1992). *Den vilda leken.* [The wild play]. Lund: Studentlitteratur.

Howes, C., Phillips, D. A. and Whitebook, M. (1992). Thresholds of quality: Implications for the social development of children in center-based child care. *Child Development, 63*(2), 449–460.

Izumi-Taylor, S., Pramling-Samuelsson, I. and Steele Rogers, C. (2010). Perspectives of play in three nations: A comparative study in Japan, the United States and Sweden. *Early Childhood Research and Practice, 12*(1), 2–12.

Johnson, J. E., Christie, J. F. and Wardle, F. (2005). *Play, development and early education.* New York: Pearson Educational.

Jones, R. and Reynolds, G. (1992). The play is the thing: Teachers' roles in children's play. *Early Childhood Education Journal, 35*(2), 199–207.

Laine, K., Neitola, M., Auremaa, J. and Laakkonen, E. (2010). Longitudinal study on the co-occurrence of peer problems at daycare centre, in preschool and first grade of school. *Scandinavian Journal of Educational Research, 54*(5), 471–485.

Lillvist, A. and Granlund, M. (2009). Preschool children in need of special support: Prevalence of traditional disability categories and functional difficulties. *Acta Paediatrica, 99*(1), 131–134.

Lindgren, A., Strömstedt, M. and Norman, J-H. (1987). *Mitt Småland* [My Småland]: Stockholm: Rabén & Sjögren Bokförlag.

Medierådet (2010). *Småungar & Medier 2010. Fakta om små barns användning och upplevelser av medier.* [Young kids and media 2010: Facts about children's use and experiences of media]. Stockholm: Kulturdepartementet.

Ministry of Education (2010). Förskola i utveckling – bakgrund till ändringar i förskolans läroplan. [Preschool in development – background to the changes in the preschool curriculum]. Solna: Government Offices.

Montessori, M. (1972). *The secret of childhood* (trans. M. J. Costelloe). New York: Ballantine.

National Agency for Education (1998/2010). *Curriculum for the pre-school, LPFÖ 98.* Stockholm: Fritzes.

National Agency for Education (2003). *Information om allmän förskola.* [Information about general preschool]. Report 03:791. Stockholm: Fritzes.

National Agency for Education (2013). *Skolverkets lägesbedömning 2013.* Raport 387:2013. [National Agency for Education, evaluation of 2013. Report 387:2013]. Stockholm: Fritzes.

Niklasson, L. and Sandberg, A. (2010). Children and outdoor environment. *European Early Childhood Education Research Journal, 18*(4), 485–496.

Nordfeldt, M. and Segnestam Larsson, O. (2011). Local welfare in Sweden: Housing, employment and child care. *WILCO Publication* no, 3.

Norling, M. and Sandberg, A. (submitted). Language learning in outdoor environments.

OECD (2007). *PISA 2006: Science competencies for tomorrow's world.* Paris: OECD.

Öhman, M. (2011). *Det viktigaste är att få leka.* [The most important thing is to play]. Stockholm: Liber.

Piaget, J. (1962). *Play, dreams and imitation* (Vol. 24). New York: Norton.

Pramling-Samuelsson, I. (2011). Förskolan i Sverige 2011. Vilka är utmaningarna? [The preschool in Sweden 2011. What are the challenges?]. *Psykisk hälsa, 3*, 25–28.

Pramling Samuelsson, I. and Johanson, E. (2009). Why do Children involve teachers in their play and learning? *European Early Childhood Education Research Journal. 17*, 77–94.

Pramling-Samuelsson, I. and Sheridan, S. (2003). Delaktighet som värdering och pedagogik. *Pedagogisk Forskning i Sverige, 8*(1–2), 70–84.

Sandberg, A., Lillvist, A., Sheridan, S. and Williams, P. (2012). Play competence as a window to preschool teachers' competence. *International Journal of Play, 1*(2), 184–196.

Sandberg, A. and Vuorinen, T (2005). *Barndomens lekarenor.* [The play areas of childhood]. Västerås:Mälardalens högskola, ISB. CHILD rapport 13.

Sandberg, A. and Vuorinen, T. (2010). Reflecting the child: Play memories and images of the child. In L. Brooker and S. Edwards (Eds.), *Engaging play.* Maidenhead: Open University Press.

Sheridan, S. and Pramling-Samuelsson, I. (2001). Children's conceptions of participation and influence in pre-school: A perspective on pedagogical quality. *Contemporary Issues in Early Childhood, 2*(2), 169–194.

Sheridan, S., Williams, P. and Sandberg, A. (2013). Systematic quality work in preschool, *International Journal of Early Childhood, 45*(1), 123–150.

Simeonsdotter Svensson, A. (2009). Lärande i förskoleklassens samling [Learning in the circletime in preschool-class], In A. Ahlberg (Ed.), *Specialpedagogisk forskning. En mångfasetterad utmaning.* Lund: Studentlitteratur.

Sommer, D., Pramling-Samuelsson, I. and Hundeide, K. (2010). In search of the features of child perspectives and children's perspectives in developmental pedagogy. In D. Sommer, I. Pramling-Samuelsson and K. Hundeide (Eds.), *Child perspectives and children's perspectives in theory and practice* (pp. 163–176). New York: Springer Verlag.

Szczepanski, A., Malmer, K., Nelson, N. and Dahlgren, L. O. (2006). Utomhuspedagogikens särart och möjligheter ur ett lärarperspektiv. *Rapport fra konferencen: Sundere, klogere og gladere børn*, 27. [The speciality and possibilities of outdoor-didactics from a teacher perspective. Report from the conference: Healthier, wiser and happier children, 27].

UNICEF (2008). *The child care transition. A league table of early childhood education and care in economically advanced countries*. Florence, Italy: UNICEF Innocenti Research Foundation.

Vickerius, M. and Sandberg, A. (2006). The signification of play and the environment around play. *Early Child Development and Care, 176*(3), 207–217.

Vygotsky, L. S. (1976). The role of play in the mental development of the child. In J. S. Bruner, A. Jolly and K. Sylva (Eds.), *Play. Its role in development and evolution*. New York: Penguin.

Vygotsky, L. S. (2012). *Thought and language*. Cambridge, MA: MIT Press.

Waite, S., Rogers S. and Evans, J. (2013). Freedom, flow and fairness: Exploring how children develop socially at school through outdoor play. *Journal of Adventure Education & Outdoor*, (ahead-of-print), 1–22.

Williams, P., Sheridan, S. and Pramling-Samuelsson, I. (2000). *Barns samlärande. En forskningsöversikt*. [The collaborative learning of children]. Stockholm: Skolverket.

Wood, E. (2004). Developing a pedagogy of play. In A. Anning, J. Cullen and M. Fleer (Eds.), *Early childhood education: Society and culture* (pp. 19–30). London: Sage.

15 The capture of play within policy discourses: a critical analysis of the UK frameworks for early childhood education

Elizabeth Wood

The following vignette was recorded in a primary school classroom in Wales and involved children aged 5–6 years. The school is located in a culturally diverse urban area and more than 20 different languages are spoken in the school. The children in this vignette are British-Somali (Muna), British-Asian (Shobna and Aamina), and British-Welsh (Bethan).

The children are playing in the home corner. Bethan is playing at parties, and is trying to get everyone organized. Shobna, Muna, and Aamina are laying on the floor, deeply engrossed in reading comics for girls, and chatting about them.

Bethan:	Hey, everyone, it's party time. Party time for girls. Let's get going then. Muna, Aamina, come and help me get ready. Shobna, let's get going with the food.
Shobna:	We are reading this, about girls and hairstyles and everything.
Bethan:	Do that later, come and get ready for the party now. It's going to be good with jellies and cakes. What sandwiches do we want?

The three girls do not answer and Bethan carries on mixing cakes and laying the table. Shobna, Muna, and Aamina continue reading.

Shobna:	(pointing to pictures of girls on the "fashion" page) I like this one, very pretty.
Muna:	I can't wear that . . . in my home . . . only trousers. I can wear trousers, not that skirt or anything like skirts and dresses, or only if they're long, down to the floor . . . or just to here (points to her knees).
Aamina:	Yeah, we always wear trousers, don't we? Like, for school and everything. (Pointing to a picture of a young girl wearing make-up) This one's nice, curly hair and everything.
Shobna:	Is that lipstick?

The girls giggle and pretend to put on lipstick and eye make-up. Bethan has gathered some clothes from the dressing-up box and goes over to the girls.

Bethan:	You can wear long dresses and some saris and some scarves, all sparkly, to come to the party.
Muna:	No we don't want to. We're reading comics. We don't have these comics at home.

Introduction

The aims of this chapter are to analyze the ways in which play has been captured within the policy frameworks for early childhood education in the United Kingdom and to consider the implications for curriculum, pedagogy and practitioners' roles, particularly in relation to culture and diversity. The UK is made up of England, Scotland, Wales, and Northern Ireland, each with its own legislature for social policy, including early childhood education (ECE). Although each nation has developed its own distinctive approaches, a common trend has been towards developing versions of "educational play," in which play "earns" its place by being aligned with curriculum goals and learning outcomes. This analysis will be juxtaposed with the more complex versions of play within international research in order to consider children's play choices and cultures, and how practitioners can remove some of the barriers to play that may be constructed as a result of policy frameworks.

Educational play

The rhetoric of "play as progress" (Sutton-Smith 2001) has been highly persuasive in justifying play within early childhood education. There is substantial research that illuminates the contribution of play to the development of children's meta-cognition and thinking skills and to domain-specific learning in, for example, mathematics, literacy and communication (Wood 2013a). The powerful discourse of developmental psychology has been extended to include cognitive neuroscience, in which play contributes to optimal brain development (Meier et al. 2010; Oates et al. 2012).

In the "play as education" discourse, early childhood practitioners are expected to use play as a means to promote learning and development. The concepts of play-based learning, curriculum and pedagogy are embedded in policy frameworks throughout the world (Hughes 2010; Saracho 2012; Wisneski and Reifel 2012; Brooker and Woodhead 2013). However, recent changes in this discourse reflect neo-liberal influences on policy-making, with increasing demands for effectiveness and accountability (where quality of provision is measured by children's outcomes) (Ruffolo 2009; Krieg 2011; Martlew et al. 2011; Pence and Pacini-Ketchabaw 2011) and for meeting the "school readiness" agenda (Brown 2010). Play has become vulnerable when exposed to performance-led policy technologies such as assessment, inspection regimes, and school-level comparative benchmarking (Walsh et al. 2011; Broadhead and Burt 2012). As Kuschner (2012) has argued, there are fundamental tensions around attempts to integrate play into the school curriculum that are theoretical, conceptual, and practical. This chapter analyses the ways in which play is constructed as pedagogic practice within the four UK policy frameworks in terms of what play is, what play is expected to do for children, and how practitioners are expected to plan for, and assess play in ways that align with curriculum goals.

It will be argued that the UK policy frameworks create versions of play that are potentially restrictive and restricting, both for children and for practitioners, whose beliefs about play are sometimes negated as they are expected to align their practices with performance goals. In contrast, the internal logic of play is related to what players do and create, and the development of themes and patterns over time. These more complex qualities are difficult to align with the logic of policy technologies, because children (like Bethan, Shobna, Muna, and Aamina in the opening vignette) bring their own choices, interests, and cultural repertoires to their play. The challenge for practitioners is to understand these interests and repertoires in order to tune their own playful/educational interactions with young children, while at the same time allowing agency in their play (Kane et al. 2013).

The performatization of play

In the UK, the capture of play within policy discourses gathered speed during the last quarter of the twentieth century. Inter-professional working was considered to deliver better outcomes for children, and play was afforded a key role in achieving government goals of, for example, raising educational outcomes, improving child and family well-being, and reducing anti-social behavior. Play and outdoor activities became embedded in preventative, reparative and restorative interventions, again linked to outcomes measures. The four UK countries all developed their own play strategies based on reviews that were intended to ensure that policy was informed by evidence-based research. However, the performativity agenda became the dominant discourse, on the assumption that specific play provision and interventions would deliver specific outcomes, in spite of the caveats noted by Lester and Russell (2008) in a review commissioned by Play England:

> It becomes difficult to make (with any certainty) specific claims for the importance of playing in the lives of children. For example, to recognize the interconnectedness of genes, brains and bodies, and physical, social and cultural environments, opens up infinite and reciprocal possibilities for influence rather than singular cause and effect, as does the recognition of children themselves as active agents in their own lives. This makes it almost impossible to make generalisations or universal claims regarding interventions.

> (2008: 14)

A further problem in making universal assumptions about educational play is the neglect of dimensions of diversity, and the ways in which these dimensions intersect to create different orientations to play. There are cultural variations in how children engage in play, how they share, negotiate and manage cultural information, and how they manage the pedagogic practices that frame and control play (Göncü and Gaskins 2007; Papadopoulou 2012; Wisneski and Reifel 2012).

In summary, although the evidence for the importance of play is persuasive, the exact mechanisms that link forms of play with areas of learning (or curriculum goals) have not been specified, and the claims that are made for play are not always realized in practice. Furthermore, the policy emphasis on educational play results in complexity reduction because the expectations for children and practitioners may not be achievable. These tensions are exemplified in the UK policy frameworks.

The UK policy frameworks

The four policy frameworks examined and analyzed for this chapter include: Early Years Foundation Stage (England, birth to age 5); Curriculum for Excellence (Scotland, ages 3–6); Foundation for N. I. (Northern Ireland, ages 4–6); and Foundation Phase (Wales, ages 3–7). Each of these frameworks specifies curriculum content (what is to be learned), pedagogical approaches, assessment procedures, progression, and continuity with primary education (including constructs of "school readiness").

Each framework supports a mixed (adult-led and child-initiated) pedagogical model: the emphasis is on planned, purposeful, structured play, in which the aims for learning are, to varying degrees, defined by practitioners. The planned activities, and adults' roles, are informed by these aims, alongside free/spontaneous child-initiated activities that reflect children's interests. There are risks and benefits in this pedagogical model. There is substantial evidence that practitioners plan activities that engage children playfully with curriculum content, in ways that are imaginative and appropriate for different age groups and abilities (Broadhead and Burt 2012). They offer children experiences that may not be available in their homes, and use play themes (such as shops, explorers, veterinary clinic, hospital) that enable children to apply their skills and subject knowledge in, for example, literacy, mathematics and science. Structured play provides opportunities for teaching knowledge, skills and concepts, and for ensuring access to activities and resources for all children. The policy interpretation of structure implies that all children have (or will acquire) the skills to benefit from play that incorporates curriculum goals. However, play cannot easily be aligned with these goals because it is not a reliable means by which children learn defined curriculum content, or use and apply that content in systematic ways. For example, in the context of teaching and learning mathematics in the Early Years Foundation Stage (EYFS) in England, Aubrey and Durmaz (2012) report a small-scale study of policy and practice in which different pedagogical approaches resulted in wide variations in children's responses related to their mathematical understanding. Aubrey and Durmaz identified multiple and contradictory demands, including the "unchallenged assumptions about connections between play, standards of achievement and learning" (2012: p. 74). Practitioners therefore have to extend the range of activities and interactions beyond play to accomplish curriculum goals.

There are other contradictory demands regarding cultural and linguistic diversity. The UK frameworks acknowledge that children learn in different ways and that development is not evenly paced. For example, in the Early Years Foundation Stage (England), linguistic diversity is recognized, but the emphasis is on ensuring that "children have sufficient opportunities to learn and reach a good standard in English language . . . ensuring that children are ready to benefit from the opportunities available to them when they begin Year 1" (Department for Education 2012: 6). In contrast, more complex understandings of diversity are evident in research. Play, learning and development are socially and culturally situated processes. Children engage in different repertoires of play activities in their homes and communities, which often include different orientations to time, space, and routines within everyday cultural practices. Play may be used as preparation for participation in family/community practices, for teaching children cultural knowledge, and for teaching school readiness skills (Göncü and Gaskins 2007; Brooker and Woodhead 2013). Families also have different orientations to schooling, such that the idea of "play-based learning" may be unfamiliar and inconsistent with parental expectations (Brooker 2011; Chen et al. 2011). Furthermore, there is little understanding in the policy frameworks of how dimensions of diversity intersect and are manifest in different cultural systems and how this influences children's abilities to learn curriculum content through play. In a study of the ecology of role play, Papadopoulou (2012) theorizes cultural systems as open, complex, dynamic, variable and constantly evolving over space and time. She argues that children constantly encounter different manifestations of their culture in different settings: different groups of individuals (adults and children) can innovate, share, negotiate and even challenge cultural information. In play, new events that occur in children's lives are brought into the mix, as evidenced by Bateman et al. (2013) in their study of children playing with and playing out their experiences of the earthquake in Christchurch, New Zealand. Play therefore becomes the bridge that children use to connect their home and school experiences and the way in which they create their own play cultures.

So what are the implications for practitioners' roles of both interpreting and responding pedagogically to children's freely chosen play in ways that reflect diversity? Returning to the opening vignette, the teacher had planned the home corner around the topic of festivals and celebrations in different cultures and was engaging children with curriculum content in playful and imaginative ways. She enabled the children to develop their own play themes, and to accomplish social and cognitive goals. In analysing this episode, the teacher commented that the British-Asian girls used the comics as a bridge between their different cultural home and school repertoires, and could easily read the visual content. Comics were not typical in their homes, but provided access to different ways of understanding "being a girl." Shobna, Muna, and Aamina, therefore, had a different agenda from Bethan, and enacted their choices in different ways: party play was of no interest at that time because the comics held important information that enabled them to make sense of different cultural repertoires and how aspects of social identities are performed. The choices for the teacher were multiple, based on recognizing and utilizing these cultural repertoires. First, the children's literacy development could be supported by the provision of different literacy resources that could become the focus for discussion and exploration of images and texts. Second, the teacher could play alongside Shobna, Muna, and Aamina to develop imaginative role play that would enable them to mix home, school and popular cultures.

From a socio-cultural perspective, the policy emphasis on educational play is implicated not just in complexity reduction, but in reinforcing cultural distance or dissonance. If children's cultural repertoires are not understood, they will not have the opportunities noted by Papadopoulou (2012) to innovate, share, negotiate and even challenge cultural information.

Policy-practice dilemmas

If, as Lester and Russell (2008) have argued, it is difficult to make (with any certainty) specific claims for the importance of playing in the lives of children, then aligning play with a policy-led performance agenda creates a number of dilemmas. First, practitioners may err on the side of caution in their provision in order to conform to the discourse of "planned and purposeful play," where structured activities produce tangible evidence of learning in line with curriculum and assessment frameworks. From this pedagogical perspective, play that is adult-led may limit the opportunities for children's active involvement and agency. Furthermore, there will be less time and space for children to demonstrate their cultural competencies as knowers of their own childhoods, to express their interests and cognitive concerns, or to reveal themselves as skilled players.

Free play sits even more uneasily within the performance agenda because the outcomes may not be immediately evident, and the meanings and purposes may not be visible to adults. As Broadhead and Burt (2012) have shown, children's plans and motivations emerge in complex ways as play narratives and themes develop over time. Children make their own distinctions between work and play, with consistent emphasis on play being chosen, led and controlled by the children themselves. Thus, the mixed pedagogical model in the four UK frameworks is not the same as the more complex integrated pedagogical model, in which there is a continuum between adult-led activities (both formal and play-based) and children's freely chosen play (Saracho 2010; Wood 2013a). In an integrated model, practitioners observe and engage in children's play, track their interests and help them to plan their own activities, based on the goals that emerge from the play. These goals may be complementary to curriculum goals, with adult-led activities providing some structure for teaching specific content. However, this is a complex and demanding pedagogical model, one which requires more flexibility than is available in the four UK frameworks.

Not surprisingly, the tenuous state of play has remained a consistent theme in research in the UK and is typically related to four issues: (1) the role of adults; (2) the efficacy of free and structured play for learning and assessment; (3) progression and continuity in play; and (4) transitions with the next stage of education. Following the introduction of the Foundation Stage in Northern Ireland, Hunter and Walsh (2013) examined teachers' beliefs about play and what changes in their practice had come about as a result of the new framework. Based on a questionnaire survey of 315 teachers, and qualitative observations in ten Foundation Stage classrooms, they found that to some extent, the policy framework drove changes in teachers' practice and made them plan for play. However, teachers remained uncertain about the learning potential of play, their role, and particularly their interactions during play. There was no consensus about the amount of teacher initiation or interaction required to ensure effective learning. Similarly, in Scotland, an exploratory study of six Primary 1 classrooms (age 5–6) (Stephen et al. 2010; Martlew et al. 2011) revealed that teachers plan for active and play-based learning, along with whole-class, teacher-led sessions, thus adopting contrasting pedagogical roles. In the former they were more facilitative and responsive, but were so within the framework of directing children towards small-group activities, with fewer opportunities for free choice and free play activities. There was "very little evidence of child-initiated tasks in any of the classrooms in the study and minimal evidence of peer interaction" (Martlew et al. 2011: 81).

The Foundation Phase in Wales incorporates play across the 3–7 age phase, drawing on a somewhat optimistic policy rhetoric:

> There should be opportunities for children to follow their interests and ideas through free play. Children's learning is most effective when it arises from first-hand experiences, whether spontaneous or structured, and when they are given time to play without interruption, and to reach a satisfactory conclusion.
>
> (DCELLS 2008: 5)

Although practitioners can exercise judgment about the balance between child-initiated and adult-led activities, evidence indicates that, in practice, this tips towards the latter. This is because practitioners continue to struggle with implementing play in ways that lead to defined learning outcomes, and with making time to observe children's free-choice activities as a way of understanding their interests and cultural repertoires (Broadhead and Burt 2012; Roberts-Holmes 2012). The concept of balance between adult-led and child-initiated activities cannot be prescribed in policy because balance is likely to vary according to the ages and capabilities of the children, their relationships with peers, access to play spaces and resources, and practitioners' own interpretations of the curriculum guidance documents. If play is overly structured, and used to accomplish curriculum goals, then there will be less attention to the goals that children set for themselves within play activities. From children's perspectives, these goals are significant: free play can involve stretching the demands or complexity of the activity to include risk and challenge, subverting adults' intentions, and challenging institutional rules (Wood 2013b). As shown in the opening vignette, freely chosen activities incorporate children's interests and personal agendas, their motivations to master aspects of their social and cultural worlds (which may not always be accessible to adults), and their expression of their cultural/ethnic heritages.

Three further problems can be identified in the performance agenda. First, using play predominantly as a form of pedagogy, or as an intervention to deliver specific benefits or outcomes, is unlikely to live up to policy expectations, not least because the solutions to so many "educational" problems lie in other areas of socioeconomic policy (e.g., housing, employment, health, and welfare). However, when play fails to deliver on the desired outcomes, then the default position is for less play and more work, notably "formal" (adult-directed) activities that are more likely to meet the "school readiness" agenda. In contrast, Ross (2013) proposes that the continued dichotomy between play and work belies the seriousness of play, notably its role in individual, social and cultural processes of learning.

Second, children's competencies as players will have little currency in assessment narratives. Practitioners are less likely to document children's play skills and repertoires, and more likely to focus on identifying the extent to which they have achieved curriculum goals, or are using and applying valued knowledge in their play (such as counting, ordering, naming colors, reading, and writing). Assessment is closely linked to progression and continuity, where the focus is on progression in learning and not on progression in play. In each of the four UK frameworks, the assumption is that transition from preschool to compulsory education is largely a matter of progressively introducing more formal, teacher-directed activities, and a concomitant reduction of time for child-directed play. For example, in England, the emphasis on school readiness means that play is gradually phased out during the Reception year (age 4–5 years) of the EYFS in preparation for Year 1 of the National Curriculum:

> As children grow older, and as their development allows, it is expected that the balance will gradually shift towards more activities led by adults, to help children prepare for more formal learning, ready for Year 1.
>
> (Department for Education 2012: 6)

Of the four UK nations, England has the lowest age of transition to compulsory education, and the policy direction here is that play can be phased out *before* this transition occurs. This links to the third point, namely that the sustainability of initiatives to develop play-based and active learning is compromised within contemporary policy technologies that focus on defining, measuring, evaluating and assuring "quality" and "effectiveness" (Cottle and Alexander 2012).

Although the policy rhetoric of play as an "effective" (or even "the most effective") way of learning is difficult for practitioners to implement and demonstrate, there is some evidence of the ways in which practitioners manage these difficulties. Kane et al. (2013) describe a small-scale action research study involving practitioners from England and Sweden. The study focused on play facilitation and intervention, and explored the tensions between children's agency and the constraints of the setting. Five key themes were identified: (1) creating space for play; (2) finding where to "draw the line"; (3) controlling children's activities; (4) playing with the children; and (5) avoiding judgment (2013, p. 13). In the theme of finding where to "draw the line," the participants expressed uncertainties about the ways in which they interpret play activities, particularly the types of play that are repetitive, push boundaries, or are "disruptive," "destructive" or "chaotic." Through focus group discussions, the practitioners were able to articulate their interpretations and question the nature and intentions of their interventions. What seems "chaotic" or "disruptive" to adults may be part of the children's play frame and not intentionally disruptive to institutional order. The authors also raise the issue of whether practitioners "use their own agency and professional understanding to contest and resist the limitations of the setting when it comes to providing for children to exercise agency" (Kane et al. 2013: 19).

Research with children who have special educational needs and disabilities reinforces the need for professional decision-making that does not conform either to an orthodoxy of non-intervention, or to policy emphases on adults' purposes. In an ethnographic study of autistic children's play, Kangas et al. (2012) emphasize the importance of observing play over time to discern patterns and events, to dispel myths and assumptions about play and autism, and for practitioners to facilitate interactions accordingly. Chazan (2012) also advocates observing and recording play over time. She developed the Children's Play Therapy Instrument and the Children's Developmental Play Instrument to identify children's play styles, and to enable the observer to integrate an understanding of the child's play activity that includes affective, cognitive, narrative, social level, developmental level, and the interaction between players (p. 298). The instruments also aid parents' and practitioners' understanding of children's play activities and play styles, and develop their skills of observation and analysis across home and pre-school/school settings. The evidence generated from practice concurs that professional knowledge and agency remain critical to decision-making in the context of play (Cottle and Alexander 2012). Practitioners have a role in removing both policy barriers and institutional barriers to play as a means of ensuring access and inclusion and supporting children's participation in playing and learning.

Conclusion

The capture of play within policy frameworks can be seen as a mixed blessing. On the one hand, early childhood practitioners are able to work with familiar values and principles, with the expectation that play activities will be embedded within their practice. On the other hand, the requirement to demonstrate effectiveness and outcomes may result in a default position of predominantly adult-led structured play, or a dichotomy between play and work. Although play is linked to the overall quality of provision, the forms and functions of play are distinctly educational in order to meet the performance agenda. Not surprisingly, play does not always sit comfortably within these discourses, and the international evidence indicates that practitioners engage in a continuous balancing act between their own beliefs, and pragmatic approaches to educational play. Inevitably there are trade-offs between freedom and structure, and between play and work.

From post-structural perspectives, researchers are asking critical questions about claims for the universal efficacy of play in relation to multiple dimensions of diversity and the ways in which discourses of effectiveness, quality and child development all contribute to the normalization and regulation of children and practitioners (Ruffolo 2009; File et al. 2012). A response to these challenges is that arguments for play must be informed by detailed knowledge about, and responsiveness to, the different cultural practices, values and beliefs found within pluralistic societies. Deeper knowledge of play and diversity is needed and must come from within families and communities as a means of constructing culturally situated understanding of play that can inform equitable practices and policies. The knowledge and beliefs of practitioners are crucial in implementing policy frameworks in ways that are responsive to children, and maintain a commitment to adult-led and child-initiated activities as integrated (and not opposing) strands of curriculum planning.

References

Aubrey, C. and Durmaz, D. (2012). Policy-to-practice contexts for early childhood mathematics in England. *International Journal of Early Years Education, 20*, 59–75.

Bateman, A., Danby, S. and Howard, J. (2013). Living in a broken world: How young children's well-being is supported through playing out their earthquake experiences. *International Journal of Play, 3*, 201–219.

Broadhead, P. and Burt, A. (2012). *Understanding young children's learning through play.* London: Routledge.

Brooker, L. (2011). Taking children seriously: An alternative agenda for research? *Journal of Early Childhood Research, 9*, 137–149. doi: 10.1177/1476718X10387897.

Brooker, L. and Woodhead, M. (Eds.) (2013). *The right to play.* Early Childhood in Focus, 9. Milton Keynes: Open University Press/Bernard van Leer. www.bernardvanleer.org.

Brown, C. (2010). Balancing the readiness equation in early childhood education reform. *Journal of Early Childhood Research. 8*, 133–160.

Chazan, S. (2012). The children's developmental play instrument (CDPI): A validity study. *International Journal of Play, 1*, 297–310.

Chen, J-Q., Masur, A. and McNamee, G. (2011). Young children's approaches to learning: A socio-cultural perspective. *Early Child Development and Care, 181*, 1137–1152. doi: 10.1080/03004430.

Cottle, M. and Alexander, E. (2012). Quality in early years settings: Government, research and practitioners' perspectives. *British Educational Research Journal, 38*, 635–654. doi: 10/1080/01411926.2011.571661.

DCELLS (Department for Children, Education, Lifelong Learning and Skills) (2008). *Play/ active learning overview for 3–7 year olds.* Crown Copyright. Available at: www.wales. gov.uk.

DfE (Department for Education) (2012). *The statutory framework for the early years foundation stage: Setting the standards for learning, development and care for children from birth to five.* Available at: www.education.gov.uk/publications/standard/All Publications/Page1/DFE-00023-2012. (accessed 15 April 2013).

File, N., Mueller, J. and Wisneski, D. (2012). *Curriculum in early childhood education: Re-examined, rediscovered, renewed.* New York: Routledge.

Göncü, A. and Gaskins, S. (Eds.) (2007). *Play and development: Evolutionary, sociocultural and functional perspectives.* Mahwah, NJ: Lawrence Erlbaum.

Hughes, F. P. (2010). *Children, play and development* (2nd ed.). Thousand Oaks, CA: Sage.

Hunter, T. and Walsh, G. (2013). From policy to practice: The reality of play in primary school classes in Northern Ireland. *International Journal of Early Years Education.* Published online 22.8.13, pp. 1–18. doi: 10.1080/09669760.2013.8305.

Kane, E., Ljusberg, A-L. and Larsson, H. (2013). Making magic soup: The facilitation of play in school-age children. *International Journal of Play, 2,* 7–21.

Kangas, S., Määttä, K. and Uusiautti, S. (2012). Ethnographic research on autistic children's play. *International Journal of Play, 1,* 37–50.

Krieg, S. (2011). The Australian early years learning framework: Learning what? *Contemporary Issues in Early Childhood, 1,* 46–55. doi:10.2304/ciec.2011.12.1.46.

Kuschner, D. (2012). Play is natural to childhood but school is not: The problem of integrating play into the curriculum. *International Journal of Play, 1,* 242–249.

Lester, S. and Russell, W. (2008). *Play for a change: Play, policy and practice: a review of contemporary perspectives, summary report.* London: Play England/National Children's Bureau.

Martlew, J., Stephen, C. and Ellis, J. (2011). Play in the primary school classroom? The experience of teachers supporting children's learning through a new pedagogy. *Early Years: An International Journal of Research and Development, 31,* 71–83. doi: 10.1080/09575146. 2010.529425.

Meier, E., Engel, B. and Taylor, B. (2010). *Playing for keeps: Life and learning on a public school playground.* New York: Teachers College Press.

Oates, J., Karmiloff-Smith, A. and Taylor, M. H. (2012). *Developing brains.* Early Childhood in Focus, 7. Milton Keynes, Open University Press/Bernard van Leer. www.bernardvanleer.org.

Papadopoulou, M. (2012). The ecology of role play: Intentionality and curricular evolution. *British Educational Research Journal, 38,* 575–592.

Pence, A. and Pacini-Ketchabaw, V. (2011). The postmodern curriculum: Making space for historically and politically situated understandings. *Australian Journal of Early Childhood, 36,* 4–8.

Roberts-Holmes, G. (2012). 'It's the bread and butter of our practice': Experiencing the Early Years Foundation Stage. *International Journal of Early Years Education, 20,* 31–42.

Ross, D. (2013). Ambiguity and possibility: Cognitive and educational grounds for play. *International Journal of Play, 1,* 22–31.

Ruffolo, D. V. (2009). Queering child/hood policies: Canadian examples and perspectives. *Contemporary Issues in Early Childhood, 10,* 291–308. doi.org/10.2304/ciec.2009.10.3.291.

Saracho, O. (2010). Children's play in the visual arts and literature. *Early Child Development and Care, 180,* 947–965. doi: 10.1080/03004430802556356.

Saracho, O. (2012). *An integrated play-based curriculum for young children.* New York: Routledge.

Stephen, C., Ellis, J. and Martlew, J. (2010). Taking active learning into the primary school: A matter of new practices? *International Journal of Early Years Education, 18,* 315–329.

Sutton-Smith, B. (2001). *The ambiguity of play* (2nd ed.). Cambridge, MA: Harvard University Press.

Walsh, G., McGuinness, C., Sproule, L. and Trew, K. (2010). Implementing a play-based and developmentally appropriate curriculum in Northern Ireland primary schools: What lessons have we learned? *Early Years: An International Journal of Research and Development, 30*, 53–66.

Walsh, G., Sproule, L., McGuinness, C. and Trew, K. (2011). Playful structure: a novel image of early years pedagogy for primary school classrooms. *Early Years: An International Journal of Research and Development, 31*, 107–119.

Wisneski, D. and Reifel, S. (2012). The place of play in early childhood curriculum. In N. File, J. Mueller and D. Wisneski (Eds.), *Curriculum in early childhood education: Re-examined, rediscovered, renewed* (pp. 175–187). New York: Routledge.

Wood, E. (2013a). *Play, learning and the early childhood curriculum* (3rd ed.). London: Sage.

Wood, E. (2013b). Free play and free choice in early childhood settings: Troubling the discourse. *International Journal of Early Years Education*. Published online 2.9.13. 1–15. doi:10.1080/09669760.2013.830562.

16 Children's play in the Estonian context

Aino Ugaste and Rain Mikser

> Kalev (4 years) is building, together with other players, constructing a road for cars, on which they start driving. Kalev says that there is a cage in front of his car. Kalev points at his own car and says: "This cage is playfully."
>
> The friend goes away. Meanwhile Kalev continues building the road alone, driving his car around. The friend comes back and takes a motorcycle from the garage.
>
> Kalev turns towards his friend: "I have got one road, I am going fishing and . . ." After a while he says: "I am fishing here."
>
> *The friend*: "But I am fishing here."
> *Kalev*:   "But there is no water there."
> *The friend*: "All right; I will come fishing with you there then. Is there anything there?
>
> Kalev answers in a firm tone of voice: "Yes, there, is."
>
> The boys are fishing for some time. Then Kalev says: "Now fish is caught, let's put the cars away." They start to build the motorway.

Introduction

Estonia is a small north-eastern European country with a total population of 1.3 million. Ethnic Estonians make up 68.7 percent of the country's population, ethnic Russians 24.8 percent, and other ethnic populations 6.4 percent. Estonians are Finno-Ugric people linguistically and ethnically closely related to the Finns. The Republic of Estonia borders with Finland across the Finnish Gulf to the north, with Sweden across the Baltic Sea to the west, with Latvia to the south and with Russia to the east.

In the thirteenth century, the Estonian territory was occupied and Estonians were forcefully Christianized by the German military orders. After centuries of being dominated by foreign rulers, Estonia first gained independence in 1918. From 1940–1991, Estonia was occupied by the Soviet Union. In 1991, Estonia again became an independent country and joined the European Union in 2004.

During the last two decades Estonia, like all other former communist Eastern European countries, has experienced profound social, political, and cultural changes. These changes are related to the integration of the country into the European democratic and humanistic value system. These attempts have contributed to the development of a new educational paradigm, one which holds central the concept of lifelong learning, a concept focused on creating learning opportunities for all people from early childhood to old age. Consequently, attempts have been made to connect play as a child's independent creative activity to the overall concept of education.

In this chapter, the meaning of children's play in Estonian education is analyzed from an historical perspective and also from the perspective of how play may fit into the curricula of early childhood education and general education institutions. Additionally, teachers' beliefs about children's play and its place in the curricula are discussed. Adults' roles in creating conditions for the child's play at home and the opportunities for further study are also examined.

A historical overview of children's play in Estonia

Even before the occupation and Christianization of Estonia, children's play already had an essential role in forming and maintaining the Estonian national identity and preparing children to fulfill their roles as adults. Boys played at imitating the obligations of adult men such as fighting and hunting, while girls imitated the traditional women's roles of parenting and housekeeping (Andresen 1997). To keep expenditures for childrearing minimal, children were engaged in work from as early an age as possible and generally were not provided a special time for play. Play had to be directly connected with the tasks children were expected to fulfill as adults. In order to shape and maintain the Estonian cultural identity, games were connected to certain socially and culturally important ceremonies such as initiation rites, weddings, or feasts of the national calendar. Such games, which included elements of singing, dancing, and performing, were considered "pagan" by the Christian Church authorities. Despite the many attempts to prohibit them, these games persisted until the eighteenth century (Andresen 1997). Gradually merged into the Christian customs, children's play traditions thus had an essential role in shaping the Estonian national and cultural identity.

As a conscious means of making learning easier and more interesting, emphasizing children's play as a pedagogical approach first gained attention in Estonia from the late nineteenth century onward. During that period, the first nursery schools were established in Estonia and the ideas of Froebel, the great advocator of children's play for educational purposes, began to have an influence (Torm 2011). In the early twentieth century, the ideas of Montessori, another internationally important advocate of children's play, gained popularity in Estonia (Torm 2011: 93). During the first period of independence (1918–1940), however, early childhood education was not officially regulated at a national level in Estonia. As a result, there were no official policy statements on children's play.

In 1940, Estonia was forcefully incorporated into the Soviet Union. The Sovietization of education in Estonia and elsewhere in Eastern Europe introduced many negative consequences such as extreme ideologization, centralization and standardization

(Cerych 1997). However, the importance of play—as a free time activity as well as a didactic means for achieving important curricular aims—was strongly emphasized alongside the growing importance of preschool education. This was mostly due to the fact that the level of women's participation in the active workforce was very high (Tuul et al. 2011). Early childhood education formed the initial stage of the Soviet education system. A lot of attention was paid to educating and teaching children before they began their formal schooling. Official study programs for early childhood education institutions were elaborated, focusing on children's all-round development through various activities (play, learning, academic activities). Through play, children could begin to understand their surrounding environment, develop empathy, and imitate adults' work and activities (*Koolieelsest Kasvatusest Lasteasutuses* 1979). The programs also stressed that time and space (indoor and outdoor) had to be provided for children in order to create opportunities to play with various toys.

Teachers had a definite role in preschool education, both as mediators of knowledge and organizers of the children's lives. During the time of the Soviet occupation, a great deal of attention was paid both in initial and in-service teacher education to the theoretical and didactic aspects of children's play.

At that time, the theoretical foundations for an emphasis on the importance of children's play mostly originated from cultural-historical theory as articulated by the Russian psychologists Vygotsky (1976), Leontjev (1981), and Elkonin (1978), among others (Ugaste et al. 2014). Play was seen as a leading activity for children of preschool age, an activity that creates a zone of proximal development. According to cultural-historical theory, children's play develops in social contexts during interaction with adults (Berk and Winsler 1995; Bodrova and Leong 2007).

In the late 1980s, hope of restoring national independence emerged in Estonia. At the Estonian Educationalists' Conference in 1988, the main ideas of educational innovation were formulated, aiming to develop a new generation that would be able to act democratically in a democratic society. Conference participants also discussed the goals and objectives of early childhood education and the importance of the play environment. There were arguments among the participants about whether to adopt Western educational models, how much to preserve of the existing education system and how much to change. All parties agreed that extensive changes were necessary.

Immediately after the Estonian re-independence in 1991, legal measures were taken to accentuate children's rights to education and play, based on the recognition of basic human and national values and the freedom of personality, religion, and consciousness. In 1991, Estonia ratified the United Nations Convention on the Rights of the Child. On the basis of the aforementioned convention, the Child Protection Act (Eesti Vabariigi Lastekaitse Seadus 1992) was written and adopted in Estonia in 1992. The Child Protection Act affirmed children's right to free time and play (Figure 16.1). The convention brought a major change in the previously dominant perspective of the child as a passive learner and listener. Children came to be recognized more as active agents with their own rights, interests, and wishes. Local and nationwide discussions on children's rights among various professional and social groups supported the spread of ideas of child-centeredness and a new approach to children and to childhood.

Figure 16.1   Under the new early childhood initiatives in Estonia, children are encouraged to play freely.

Children's play and the curriculum

The reform and elaboration of national curricula for preschool as well as general education was decisive; there was overwhelming support for the reorganization and innovation of Estonian education. The first national framework curriculum for preschool education after re-independence came into force in 1999. It met the needs of a democratic society and gave every preschool institution the right to develop its own curriculum, taking local circumstances into account (*Alushariduse Raamõppekava* 1999). According to the curriculum, an early childhood institution offers care and education for children before the compulsory school age (7 in Estonia). It was stated that the basic aim of early childhood education is to foster good opportunities and a stimulating environment for each child's well-being and holistic development.

But it was soon realized that the curriculum did not meet the needs of a rapidly developing society, nor did it meet the expectations of the public and teachers. In 2008, a new national curriculum came into force, one which gave more decision-making opportunities to the preschools, parents and children (*Koolieelse Lasteasutuse Riiklik õppekava* 2008). The new curriculum enabled education professionals to make the organization of schooling and education more flexible. It also placed more emphasis on the importance of facilitating children's comprehensive development.

The new national curriculum differed from the previous curricula because it discussed children's play in a separate paragraph within the document. It was stated that play is the main activity of preschool-aged children. The rationale for this was that through play children acquire and consolidate new information and skills, express emotions and desires, learn to communicate, engage in new experiences, and internalize rules of conduct. Play skills were described as the basis for the development of all general skills, as well as skills and knowledge for the different subject areas of the school curriculum. Areas emphasized included the joy of play, the connection between creativity and play, and children's joint play activities. The role of the teacher was to involve the children in the dynamics of schooling and education by asking the children about the games, toys, and activities that form their interests. It was stressed that there must be sufficient time for playing in the daily schedule. According to this curriculum, the teacher's role was to direct the children's development and to create environments that promote their development. Teachers were to help children with their games and activities but only when the children could not manage without the teacher's intervention.

Children's play had been regarded as important in Estonia during the Soviet period as well but there were essential differences between how play was conceptualized then and after independence was regained. Examining teachers' perceptions of the differences between the preschool education curricula of the two periods, Tuul et al. (2011) found that while play was regarded as important during the Soviet period, it was over-regulated, leaving little room for free choice by the children and by teachers. Additionally, play was regarded as an isolated activity, detached from other important activities such as learning or practicing self-help skills. Nowadays, play is related to the achievement of a broad range of educational aims, whereby children's activity, self-determination, and freedom of choice are emphasized.

Children's play and the Step-by-Step program

The Step-by-Step program

In 1994, the Step-by-Step (SbS) program (in Estonian, Hea Algus) was introduced and subsequently widely employed in Estonian early childhood education (Õun et al. 2010). It is aimed at children from birth to 10 years of age and is based on the developmentally appropriate approach to teaching (Bredekamp and Copple 1997). The SbS program emphasizes that learning in early childhood takes place in the form of play. Theoretically, the program is based on the approaches to child development of Dewey, Erikson, Piaget, and Vygotsky. The program also includes the principles of democratic education that encourage children to make choices and to take responsibility, to act independently as well as cooperatively, and to respect differences among people (Hansen et al. 1997; Klaus 2004).

Preliminary findings on the SbS program

Attempts have been made to discover whether there are any differences in the attitudes of SbS teachers regarding their child-centered approach to education compared to teachers of traditional preschools (e.g., Õun et al. 2010). By a traditional preschool institution, we mean a modern Estonian preschool institution, where teaching and educational activities are in compliance with current education legislation. Teaching and educational activities in the SbS preschools are also based on

Estonian education legislation, but special guidelines developed for the program are also employed. Comparisons of teachers in SbS and traditional programs indicated that SbS teachers tend to use more teaching methods that support a child's meaningful learning and pay more attention to the creation of a learning environment that takes the child's development into account. SbS teachers try to create more activity centers and possibilities for diverse games for both solitary and group play. SbS teachers also employ a greater variety of play activities in their teaching approaches. They create conditions whereby diverse play materials would be available for the children in their group room. They also involve parents and encourage them to play with their children. In designing the learning environment, the SbS teachers place value on children's self-directed and active learning more so than do the teachers in the traditional kindergarten.

Kuimet and Ugaste (2012) also interviewed teachers in SbS preschools and traditional preschools, aiming to understand teachers' concepts about play and the meaning they assign to children's play and play environment. The results showed that the teachers of both groups consider play to be primarily imitation, be it the imitation of adults' activities, the contents of films and books, or of heroes and animals. Many teachers mentioned that it is difficult to explain play, as it includes almost all the situations that children encounter during the day. The interviewees regarded play as important for the child's development because it is connected principally with social skills, interaction, and learning. The traditional preschool teachers connected games with certain activities and often described play using concrete examples of games that children participated in, games where rules were considered important. The SbS teachers emphasized children's multipurpose activities and their choices of diverse play materials. The traditional preschool teachers focused on following rules in their play with the children. The SbS teachers only involved themselves in the play if deemed necessary, for example, when problems emerged between children or when they asked for help. In their opinion, the adult's role is to be the supporter of the children's independent games and to be more of an observer and follower of the playing children.

Traditional preschool teachers considered the following of rules as important because this was a way to help the children avoid and/or solve problems that occur during play. The SbS teachers emphasized the importance of creating an environment for play and learning that is beneficial for the development and socialization of children. Accordingly, activity centers are used in play and learning processes in the SbS classrooms to help children develop their skills for making choices and taking responsibility for those choices. Activity centers also existed in traditional preschool groups, but the interviewees did not explain comprehensively how they were used. Thus, these teachers understood the significance and essential role of play in the children's lives, but the SbS teachers perceived play more widely and more diversely than did traditional preschool teachers. The latter emphasized the existence of rules and their application, and considered the adult's participation in children's play as necessary. SbS teachers emphasize the meaning of the children's choices and initiative in play.

Play and parenting

The social and political changes in Estonia in the late 1980s and early 1990s have also brought about changes in the relationship between parents and children which, in turn, affect parental attitudes towards children's play. In the wake of the political democratization, parental educational values are not so clearly defined as they once were and this uncertainty has led to increased feelings of insecurity regarding children's futures. Play, therefore, is increasingly seen as a necessary didactic means of achieving academic aims and securing children's future success in school (Ugaste 2005).

Using a questionnaire developed by van der Kooij and Neukäter (1989), Saar and Niglas (2001) examined differing parental attitudes towards childrearing and play. Studying parents in four European countries (the Netherlands, Germany, Norway, and Poland) in the late 1980s, van der Kooij and Neukäter concluded that in the democratic countries, young parents were much more oriented to respecting their children's autonomy than were parents living in totalitarian societies (i.e., Poland). The authors suggested that the social-political context has an impact on parental attitudes towards childrearing and play. In Saar and Niglas's (2001) study, ethnic Estonian mothers, non-ethnic Estonian mothers in Estonia, and ethnic Russian mothers from Moscow, all with preschool-aged children, were surveyed in the late 1990s. It was hypothesized that there would be no significant differences in attitudes towards play among the three groups studied since all the groups had grown up in a unitary society where the upbringing and education of children were the function of the social system. The results, however, revealed that while Estonian mothers were indeed less controlling than the Moscow mothers were when supporting their children's play, the most controlling of the three groups were non-Estonian mothers living in Estonia. Saar and Niglas posit that while democratization of the society indeed has a positive impact on the parental attitudes towards childrearing and play (particularly for younger parents), these changes may occur differently in different social and ethnic groups. Although the democratization and liberation process in the late 1980s and early 1990s was generally welcomed by the ethnic Estonians, some non-ethnic groups such as ethnic Russians had concerns with the outcomes of this process in terms of their future, which may have caused resistance to changes in attitudes towards childrearing.

Play as a means for language instruction and social integration

Language immersion, particularly at early stages of development, has been regarded as paramount for achieving social cohesion in the Estonian society, especially the integration of ethnic Russians, the largest ethnic minority group in Estonia (Eesti Lõimumiskava 2008–2013). As with other multicultural societies, Estonia pays significant attention to maintaining and developing the resources and mechanisms needed to preserve and develop the cultures and languages of the various ethnic groups represented within its borders. Language immersion as a form of learning was implemented as a national program in Estonia to promote the effective acquisition of Estonian and other languages. Inplementation begins at the preschool stage. The basic principle of language learning program is that a language is acquired most effectively when a student is interacting in meaningful and essentially social situations; during childhood these situations often occur during play. Teachers have learned that a child can be encouraged to talk while playing with the help of a variety of games and pictures. Many types of games and other play forms have been created so that the language learning is child-centered and playful.

There is not yet a great deal of research on how well play supports language immersion in Estonia. There has been research, however, that investigated the differences between teachers' attitudes towards play as a means for learning in preschool when the focus language is either Estonian or Russian (Ugaste et al. 2014). The results of this study showed that teachers in preschools where Estonian is the focus language placed more emphasis on the children's own activity and learning from one another, and on play. Teachers from preschools with Russian as the focus language, while also emphasizing various activities and games in children's learning, indicated that these activities were more often initiated and carried out by grown-ups. The different approaches of the two groups of teachers led to differences in the planning and carrying out of the learning process, to the use of different learning methods, and to differential expectations on the part of the teachers (Ugaste et al. 2014).

Play and the education of values

Education professionals have recognized that the Estonian education system has paid too much attention to the acquisition of academic knowledge while the education of values has been largely neglected. This recognition led to the creation of the National Programme: Value Development in the Estonian Society 2009–2013. The aim of this program is to promote the development of those values that form part of the foundation for a happy personal life and that also enable successful cooperative integration into society. As values are formed primarily during childhood and the school years, it is reasonable to lay emphasis on preschool and school children's value education. A research compendium, "Values in preschool age: Value education in preschools" (Väärtused koolieelses eas. Väärtuskasvatus lasteaias 2010), was created with the aim of describing the possibilities of values education in different educational areas and activities. The collection highlights the descriptions of various games and how these enable joint interactions among children. In order to improve the quality of education, the school culture and children's well-being, a "values game" has been developed. The game, with a serious and cheerful format, helps to enhance teachers' dialogues about different behavioral situations and possible conflicts regarding values.

Conclusion

The development of Estonia during the period of independence has often been regarded as a success story. Estonian students have done well in various international tests of school achievement. As early childhood education is seen as the first step of lifelong learning and a preparation for further studies, these results are also credit to the quality of early childhood education opportunities in Estonia. Yet this story has its difficulties and serious problems. One of the most essential changes in education reflects the increased awareness of the importance of children and childhood in Estonian society. As a result, a movement towards more child-centered approaches to education has developed.

Much discussion has focused on how to facilitate a child's participation in society, how to ensure children's well-being and happiness, and how society can guarantee that every child will enjoy the right to rest, free time, and play. At the same time, as teachers have found in their everyday work, early childhood education is more oriented to children's academic activities and preparation for school (e.g., development of reading and writing skills). Consequently, children have less time for free play. Paradoxically, play is often seen, on the one hand, as a child's leisure time activity and is engaged in simply for entertainment and pleasure. On the other hand, play is seen as an activity organized by adults and having a clearly defined educational purpose. Teachers, aware of the importance of play activities in a child's development, have been placed in a conflictual situation between their educational ideology and the values of society.

Children's development is largely determined by the cultural context, and play is a culturally mediated activity, influenced by a culture's norms, values, beliefs, and traditions (Sutton-Smith 1998; Göncü et al. 2000). In 2013, Tallinn University organized an international conference, "Providing for play: Applications for policy and practice from research." A common theme across the conference presentations was that there is an urgent need to investigate children's play more broadly. Up to now in Estonia, children's play has been studied mostly from the adult's standpoint. By considering children to be agents of their own activity, children's play and play environments should be studied from the child's own perspective as well.

Acknowledgements

This article was supported by European Social Fund, grant number TA/7610.

References

Alushariduse Raamõppekava (1999). [Framework curriculum of preschool education]. Riigi Teataja: I, 80, 737.

Andresen, L. (1997). *Eesti rahvakooli ja pedagoogika ajalugu* [The history of Estonian national school and education]. I. Tallinn: Avita.

Berk, L. E. and Winsler, A. (1995). *Scaffolding children's learning: Vygotsky and early childhood education.* NAEYC Research and Practice Series, 7. Washington, DC: National Association for the Education of Young Children.

Bodrova, E. and Leong, D. I. (2007). *Tools of the mind: A Vygotskian approach to early childhood education.* Columbus: OH: Merrill/Prentice Hall.

Bredekamp, S. C. and Copple, C. (1997). *Developmentally appropriate practice in early childhood programs*. Washington, DC: National Association for the Education of Young Children.

Cerych, L. (1997). Educational reform in Central and Eastern Europe: Processes and outcomes. *European Journal of Education, 32*(1): 75–97.

Eesti Lõimumiskava 2008–2013. [Estonian Integration Strategy, 2008–2013]. Available at: http://www.kul.ee/webeditor/files/mitmekesisus/Estonian_Integration_Strategy_2008-2013_ENG_VV_11.06.09_nr_236.pdf (accessed 21 Nov. 2013).

Eesti Vabariigi Lastekaitse Seadus (1992). [The Child Protection Act of the Republic of Estonia]. *Riigi Teataja, 28,* 370.

Elkonin, D. B. (1978). *Psichologija igry*. [The psychology of play]. Moscow: Pedagogika.

Göncü, A., Mistry, J. and Mosier, C. (2000). Cultural variations in the play of toddlers. *International Journal of Behavioral Development, 24*(3): 321–329.

Hansen, K., Kaufmann, A. and Walsh, K. R. (1997). *Hea Alguse lasteaedade programm* [Step by Step kindergarten program]. Tallinn: Avatud Eesti Fond.

Klaus, S. (2004). Stepping into the future: A history of the Step by Step program. *Educating Children for Democracy, 8*: 3–14.

Koolieelse Lasteasutuse Riiklik õppekava. (2008). [National Curriculum for Pre-school Child Care Institutions]. *Riigi Teataja*, I: 23, 152.

Koolieelsest Kasvatusest Lasteasutuses. (1979). [About preschool education in a childcare establishment. program and instructions]. Tallinn: Valgus.

Kuimet, M. and Ugaste, A. (2012). Preschool teachers' perceptions of democratic principles and play. Unpublished manuscript.

Leontjev, A. N. (1981). *Problemy razvitija psichiki*. [Problems of psychological development]. Moscow: IMGU.

National Programme: Value Development in Estonian Society 2009–2013. Available at: http://www.ethics.ut.ee/orb.aw/class=file/action=preview/id=802621/Value+Development+in+Estonian+Society+2009%962013.pdf (accessed 20 Oct. 2013).

OECD (2013). *PISA 2012 Results: Ready to learn – students' engagement, drive and self-beliefs* (Vol. III). PISA, OECD Publishing. Available at: http://dx.doi.org/10.1787/9789264201170-en (accessed 18 January 2014).

Õun, T., Ugaste, A., Tuul, M. and Niglas, K. (2010). Perception of Estonian preschool teachers about the child-centred activities in different pedagogical approaches. *European Early Childhood Education Journal, 18*(3): 241–256.

Saar, A. and Niglas, K. (2001). Estonian and Russian parental attitudes to childrearing and play. *Early Child Development and Care, 168,* 39–47.

Sutton-Smith, B. (1998). *The ambiguity of play*. Cambridge, MA: Harvard University Press.

Torm, M. (2011). 170 years of development in Estonian preschool institutions: Historical trends in preschool education. In M. Veisson, E. Hujala, P.K. Smith, M. Waniganayake and E. Kikas (Eds.), *Global perspectives in early childhood education: Diversity, challenges and possibilities* (pp. 81–104). Frankfurt am Main: Peter Lang Verlag.

Tuul, M., Ugaste, A. and Mikser, R. (2011). Teachers' perception of the curricula of the Soviet and post-Soviet eras: A case study of Estonian pre-school teachers. *Journal of Curriculum Studies, 6*: 759–781.

Ugaste, A. (2005). The child's play world at home and the mother's role in the play. *Jyväskylä Studies in Education, Psychology and Social Research*, 259. Jyväskylä.

Ugaste, A., Tuul, M., Niglas, K. and Neudorf, E. (2014). Estonian preschool teachers' views on learning in preschool. *Early Child Development and Care, 3*: 370–385.

Väärtused koolieelses eas. Väärtuskasvatus lasteaias. (2010). [Values in preschool age. Value education in preschools]. Tartu Ülikooli eetikakeskus. Tallinna Ülikooli kasvatusteaduste instituut.

Van der Kooij, R. and Neukäter, H. (1989). Elterliches Erzieherverhalten und Spiel im internationalen Vergleich. *Zeitschrift für Pädagogische Psychologie, 3*: 259–263.

Vygotsky, L. S. (1976). Play and its role in the mental development of the child. In J. Bruner, A. Jolly and K. Sylva (Eds.), *Play: Its role in development and evolution* (pp. 537–554). New York: Basic Books.

17 Play in a Turkish cultural context

Asiye Ivrendi and Nesrin Isikoglu Erdogan

It used to be an unspoken rule for children to play together in front of their houses or in empty spots available around their neighborhood. Nearly three decades ago, the neighborhoods were filled with children's voices. Energetic boys played with steel-skittles, girls jumped rope and played hopscotch. As soon as these games ended, with an inexhaustible energy, boys and girls got together to play "seven tiles," "hide and seek" and "froze-melted." When children decided to play "seven tiles," they sang rhymes to choose who would start first to play. During the game, players threw the ball to hit the tiles and built them again before the "It" hit them with the ball. After the game was over, the winner of "seven tiles" determined what to play next or prepared the playground for another game. These games lasted until mothers called their children in either for lunch or supper. Nowadays, children play less of these games. Even children living in small cities usually prefer to play inside with manufactured toys and/or computer games.

Introduction

Young children's play is considered both a universal and culture-specific activity. Play is universal because all children engage in such behaviors. The feature that makes play a cultural activity is its varying and unique forms of expressions across cultures. Examining the culture-specific nature of play requires three interactive factors to be taken into account. The first considers the physical and social surroundings in which children live. The second includes how adults conceive of play as a result of historical influences. The third points to the ideological beliefs about the meaning of play held by the particular culture (Roopnarine et al. 1994). What is happening socially, economically and politically in a culture influences both the immediate settings for children's play and their play behavior. Thus play reflects features of children's particular environments. With these points in mind, this chapter examines children's play in Turkey by focusing on the following issues: (1) Turkish society and its views of children; (2) play in the family; (3) play in early childhood education; (4) research on play; and (5) implications and suggestions for further research and policy considerations.

Turkish society and views of children

From the early 1970s, increasing industrialization, economic growth and women's entry into the workforce represent some of the major changes that have taken place in Turkish society. With increasing industrialization, migration from rural to urban areas is an ongoing phenomenon (UNICEF 2011). The Turkish economy is the world's third fastest-growing economy after China and India (World Economic Outlook 2012). With respect to women's entry into the workforce, the Turkish Statistical Instate Survey (TUIK 2011) reports that female labor force participation increased from 23.3 percent to 28.8 percent in 2011. These recent social changes have influenced both family structures and family relations. Specifically, women's workforce participation has led to an increase in single child and two-child families (Tezcan 2000; Kağitcibaşi and Ataca 2005). About 6 percent of Turkish households are headed by a single parent; 80 percent of households are composed of nuclear families; 13 percent of households consist of large families; and 3 percent of households are composed of students and workers (TUIK 2006).

Turning to the types of family relationships, the Turkish family is described as evidencing "interdependence," "independence", and "psychological (emotional) interdependence" (Kağitcibaşi and Ataca 2005). Known also as collectivism, the model of interdependence refers to familial social connections and ties in both psychological and material areas. It is widespread in rural settings. The independence model reflects the characteristics of an individualistic culture that is seen more in urban than in rural contexts. The psychological (emotional) interdependence model consists of the combination of interdependence and independence models and is more likely to be seen in urban and high socioeconomic settings. Hence, as socioeconomic status increases, the emerging change is not about separation and independence, but it encompasses "interdependence in the emotional realm with independence in the material realm" (Kağitcibaşi and Ataca 2005: 320). That is, family relationships reflect both relatedness and autonomy.

Evidence of the changing dynamics in Turkish society comes from a longitudinal study examining the value of children (VOC) over a 30-year time span (Kağitcibaşi 2007). The results of the VOC study demonstrated a change both in the value of children and in parental goals, which were defined as the qualities mothers desire to see in their children. With respect to the value of children, utilitarian expectations such as gaining material benefits from children and financial assistance in old age have decreased, while psychological expectations such as joy and companionship of having a child have increased. Decreasing utilitarian expectations from children have also resulted in decreasing preferences for sons as compared to three decades ago (Kağitcibaşi and Ataca 2005).

Within the Turkish family context of having close relations and increasing psychological expectations from children, parents tend to create more opportunities for child play. Playing with children is perceived as a valuable way of spending time with children. Depending on the value given to play in a community, play experiences offered to children may differ in terms of the physical environment in which play occurs, the materials and time provided for play, and the availability of play partners (Göncü 2001; Kalliala 2006).

Along with the changing value of children in families, transformations in children's and parent–child play are also evident. Games such as steel-skittles, hopscotch, nine tiles, skipping rope, tag, games with knucklebones and marbles have been among the best known outdoor play from the past to the present. Traditionally, children and adults used to make toys from natural materials, for example, dolls were made out of stone, fabric, wood, corncob, pine bark, and dried squash. Sheepskin and clay were used to make toys like spinners and windmills. Although a survey on traditional toys indicated the most common ones included dolls, cradles, miniature home objects, transportation vehicles, toys with music and sound, and toy animals (Onur 2002), there has been a decline in traditional children's play and hand-made toys (Onur et al. 2004; Basal 2007).

The most important reasons behind the decrease in the use of traditional hand-made toys and lessening outdoor play are rapid urbanization and technological developments related to the access of commercially manufactured toys. Rapid urbanization in Turkey has led to dense residential systems in cities, leaving less room for empty spaces that can be used as play areas (Basal 2007). Research on children's outdoor play indicates that children play less in the streets and schoolyards, and as the socioeconomic status of children increases the total time for outdoor play decreases (Ahioglu 2012; Onur et al. 2004). Emphasizing play as a natural need of children, Oguz and Ersoy (2005) suggested that outdoor play could help children develop friendships and also allow for the transmission of traditional games from generation to generation.

Concerns over losing traditional play and toys in Turkey have led to research on and the documentation of the existence of traditional toys and play (Demircioğlu 1934; Baran 1993; Onur 2002; Onur et al. 2004; Oguz and Ersoy 2005; Basal 2007). For instance, in their descriptive study, Oguz and Ersoy (2005) conducted structured interviews with adults from different regions of Turkey about their childhood games. They documented 144 games and categorized them into 30 groups according to materials, such as ball games, knucklebone games, and marble games. Further, one way of protecting traditional toys and games has been the establishment of toy museums. Currently in Turkey, there are four toy museums located in Istanbul, Ankara, and Izmir. Bekir Onur established Turkey's first toy museum in 1990. Another well-known museum was established by Sunay Akın in 2005 as the Istanbul Toys Museum. This museum features toy exhibits from different countries and offers a variety of toy making activities, including the construction of wooden toys and model aircraft. These attempts have increased public awareness about the importance of play and play materials in the lives of children and adults. Moreover, toy museums have provided opportunities to compare past and present play in Turkish society. In addition to protecting culture-specific toys, these museums aim to facilitate research studies dealing with the history of childhood culture (Basal 2007) and provide enriched activities for educational purposes.

Play in the family

Parental beliefs

Parental beliefs are constructed within a cultural context, and ways of communicating these beliefs to children, therefore, demonstrate great variations. These variations stem from an array of factors, including educational level, income, perceptions of sex roles, and family structure (married or separated). Within these socioeconomic factors, one's own beliefs about play seem to influence the level of engagement in play. Adults may communicate their values about play to children in various ways. One way is to directly play with the child. Another way is through messages that adults give to children (Göncü 2001); what parents prefer to do and not to do are ways in which their beliefs may be implicitly conveyed to their children (Murphy 1992). However, the relationship between parental beliefs and parental behavior is not unidirectional. Just as parental beliefs exert influence on parental behavior, the reverse is also possible. As Murphy suggests "Parents may construct beliefs in order to rationalize or justify the way they already behave" (1992: 205).

Families' economic structure determines the presence and development of children's activities. In communities where the source of living depends on agriculture and/or parents are of low socioeconomic status, parents may not provide time for children's play (Göncü 2001). Studies have demonstrated that level of education and income influence parents' views about play (Celen 1999; Ivrendi and Isıkoglu 2008) and participation in their children's play (Isıkoglu and Ivrendi 2008). For example, a survey study of Turkish fathers' views and participation in play showed that high-income fathers and those from two-parent families had supportive views about play and demonstrated more participation in their children's play. Fathers who believed that play was a means of learning engaged more often in their children's academic, sociodramatic and physical play than did fathers who did not share this belief (Ivrendi and Isıkoglu 2010) (Figure 17.1).

Figure 17.1 Turkish fathers are assuming an increasing role in parent–child activities.

Play in Turkish early childhood education and teacher training

To better understand the role of play in the Turkish educational system, we provide a brief description of the early childhood educational services available in Turkey. Although Turkey does not have a widespread standardized system of early education, there is a national early childhood curriculum guide. Early childhood education (ECE) programs either belong to or are under the supervision of the Ministry of National Education (MONE) or the general directorate of the Social Welfare and Child Protection Agency (Bekman 2005). Because early childhood education is not mandatory, parents elect to use these services when their children are under 6 years of age.

Due to the prioritization of primary education, early childhood education began to receive public attention in the early 1960s (Bekman 2005). As seen in Table 17.1, the schooling rate of young children has increased over the years. Table 17.1 shows a sharp increase in early education programs between 2009 and 2013. Roughly 44 percent of the 4–5-year-olds and 55 percent of 5–6-year-olds received early childhood services in 2013 (MONE 2013). There is a limited number of early childhood programs serving children under 3. These children are usually cared for by extended family members or nannies.

Based on age, Turkish early childhood services are divided into three categories: (1) crèches that serve children from birth to 3 years; (2) preschools that serve children from 3–6 years; and (3) kindergartens that serve 5- and 6-year-old children. The focus of these early childhood programs varies. Kindergartens and preschools mainly emphasize education whereas the crèches focus on both care and education. From the beginning of the 1990s, public kindergartens and preschools have implemented a mandatory national ECE curriculum across the country. In 2002, 2006, and 2013, Turkey revised its national ECE curriculum guidelines for 36- to 72-month-old children.

Table 17.1 Number of children attending early childhood education

Academic year	Age	Percentage of children attending ECE programme
2009–2010	3–5 years old	26.92
	4–5 years old	38.55
2010–2011	3–5 years old	29.85
	4–5 years old	43.10
2011–2012	3–5 years old	30.87
	4–5 years old	44.04
2012–2013	3–5 years old	30.93
	4 years old	44.04
	5 years old	55.39

Population of children aged from 3–5-years old

Source: Ministry of National Education (MONE), 2011–2012 and 2012–2013 Academic Year National Statistics.

The Early Childhood Education Curriculum and Teacher Handbook were published by the MONE to give teachers a better foundation for understanding and implementing the curriculum guidelines (MONE 2013).

The purpose of the current curricula is to provide early childhood educational opportunities based on the child-centered and constructivist learning principles. Early childhood curricula, therefore, should stimulate play, creativity and joyful learning experiences. Mathematics, language, science, music, art and indoor and outdoor play are the main daily activities. However, within the current curricula, play has gained an essential role. Play is increasingly viewed as the most important work of children and as an inseparable part of their lives (MONE 2013). This point of view has placed play at the center of the curriculum as a primary strategy for learning and teaching (Figure 17.2).

Traditionally, play and other learning activities, including mathematics, science, and language, have been viewed as distinct activities in Turkish early childhood schools. Generally, play was considered the child's own world, and teachers usually let children play by themselves. Aside from play, teachers strictly planned other learning activities. As a result of curriculum revisions (MONE 2002, 2006, 2013), this paradigm came to an end and play has been integrated into all activities. Thus, play is subtly woven into the curriculum as a way of promoting learning. The role of the teacher has become one of supporting children's play by providing appropriate play areas, materials and opportunities for children to play and learn. For instance, teachers organize learning centers with appropriate materials, take observational notes and even become a play partner while children play in different areas.

Figure 17.2 Children's play is at the center of the Turkish early childhood curriculum.

In the Turkish curriculum, children's play activities are divided into three main categories: unstructured, semi-structured and structured play. Unstructured play (free play) can be defined as play in which children select what to play, how to play and with whom they want to play. This type of play usually occurs during the free play activity time which lasts at least an hour each day. Teachers usually take on an observer role in these play activities. By contrast, semi-structured play aims to accomplish certain learning goals. The teacher initiates this type of play and children then lead the rest of the play process. If the goal is to support the development of throwing and catching skills of children, for example, then the teacher will provide different sizes and kinds of balls for children. Afterwards, children will create their play that includes throwing and catching. Semi-structured play activities have important educative roles in supporting children's creativity and involving them in the decision-making process. In structured play teachers predetermine the goals, rules, materials, and processes of play. Both teacher and children actively participate in such play. Finger play and games with rules are examples of structured play. This type of play has educational value in accomplishing certain academic goals, such as learning how to count numbers. The early childhood curriculum guidelines stress that these three types of play should be integrated into the daily activities of children in a balanced way (MONE 2013).

As play has taken its valuable place within the Turkish early childhood curriculum, research results show that teachers demonstrate deficiencies when it comes to providing play opportunities in actual classrooms (Ersan 2011; Kadim 2012). Kindergarten teachers' self-efficacy about planning, implementing, and evaluating play activities was lower than preschool teachers' and in-service training related to play activities was suggested for both groups of teachers (Kadim 2012). A qualitative study also indicated that although teachers allocate an hour every morning for free play activities, they consider this a time when children should play freely without any educational purpose (Ersan 2011).

Research on play

Although Turkish early childhood research is not well developed, it has nonetheless addressed some of the significant concerns in young children's education. The development of early childhood education as an academic discipline does not have a long history in Turkey. For a long time, child development programs trained ECE teachers and researchers within this field (Bekman 2005). However, since the 1980s, Turkish universities and graduate schools have opened ECE teacher training programs. These departments are in their relative infancy but they have made valuable contributions to national and international research on ECE.

Children's play has received special attention from Turkish researchers at the Center of Child Culture and Research (Onur 2004). One of the important functions of this center is to collect publications focusing on play. Examination of these publications indicates that the study of play has increased since the late 1990s, but at this time it is not possible to identify common trends, debates or research orientations in Turkish play research. The studies are either descriptive in nature or small-scale comparison studies (Bekman 2005) that are greatly influenced by the work of such play theorists and researchers as Parten, Piaget, Vygotsky, and Smilansky (Onur 2004; Guler 2007; Ahioglu 2012). Thus, the conceptual frameworks of these theorists have provided a basis for understanding Turkish children's play. Researchers find common patterns in children's play trends, parent–child play, and teachers' role in play when compared to families and children in Western cultures (Göncü 2001; Ahioglu 2012). Similarly, the relationships between play and development, parent–child play, educative play, and traditional play are among the major issues in Turkish play research. Although there is a limited number of research studies directly indicating the influence of play on children's development, some studies have found that play supports children's physical, cognitive, social, and language development (Celen 1992; Baykoç Dönmez 1992; Ahioglu 1999; Sevinc 1999; Ulutas 2011).

In terms of parent–child play, most of the studies have examined parental behaviors, attitudes, and beliefs about play. For example, a small-scale investigation of child–mother play conducted by Akgun and Yesilyaprak (2011) examined mothers' behavior during a free play session. Mothers had difficulty in allowing children to lead play. Mothers tended to emphasize teaching concerns and tended to transmit information to their children while they played together. A cross-cultural study conducted by Göncü et al. (2000) focused on the disparities in toddlers' social play in four cultural communities: Dhol-Ki-Patti, Rajasthan, India, Salt Lake City, USA, San Pedro, Guatemala, and Kecioren, Ankara, Turkey. Findings indicated that Turkish and European-American parents participated in their toddlers' play whereas Guatemalan and Indian parents were not as likely to engage in play with their toddlers.

There is evidence of differences in Turkish mothers' and fathers' participation in play. In their survey study, Isıkoglu and Ivrendi (2008) found that fathers were more likely to engage in their children's sociodramatic and physical play than were mothers, and parents who had a single child participated more in their children's academic play than did parents who had more than one child. As discussed in a previous section, considering the trend towards having a single child or two children in Turkish families (Tezcan 2000; Kağitcibaşi and Ataca 2005), parents with fewer children may have more time to spend with them in play and academic activities. In another study (Ozgun and Honig 2005) that involved Turkish parents with typically developing children and children with special needs, it was demonstrated that mothers still assumed primary responsibility for childcare, and that fathers played with their typically developing children more than mothers did.

Studies centered on the educative value of play are also very important for understanding play in school settings. A descriptive study conducted by Demir (2004) surveyed teachers and administrators about play approaches in early childhood settings. This study demonstrated that schools allocated an average of two hours per day for play. Children mostly preferred constructive play, and dolls, stuffed animals, and blocks were the favorite toys at school. Another descriptive study revealed that teachers ignored the educative value of free play activities as their interactions with children during free play were very limited (Ersan 2011). Other studies have examined the impact of play-based intervention and educational programs on children's development. For example, Ilgaz and Koc (2005) found that pretend play facilitated narrative production in 3- to 5-year-olds and Durualp and Aral (2010) in their experimental study showed that children who participated in a play-based intervention program that focused on improving social skills had better scores on social skills measures compared to the children in the control group.

In addition to exploring the educational benefits of play, Turkish researchers are also concerned about changes in children's play over time and the state of traditional games. Artar et al. (2004) conducted interviews with children, parents, and grandparents about play. They found that involvement in group games has decreased, girls' play seems to have become more feminine, and the use of plastic toys has increased. It was concluded that even in the villages, the impact of urbanization, the media, economic growth, and schooling has gradually prevented the transmission of traditional games to new generations. In another study that looked at changes in play culture, Ahioglu (2012) interviewed 30 children and their grandparents. She further confirmed that the contents and structures or types of play have changed over time. Relative to the past, individual play and adult participation in play have increased, but large group outdoor free play has decreased. At the same time, individual play with computer games has increased. While grandparents of children made their own toys with natural materials such as mud or sticks, the children in the latter study reported spending more time playing with prefabricated toys. Investigating similar concerns, Basal (2007) concluded that traditional games were usually played by large groups of children in the yards, streets and empty areas in neighborhoods across Turkey.

In conclusion, even though Turkish play research is still in its early stages, significant attempts have been made to understand children's play at home and in early childhood settings. Turkish research aligns with Western research in finding that play is valuable and important for childhood development. Differences between Turkish and Western research are shown in how parents and teachers participate and encourage play as well as in how and what children play. Turkish researchers value cultural aspects of play and have concerns about the transmission of traditional play and play materials to new generations. We believe that the positive attempts of such institutions as the Child Culture Center and universities will expand and improve on play research in Turkey.

Implications and suggestions

Signs of change are clear regarding the importance of play both in Turkish family contexts and in early childhood educational settings. Following this awareness, children can be guided to learn traditional games as a way to maintain the cultural values of Turkish society. Newly emerging views of play in Turkish ECE curriculum are noteworthy since they emphasize play as a means of promoting learning. Application of such contemporary practices through a national curriculum is an important step to promote child-centered education. Research has shown, however, that teachers have difficulties in implementing this new paradigm into their classroom practices. There is an urgent need to create awareness of the new view of play among Turkish ECE teachers. Fortunately, after the curriculum revision in 2002, early childhood teacher education programs have been reformed. Currently, these programs have courses, such as "Development of Play," "Physical Education and Play Activities" and "Drama" that promote using play as a means to learn and to teach. Furthermore, the new role of play is promoted through methods courses including mathematics, science and art. ECE teachers working in classrooms need in-service education to better learn how to implement the new curriculum; and both families and educators should provide contemporary play opportunities in order to respond to the changing needs and interests of children.

References

Ahioglu, N. (1999). The influence of symbolic play on 4 year old children's language acquisition. Unpublished Master's dissertation, Ankara University.

Ahioglu, L. N. (2012). Changes in play over two generations. *International Online Journal of Educational Sciences*, 4(2), 395–410.

Akgun, E. and Yesilyaprak, B. (2011). The qualitative dimension of mother–child play interaction: An evaluation of mother–child play. *H.U. Journal of Education*, 40, 11–20.

Artar, M., Onur, B. and Celen, N., (2004). Changes in children's games through three generations: A study in rural setting in Turkey. In B. Onur and N. Guney (Eds.), *Research on children's games in Turkey*. Ankara: KOK.

Baran, M. (1993). *Child games*. Ankara: Publications of Ministry of Culture.

Basal, H. A. (2007). Turkish children's play from past to present. *Uludag University Journal of Education*, 20(2), 243–266.

Baykoç Dönmez, N. (1992). Role of play in children's social and emotional development. *Okul Oncesi Dergisi* [Journal of Preschool], 43, 10–12.

Bekman, S. (2005). Early childhood education in Turkey. In B. Spodek and O. N. Saracho (Eds.), *International perspectives on research in early childhood education*. Greenwich, CT: Information Age Publishing.

Celen, N. (1992). Role of symbolic play on 4-6-year old(s) children's acquisition of number and spatial concepts. Unpublished doctoral dissertation, Ankara University.

Celen, N. (1999). Mothers' and fathers' attitudes about children's right to play. In B. Onur (Ed.), *Republic and child: 2nd National Child Culture Congress Proceedings*. Ankara: Ankara University Press.

Demir, T. S. (2004). The play policies in preschools in Ankara. In B. Onur and N. Guney (Eds.), *Research on children's games in Turkey*. Ankara: KOK.

Demircioğlu, Y. Z. (1934). *Ancient child games in Anatolia*. Istanbul: Milli Mecmua Matbaası.

Durualp, E. and Aral, N. (2010). A study on the effects of play-based social skills training on social skills of six-year-old children. *Hacettepe University Journal of Education*, 39, 160–172.

Ersan, S. (2011). An analysis of preschool teachers' ideas and practices about free play activities on the activity centre. Unpublished doctoral dissertation, Gazi University.

Göncü, A. (2001). Place of societal and cultural context in child's play. In B. Onur (Eds.), *Changing childhood in the World and in Turkey, 3rd. National Child Culture Congress Proceedings*. Ankara: Ankara University Press.

Göncü, A., Mistry, J. and Mosier, C. (2000). Cultural variations in the play of toddlers. *International Journal of Behavioral Development, 24*(3), 321–329.

Guler, T. (2007). "Play Planning" model in early childhood. *Education and Science, 32*(143), 117–128.

Ilgaz, H. and Koc, A. A. (2005). Episodic development in preschool children's play-prompted and direct-elicited narratives. *Cognitive Development, 20*, 526–544.

Isıkoglu, N. and Ivrendi, A. (2008). Mothers' and fathers' participation in play. *Pamukkale University Journal of Education, 24*(2), 47–57.

Ivrendi, B. A. and Isıkoglu, N. (2008). Mothers' and fathers' beliefs about play in early childhood period. *Cagdas Egitim, 33*(355), 4–12.

Ivrendi, B. A. and Isıkoglu, N. (2010). A Turkish view on fathers' involvement in children's play. *Early Childhood Education Journal, 37*(6), 519–526.

Kadim, M. (2012). Examining the preschool teachers' self-efficacy about the game activities according to the type of school. *Nevsehir University Social Sciences Institutes Journal, 2*(1). Available at: http://edergi.nevsehir.edu.tr/index.php/sbe/issue/view/10 (accessed 14 September 2013).

Kağitcibaşi, C. (2007). *Family and human development across countries: A view from the other side* (2nd ed.). Hove: Psychology Press.

Kağitcibaşi, C. and Ataca, B. (2005). Value of children and family change: A three-decade portrait from Turkey. *Applied Psychology: An International Review, 54*(3), 317–337.

Kalliala, M. (2006). *Play culture in a changing world*. New York: Open University Press.

MONE (Ministry of National Education). (2002). *Curriculum for 36–72-month-old children*. Ankara: MEB.

MONE (Ministry of National Education). (2006). *Curriculum for 36–72-month-old children*. Ankara: MEB.

MONE (Ministry of National Education). (2013). *Curriculum for 36–72-month-old children*. Ankara: MEB.

MONE (Ministry of National Education). (2013). *National Educational Statistics for Formal Education 2012–2013*. Available at: http://sgb.meb.gov.tr/istatistik/meb_istatistikleri_orgun_egitim_2012_2013.pdf (accessed 14 September 2013).

Murphy, D. A. (1992). Constructing the child: Relations between parents' beliefs and child outcomes. *Developmental Review, 12*, 199–232.

Oguz, O., and Ersoy, P. (2005). *Living Turkish traditional child games in 2004*. Ankara: Gazi University Turkish Folklore Research and Practice Centre.

Onur, B. (2002). *World with toys*. Ankara: Dost Kitapevi.

Onur, B. (2004). Preface. In B. Onur and N. Guney (Eds.), *Research on children's games in Turkey*. Ankara: KOK.

Onur, B., Artar, M. and Celen, N. (2004). Traditional toys in Turkey: Comparison in a rural and urban setting. In B. Onur and N. Guney (Eds.), *Research on children's games in Turkey*. Ankara: KOK.

Onur, B., Cok, F., Artar, M., Sener, T. and Bagh, M. (2004). Children's outdoor games in big cities. In B. Onur and N. Guney (Eds.), *Research on children's games in Turkey*. Ankara: KOK.

Ozgun, O. and Honig, A. S. (2005). Parental involvement and spousal satisfaction with division of early childcare in Turkish families with normal children and children with special needs. *Early Child Development and Care, 175*(3), 259–270.

Roopnarine, J., Johnson, J. and Hooper, F. (Eds.) (1994). *Children's play in diverse cultures*. Albany, NY: State University of New York Press.

Sevinc, M. (1999). Role of symbolic play on children's cognitive and social development. Paper presented at 3rd International Early Childhood Education Congress, Warwick.

Tezcan, M. (2000). *Turkish family anthropology*. Ankara: Imge Kitabevi Yayınları.

TUIK (2006). Family structure survey. Available at: http://www.ailetoplum.gov.tr/upload/athgm.gov.tr/mce/2013/taya_kitap_butun.pdf (accessed 10 May 2013).

TUIK (2011). Women in statistics. Available at: www.tuik.gov.tr/jsp/duyuru/upload/Duyuru_070312.pdf (accessed 4 June 2013).

Ulutas, A. (2011). The effects of games on children's psychomotor development at the preschool period. Unpublished Master's thesis. Malatya: Inonu University, Turkey.

UNICEF (2011). *Report on children in Turkey*. Available at: http://panel.unicef.org.tr/vera/app/var/files/s/i/sitan-tur.pdf (accessed 20 June, 2013). World Economic Outlook: Coping with high debt and sluggish growth (2012). http://www.imf.org/external/country/tur/rr/2012/100112.pdf (accessed 8 March 2013).

World Economic Outlook (WEO) (2012). *Growth resuming, dangers remain*. Washington, DC: International Monetary Fund.

Part V

Synthesis

18 Synthesis and perspectives on twenty-first-century play around the world

David Kuschner

Introduction

As the chapters of this volume illustrate, the play of children is a universal phenomenon, one that crosses borders and is expressed and realized within a variety of landscapes. Whether it is by a riverbank in Kenya, on a migrant farm in the United States, or in a forest in Sweden, children seem to have an intrinsic drive to manipulate their physical environments, interact with peers and adults, and engage in imaginative activities, all in ways that are freely chosen and playful.

Although the play instinct or drive may be considered universal, the chapters in this book illustrate that the manifestation of play always occurs in a particular context. Just as "all politics is local," in many ways, all children are local; they live and develop in given physical and social geographies, as part of special histories, as members of particular family structures, and within specific cultural communities. The study of any aspect of children's development, play in the case of the present book, requires that we consider both the *universal* (but not uniform) child and the *culturally constituted* child (Lubeck 1996).

Focusing on the culturally constituted child, the essence of this book entitled the *International Perspectives on Children's Play* suggests that the study of children's play is perhaps more a search for generalizable issues and questions than it is a search for generalizable answers. It may be a given that children play—but how they play and what shapes and influences their play are questions that can be answered only by examining real children in real times and places. Taken as a whole, the international perspectives presented in this volume point to a number of interesting aspects of children's play that may be differentially realized depending on cultural contexts. The remainder of this chapter selects and highlights just a few of many important questions and issues that could be raised.

The nature of pretend play

Pretend play is generally considered to be a common form of children's play and one that is positively related to emotional, social, and cognitive development. As Gaskins alludes to in her description of the play of Mayan children in Chapter 2, there are at least two kinds of pretend play: (1) there is the pretend play of the imagination and fantasy; and (2) there is the pretend play that is more a reenactment or reproduction of observed life. For Mayan children, pretend play is more likely to be a reenactment or reproduction of life experiences that have been directly observed than it is expressions of purely imaginative "flights of fancy." Gaskins suggests that the tendency towards pretend play based on real life might be a result of the fact that the Mayan culture emphasizes non-fictional storytelling: "Given this cultural commitment to true narratives, it is not surprising that children limited their pretend play to interpretations of events and activities they have observed or ones that they have heard about that really happened." The same focus on "reality-based" pretend play was described as being part of the play of Brazilian children. In Chapter 3, Gosso, Bichara, and Carvalho believe that because

> [the children are] exposed to a challenging and stimulating environment [and they are] surrounded by forests to explore, trees to climb, rivers or the ocean to swim in . . . they do not need to resort to imaginary adventure scenarios because that is part of their daily reality.

It is not enough, therefore, to say that all children engage in pretend play, or that pretend play is important for all children; we must understand that pretend play may be expressed differently and serve different functions for children based on their cultural setting.

The varieties of social contexts

Another common assumption about the play of children is that their playful activity will either be solitary or social in nature. In terms of social play, children will be interacting with either members of their family (both children and adults) or unrelated peers, perhaps in the neighborhood, on a playground, or in a classroom. A number of chapters in this book raise the interesting question about the ways in which the cultural context can determine who those play partners will be. In the chapter on Indian children, for example, the authors point out that, "In family life, living spaces, sleeping arrangements, schedules, and social events, display the ideology of inclusion of members of all ages—thus, children are always in the company of others of all ages." Playgroups in the Indian culture, therefore, might be predominantly mixed-age group, at least outside of the school setting. Gaskins identifies a similar cultural context for Mayan children. She writes: "Mayan children's social worlds are made up of relatives, not friends. This social organization reflects the general cultural norm of socializing with family members and *compadres* ('ritual family')." This has the consequence, according to Gaskins, of Mayan children primarily playing within mixed-age groups. A second interesting consequence of this socialization practice, according to Gaskins, is that "playmates today are the same as yesterday and tomorrow." In Chapter 5 on the play of children of Mexican migrant farmworkers, Mathur suggests that play in mixed-age groups is also common in that cultural setting because of the expectation that children will be responsible for the care of younger siblings.

Whereas cultural factors may shape with whom children will play in social groups, there may also be cultural factors that result in less social play and more solitary play. In Chapter 10 on the play of Taiwanese children, Pei-Yu Chang suggests that when the national government of Taiwan began to encourage smaller families and there was a decline in the birth rate, there was a concomitant change in how children played, moving from social play to more solitary play. This is a good example of why it is important to study the play of real children in real places and times. Solitary play, in this case, did not increase because children were being anti-social or were lacking in social skills, but because there were simply fewer children with whom they could play.

Parental attitudes towards play

One of the common themes that emerged from the trans-national look at play presented in the previous chapters concerns the role and influence of parents (and other adults) in the play lives of children. A number of the authors, for example, addressed the question of parental attitudes towards play. In Chapter 4, Roopnarine suggested that for at least some Caribbean cultures, parents did not value play as much as they did other aspects of a child's development such as the preparation for academic achievement and the learning of manners and obedience. As a result, "there is less of an emphasis [in these cultures] on fostering curiosity and creativity through play."

Jung, in Chapter 7 on the play of Asian American children, found some of the same parental attitudes as did Roopnarine, going so far as to write that, "Some Asian American parents may even regard play as the antithesis to work and a waste of time." When it comes to the school curriculum, Asian American mothers prefer that there be greater emphasis on school readiness and academics than on play. As a result of this attitude, "Although Asian American parents . . . acknowledge the importance of play, they do not practice play with their children at home." Instead of fostering play at home, Asian parents "spend much more time on pre-academic activities such as learning letters and numbers, playing math games, and working with computers."

The parents of Brazilian, Indian, Kenyan, and Mayan children are at other points on the continuum of parental attitudes about play. For the Brazilian parents, "Play is considered a childhood activity that does not require adult stimulation and offers no reason for concern. Children play, just like adults work." Indian parents also shared this view that the work of children is to play but since children play on their own, parents believed that school should be less about play and more about learning. For the Turkana parents in Kenya, the attitude is more like benign neglect. Children play independently from adults and as long as the children do not shirk their family and work responsibilities, parents assume a fairly passive role in their play. Like the Kenyan children, Mayan children also play independently from adults, often at a physical distance. The adults are focused on getting their own work done and do not spend very much time concerning themselves with the play of their own or other children.

In Chapter 4 on Caribbean children, Roopnarine writes that, "parental beliefs represent the internal working models or schemas about the care and education of children." Play is just one aspect of that care and education; but the question of the "internal working models" of parents is a fundamental question that needs to be asked when considering the play of children in a particular cultural setting.

Cultural traditions and societal changes

Cultures are rooted in traditions but at the same time are affected by the societal changes that swirl around those traditions. This dynamic raises the question of how the play of children is shaped by these traditions, changes, and the tensions between tradition and change that often emerge.

In Chapter 8 on the play of Native American children in the United States, Buchanan and Cooney note that a reverence for nature and a world-view that emphasizes the "circularity of existence" have long been shared values held by many Native American tribes. As a result, nature-based play has been a traditional characteristic of children's experience in the Native American culture. The examination of Taiwanese children's play in Chapter 10 highlights the long-standing influence of Confucianism and its emphasis on education. This emphasis leads to a culture that may value work over play and academic achievement over children's self-initiated activity.

In Chapter 11, Izumi-Taylor and Ito discuss a number of traditional Japanese beliefs that may influence the ways in which children's play is realized in the Japanese culture. These beliefs include *jiyu hoiku* (focusing on children's freedom), *sunao* (cooperation), *ganbaru* (persistence), *gamansuru* (enduring hardships), and *hansei* (reflection). It is easy to imagine how each of these beliefs might influence the nature of play in that culture. The authors also suggest that the concept of *pantheism*, a religious perspective that emphasizes the interrelatedness of all beings, has influenced the Japanese image of children and childhood and by implication, the view of children's play.

But countries and cultures experience changes that may come into conflict with traditions; and, as a result, attitudes towards children's play may evolve. For example, in Chapter 8, Buchanan and Cooney write that when Native American peoples were forced off their lands and pressured to assimilate into and accept the ways of the dominant, Anglo culture, the "nature-based play of traditional Native children lost its relevance." Pei-Yu Chang provides an interesting description of the shifts in Taiwanese culture just since the end of World War II and how those shifts have affected children's play, particularly in terms of the availability of toys. In Chapter 13, Davey notes how housing trends in Australia may have affected children's play due to the loss of space in which the play can occur. In Estonia, regaining independence in 1991 was a significant societal change and "like all other once communist Eastern European countries, [Estonia] has experienced profound social, political, and cultural changes with the overall aim to integrate the country into the European democratic and humanistic system." In Chapter 16, Ugaste and Mikser also detail how this societal upheaval led to a number of initiatives in education that have had consequences for the social landscape of children's play in Estonia. In Chapter 17 on play in Turkey, Asiye Ivrendi and Nesrin Isikoglu Erdogan point to such societal changes as increased industrialization and the entrance of women into the workforce as factors that have affected the nature of children's play in that country. As result of these and other societal changes, the authors believe that there has been a dip in time provided for outdoor play and a decrease in the use of traditional play, games, and toys in Turkey.

Another societal change that was mentioned in a number of the chapters relates to the migration of people out of, and the immigration of people into, a particular country or culture. The beliefs, values and practices of a culture—and the individuals within it—can change when it comes into contact with alternative beliefs, values and practices. For example, Roopnarine writes that Caribbean families that have immigrated to the United States hold somewhat more diverse views about play than the families that remained in their home countries. Similarly, Gosso and colleagues write that for some of the indigenous peoples of Brazil, contact with the larger culture results in "play themes [that] still largely mirror the local culture and habits [but] reflections of mainstream industrialized culture on children's play can occur." In terms of Kenya, it was noted that "Contemporary Turkana nomadic communities . . . have undergone significant changes due to western religious influences, exposure to educational activities, [and the] impact of urbanization."

People who change cultural contexts may also hold on to aspects of their home cultures despite contact with alternative belief systems. Research by Farver and colleagues, cited in Jung's Chapter 7 on the play of Asian American children, found that the pretend play of Korean American children differed from the pretend play of American children. Jung also highlights the fact that research has found differences between Asian American parents and American parents in terms of how they play with their children and differences between Asian American teachers and American teachers concerning the way in which they incorporate play into their classrooms. As Jung points out, "Even though the Korean-American teachers in the study are born in the United States and trained in American colleges, their teaching styles and academically-oriented curricula reflected traditional Korean values, expectations, and educational goals for children."

Play, education, and schooling

Many of the authors who contributed to this volume addressed what seems to be an ongoing tension between the nature of play and the realities of the school curriculum. In Chapter 6, Hale and Bocknek discussed how play may (or may not) relate to the educational goal of closing the achievement gap that exists for many poor, African American children in American schools. In writing about the children of Mexican migrant farmworkers in the United States, Mathur sees a tension between the value of play for children's development and parental expectations for school. Mathur states that the parents "often express frustration and displeasure when they discover that children are allowed to play at preschool for a majority of the day and would clearly prefer a traditional structured, teacher-directed preschool experience for their children." She also suggests that an emphasis on play runs counter to the current context of high stakes testing and teacher accountability that characterizes much of American education today.

It turns out that the United States may not be the only culture that is experiencing the tension between play and the school curriculum. Ugaste and Mikser suggest that real play has been marginalized within the education system of Estonia; Davey takes the fact that the study of play is not represented very well in the teacher education programs in Australia as evidence of this tension or problem. In India, the fact that children naturally play outside of school leads to the attitude that school should be a place where children learn how to read and write and is not a place where they need to play. Even in Sweden, where play has a long tradition of being valued, Lillvist and Sandberg write in Chapter 14 that over the past decade a change has occurred in that play has become viewed as a tool for reaching developmental goals rather than being valued for its own sake. Pei-Yu Chang writes that the play that occurs in Taiwanese schools is usually directed by adults and there is little freedom for self-initiated exploration on the part of children. In Chapter 15 on play in the United Kingdom, Wood discusses how governmental agencies which attempt to set educational policy are challenged by the tension between play and the school curriculum.

As I have previously written (Kuschner 2012), there may be some inherent characteristics of play and school that inevitably produce the difficult challenge and make melding the two together virtually impossible. My arguments were theoretical and based on my experiences with schooling in the United States. The international perspectives presented in this volume suggest that the tension between play and school, and the challenge to incorporate play into the school curriculum, are found in other countries as well.

Final thoughts

In a previous book about play and cultural differences, Roopnarine and Johnson wrote:

> Children's play . . . is an outcome of being a participant within a particular cultural or subcultural milieu. Cultural-ecological frameworks subscribe to the notion that the kinds of immediate contexts that children experience is also constrained and moderated by broad cultural forces and available toys and other play items within the culture.
>
> (1994: 4)

This present volume continues and extends upon this perspective that the actualization of a child's self-motivated drive to play does not occur in a vacuum. As Urie Bronfenbrenner (1979, 2005) described in his *ecological systems theory* of human development, a child's interaction and involvement with her environment are embedded in a series of contexts, some of which are immediate to the child's experience and others with which the child does not have direct contact. All of the contexts, however, can have an impact on the child's experience, in our case, the experience of play. A child, for example, has direct experience in her preschool classroom and the space, time, and materials provided by that classroom influence her play choices and activity. On the other hand, that child does not have direct interaction or experience with the board of directors that governs the preschool, the governmental agencies that set policies and allocate resources for early childhood education, or the value system of her culture that may or may not emphasize the importance of early education. Even though the child does not have direct experience with these contexts, they, too, can have an impact on the ways in which the universal drive to play is actualized by that particular child.

As Tudge et al. (2009) point out, however, it is a mistake to focus solely or too heavily on the impact of the contexts on children's development; there is always an interaction between the individual and the forces represented in those contexts. The international perspectives presented in this book help us to understand the cultural constraints within which children's play lives: the histories and traditions, the parental attitudes, the economic conditions, the governmental policies, and the changing societies. Understanding the play of the children in any particular culture requires an understanding of those constraints. But just as the universal drive to play does not freely determine how a child plays, these constraints do not fully determine the nature of the play either. In the end, it is the child who plays and that play never ceases to amaze us.

References

Bronfenbrener, U. (1979). *The ecology of human development: Experiments in nature and design*. Cambridge, MA: Harvard University Press.

Bronfenbrenner, U. (2005). The bioecological theory of human development. In U. Bronfenbrenner (Ed.), *Making human beings human: Bioecological perspectives on human development* (pp. 3–15). Thousand Oaks, CA: Sage.

Kuschner, D. (2012). Play is natural to childhood but school is not: The problem of integrating play into the curriculum. *International Journal of Play, 1*(3), 242–249.

Lubeck, S. (1996). Deconstructing "child development knowledge" and "teacher preparation." *Early Childhood Research Quarterly, 11*, 147–167.

Roopnarine, J. L., and Johnson, J. E. (1994). The need to look at play in diverse cultural settings. In J. L. Roopnarine, J. E. Johnson and F. H. Hooper (Eds.), *Children's play in diverse cultures* (pp. 1–8). Albany, NY: State University of New York Press.

Tudge, J. R. H., Mokrova, I., Hatfield, B. E. and Karnik, R. B. (2009). Uses and misuses of Bronfenbrenner's bioecological theory of human development. *Journal of Family Theory & Review, 1*, 198–210.

Index

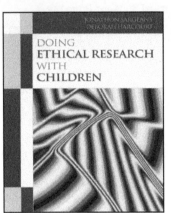

DOING ETHICAL RESEARCH WITH CHILDREN

Deborah Harcourt and Jonathon Sargeant
9780335246427 (Paperback)

August 2012

eBook also available

Doing Ethical Research with Children introduces students to the key considerations involved when researching with children and young people, from both a methodological and ethical perspective. It will assist students as they develop, conduct and disseminate research that relates to children and childhood.

Key features:

- Combines appropriate and supportive information to offer a guide through the issues and essential elements of conducting ethical research with children
- Includes pedagogical features throughout to develop understanding
- Different stages of research are covered, from planning the research to carrying out the study

www.openup.co.uk

INTERNATIONAL PERSPECTIVES ON EARLY
CHILDHOOD EDUCATION AND CARE

Jan Georgeson and Jane Payler (Eds)

9780335245918 (Paperback)
February 2013

eBook also available

There is a growing interest in understanding how early years care and
education is organised and experienced internationally. This book examines
key influential approaches to early years care as well as some less well-
known systems from around the world.

Key features:

- Informs those studying early years about perspectives in other countries
- Encourages critical thinking about issues, influences and the
  complexities of early years provision around the world
- Promotes critical reflection on students' own provision and the current
  context of that provision

www.openup.co.uk

OPEN UNIVERSITY PRESS
McGraw - Hill Education

ENGAGING PLAY

Liz Brooker and Suzy Edwards (Editors)

2010
978-0-335-23586-5 *(Paperback)*

eBook also available

This insightful edited collection brings together the perspectives of leading and emerging scholars in early childhood education and play from within Europe, the UK, Australia, New Zealand and the USA.

The chapters cover a wide range of contexts, from child-led activity in informal settings to the more formal practice of school-based learning. A range of theoretical viewpoints of play are considered and related to the experiences of today's families, children and educators across different educational settings.

Engaging Play offers an insight into the pedagogical play discourse of twenty-first century early childhood education, and in doing so offers an informative reading experience for students, researchers and policy makers alike.

www.**openup**.co.uk

OPEN UNIVERSITY PRESS
McGraw · Hill Education